SPARKS
SONG BY SONG

Promotion shot, Wi-Fi Records, 1981.

SPARKS
SONG BY SONG
VOLUME 1: 1971-1988

RUUD SWART

First published in Great Britain in 2025 by
Fonthill
An imprint of
Pen & Sword Books Ltd
Yorkshire – Philadelphia

Copyright © Ruud Swart 2025

ISBN 978-1-03615-232-1

The right of Ruud Swart to be identified as
Author of this work has been asserted by him in accordance
with the Copyright, Designs and Patents Act 1988.

A CIP catalogue record for this book
is available from the British Library.

All rights reserved. No part of this book may be reproduced,
transmitted, downloaded, decompiled or reverse engineered in any form
or by any means, electronic or mechanical including photocopying,
recording or by any information storage and retrieval system,
without permission from the Publisher in writing.
NO AI TRAINING: Without in any way limiting the Author's and Publisher's
exclusive rights under copyright, any use of this publication
to "train" generative artificial intelligence (AI) technologies
to generate text is expressly prohibited. The Author and Publisher
reserve all rights to license uses of this work for generative
AI training and development of machine learning language models.

The Publisher's authorised representative in the EU for product safety is
Authorised Rep Compliance Ltd., Ground Floor, 71 Lower Baggot Street,
Dublin D02 P593, Ireland.
www.arccompliance.com

For a complete list of Pen & Sword titles please contact

PEN & SWORD BOOKS LIMITED
47 Church Street, Barnsley, South Yorkshire, S70 2AS, England
E-mail: enquiries@pen-and-sword.co.uk
Website: www.pen-and-sword.co.uk
or
PEN AND SWORD BOOKS
1950 Lawrence Road, Havertown, PA 19083, USA
E-mail: uspen-and-sword@casematepublishers.com
Website: www.penandswordbooks.com

Acknowledgements

For their support, advice, and patience in the creation of this publication, I would like to thank Ron Meeldijk, Elizabeth Wilmot, Stef Streur, Molly Scott, John Dignan and Leslie Hanagan.

Special thanks to the following Sparks fans who generously shared their personal photos for this edition: Bart van den Hoogen, Henry Mowry, Ken Montgomery and Pody Hansbrough.

I would also like to thank those who were kind enough to send their photos, which were not used this time due to limited space. However, some of these photos will be included in the second part.

A very special thank you to Ron Mael and Russell Mael for sharing their extraordinary creations with the world. Without their exceptional talents, perseverance and resilience, we would not have experienced the joy, anticipation, excitement and wit that have enriched our lives for so many years.

This publication is not authorised by Sparks or their management. No interviews were conducted with them except for one in Brussels, Belgium, on 21 March 1981. Over the past decades, I have had extensive conversations, both in person and online, with John Mendelsohn, Ralph Oswald, Larry Dupont, Harley Feinstein, Martin Gordon, Ian Hampton, Trevor White, Leslie Bohem and Jim Wilson, as well as with Bob Breeks, backline tech and assistant to the band from 1994 to 2017. Thank you all for your time and willingness to share information.

While creating this publication, I attempted to trace the origins of each photograph. Unfortunately, I was not completely successful in this, and I would therefore appreciate it if any photographers involved could contact me directly at info@fanmael.nl.

Contents

Acknowledgements		5
Introduction		9
1	Halfnelson	13
2	A Woofer in Tweeter's Clothing	34
3	Kimono My House	49
4	Propaganda	66
5	Indiscreet	79
6	Big Beat	94
7	Introducing Sparks	110
8	No. 1 In Heaven	121
9	Terminal Jive	134
10	Whomp That Sucker	144
11	Angst In My Pants	154
12	In Outer Space	166
13	Pulling Rabbits Out of a Hat	178
14	Music That You Can Dance To	188
15	Interior Design	198
Afterword		208

Introduction

'We are notorious liars,' Russell Mael once confessed to me during a rare personal encounter. 'In fact, we lie so much you can't even be sure that we're telling the truth right now,' he smiled. It is quite obvious that the Mael Brothers have always had a rather flexible approach to interpreting the truth. This, however, makes the writing of a book dedicated to the careers of the 'Instant Darlings' a risky and difficult task. Over the years, several books on Sparks have been written. However, this publication takes a different approach. Of course, attention is paid here to the story of the brothers themselves, to their various attempts to share their music with as many people as possible without making any compromises. Attention will also be paid to their influence on the music world, their inimitable image and the degree of humour they manage to bring to their creations.

But this book mainly focuses on their work: a meticulous overview of their oeuvre, spanning almost sixty years, from their first demo recordings to their most recent album. Virtually every released song is discussed, as well as many unreleased recordings.

Given the extensive body of work Sparks has recorded, it was decided to divide the publication into two parts. The first edition focuses on the period 1971–88, briefly mentioning the previous years. Part two, to be published in 2026, will cover the period 1989–2025 as well as non-album tracks and unreleased songs.

In this publication, individual songs are discussed, including both the musical input and the interpretation of the lyrics. It is possible that these interpretations may differ from what the reader personally gets from the lyrics. Ron Mael has indicated that he finds every interpretation of his lyrics acceptable as it is all about what the words evoke in the listener.

It was in 1974 that Sparks tasted their first international success, and although it was for a relatively short period, the brothers Mael were, without a doubt, the most original and refreshing bearers of New Wave *avant-la-lettre*. They combine catchy, vibrant tunes with witty, peculiar lyrics that are always good for a grin or consideration. Sparks covered subjects like sneezing, heaven, prostitution, breasts, tropical fruits and environmental conservation. Not to mention celebrities such as Albert Einstein, Joan of Arc, Adolf Hitler, Ingmar Bergman and Noah.

Fortunately, Sparks have always been able to find some outlet somewhere, sometime, as long as they kept making records. Before their definitive breakthrough during the Island years, they already had a London-based fan club with members from the United States, Britain, Germany, the Netherlands and France, even though they were an obscurity act in those days.

In the many years to come, their popularity travelled from country to country, hardly ever simultaneously but always somewhere. This climaxed during the early Eighties, when Ron and Russell had their fifteen minutes of fame in their home country, and finally received the well-deserved appreciation and respect of their fellow countrymen. Oddly enough, without having had any hits over there since that moment, Sparks have never been as popular in the USA as they are today.

Much has been written recently about the alleged influence Sparks have had on the electronic dance groups of the Eighties, and even on stars like Morrissey, Björk and Suede. This possibility should at least be taken into consideration. Instead of arguing about whether the Pet Shop Boys were consciously influenced by them, it is much more worthwhile to focus on Sparks' music itself, for it has always had an enchanting charm.

From the dusky and almost psychedelic side of the Bearsville era (although they were never a real threat to the Velvet Underground) to the brilliantly refreshing Island years, when the Maels gave the European music industry the enema it needed, 1976 and 1977 saw them flirting with the Ramones, Brian Wilson and Zorba the Greek. In 1979, after some unrewarded demo sessions for a series of record companies, including Arista Records, they discovered Dance Music, eventually becoming entrapped by it, which they then explored and perfected. By then, Ron and Russell Mael had already proven that they were a consistently important and very interesting part of the development and current state of pop music, whether one liked it or not.

Today, Sparks are regarded as trendsetters and creators of new music directions. Respected by their fellow musicians as well as the international music press, they have finally achieved the status they have been entitled to for decades. The fact that their current music is as fresh, original and inspiring as their greatest hits from nearly fifty years ago only shows that it is about time we focused our attention on what makes Sparks so special: the music.

Their fan base continues to grow daily, and there is little chance that people will drop out, as their back catalogue is so extensive and diverse. Once you are enchanted by any of their releases, you are bound to search for more.

It may have taken a while, but their sold-out performances at legendary venues such as the Royal Albert Hall and the Hollywood Bowl indicate that they are finally being recognised as the geniuses Ron and Russell Mael are—something earlier Sparks fans have always known.

Ruud Swart
July 2025

1
Halfnelson

Release date: September 1971 (reissued July 1972 as *Sparks*)
Produced by: Todd Rundgren
Engineer: Thaddeus James Lowe
Sleeve design: Ron Mael
Photography: Larry Dupont
Recorded at: ID Studios, Hollywood
Duration: 40:23
Personnel: Ron Mael: Keyboards
Russell Mael: Vocals
Earle Mankey: Guitar
Jim Mankey: Bass guitar, guitar
Harley Feinstein: Drums

Side 1
'Wonder Girl'
'Fa La Fa Lee'
'Roger'
'High C'
'Fletcher Honorama'
'Simple Ballet'

Side 2
'Slowboat'
'Biology 2'
'Saccharin and the War'
'Big Bands'
'(No More) Mr. Nice Guys'

Singles from this album:
'Wonder Girl'/'(No More) Mr. Nice Guys'

Halfnelson, the eponymous debut album of the band that would later be known as Sparks, was recorded in the spring and early summer of 1971. Recording this album was a dream come true for the band members, one they had long worked towards. Halfnelson was formed around the brothers Ron and Russell Mael.

The band also included Earle John Mankey (born in Washington on 8 March 1946), his brother James Andrew Mankey (born in Washington on 23 May 1952) and Harley Feinstein (born in Los Angeles on 10 April 1951).

Ronald David Mael was born on 12 August 1945 in Culver City, California, and was followed by his brother, Russell Craig Mael, whose first vocal efforts were heard in Santa Monica, California, on 5 October 1948. Their parents were Meyer Mael (born in Philadelphia on 25 March 1916), a cartoonist/illustrator for the local *Citizen-News*, and Miriam Irene Mael (née Moskowitz, born 6 July 1922). She was a librarian who would later play an important role in Sparks' official fan club. Meyer Mael came from a large family, having three sisters and six brothers, spread across the USA.

The Maels' parents were artistic and progressive people who encouraged the brothers to be creative. Ron began taking piano lessons at the age of 5, and after only four weeks, in June 1951, he performed his first public piano recital at the Women's Club House in Venice. Some years later, Russell, by then 17, won first prize in May 1963 at UCLA for his recitation of Shakespearean sonnets.

Visits to the local cinema with their father were frequent events during the Saturday matinée, and when Elvis Presley's single 'Hound Dog' was released, it was immediately bought by his father for Ron (then known as Ronnie). A striking choice for an 11-year-old boy, especially at a time when such a song was not received equally positively everywhere. At the time, the family lived at 1121 Washington Boulevard in Venice, California.

It is regularly suggested, mainly by the brothers themselves, that they were youth models for children's clothing and appeared in various advertising brochures. This can certainly not be ruled out, but little evidence has been found for it, apart from an advertisement by Cambell's, a clothes store on Santa Monica Boulevard, in which a photo appears that includes a teenage Russell.

Throughout their careers, the brothers have displayed a rather nonchalant attitude towards telling innocent lies or slightly twisting the truth. This is not exclusively something they do; many artists sometimes bend the truth simply because the truth is just a bit too mundane.

Both Ron and Russell went to the Westminster Elementary School in Venice, but something extremely tragic occurred when they were 11 (Ron) and 8 years (Russell) old, their father passing away of a sudden heart attack during an argument with a store owner when he wanted to buy some shirts.

This moment must have been a decisive factor in the special bond that undoubtedly already existed between the brothers, but which grew many times stronger. Meyer was a highly respected and appreciated man in his community. A memorial service was held at Ron and Russell's elementary school and a tree was planted in his honour.

Miriam raised her sons by herself for several years, but eventually remarried in 1960 to someone who made the family more or less complete again: Oscar 'Rogy' Roganson (born 1921).

Having no other siblings, the Maels grew up together and were much more alike than one would imagine after they had achieved their worldwide fame and their respective images had apparently put them as far apart as possible. In fact, they were not nearly as different as one might think, and they certainly had a common goal: to share their creations with the rest of the world.

Meanwhile, the family had moved to 915 Galloway Street in Pacific Palisades and Rogy and Miriam ran a shop at 1013 Swarthmore named Gilded Prune, in which they bought and sold an odd collection of 'posters, art prints, gifts, imports, jewelry and clothing', as was stated on their business card.

Initially, Ron went to Uni High, where he played for the school's football team. Later, he went to the same high school that Russell went to: Palisades Charter High School. Russell too played for the football team, the Dolphins, where he did quite well as a quarterback and regularly made it into the local newspapers.

Despite their musical talents, it was not at all certain that they would devote their full attention to music. Ron started studying cinema and graphic design at UCLA in 1963, and Russell went on to study theatre and film-making in 1966.

They often went to local concerts, such as those of The Doors, Love, The Turtles, The Beach Boys, Beau Brummels, The Seeds and, as a highlight, the concert of The Beatles at the Hollywood Bowl in August 1964, which they were driven to by their mother. They also saw The Beatles in Las Vegas. Other bands and performers they witnessed at the time included The Kinks, Procol Harum, Jimi Hendrix, The Standells, Canned Heat, The Who and Blue Cheer.

Los Angeles was a special place in the second half of the 1960s, the city experiencing a cultural upheaval, and the Maels were in the right place at the right time. On 29 November 1965, they went to a taping of *The Big T.N.T. Show*, a concert where several artists performed, including Ray Charles, Petula Clark, Joan Baez, The Byrds and Ike & Tina Turner. The audience shots also include Ron and Russell, both with short hair and Ron still without his iconic moustache, surrounded by only girls.

It wouldn't be long before they would enter the music industry themselves, albeit at a very modest level.

The Mael brothers' first serious venture into the world of music occurred around the time Russell began his studies at UCLA, when he and Ron formed a band called The Urban Renewal Project. It is claimed that, even prior to this, one or both of the Maels had been involved in various other bands of little significance. Moonbaker Abbey and the Belle Air Blues Band were allegedly some of their creations during the first half of the 1960s; however, those activities, if they occurred at all, were limited to the rehearsal room. It has also been suggested that the former was not a band at all, but rather a dance troupe in which Russell participated.

The Urban Renewal Project consisted of Ron, who played lead guitar; Russell, who provided vocals and played harmonica and tambourine; Ron's friend, Fred Frank, on rhythm guitar; and his wife, Ronna, on backing vocals. Other band members included 16-year-old Raymond Clayton on drums and Harold Zellman on bass guitar. Ron and Fred were close friends, with Ron having served as Fred's best man at his wedding to Ronna on 11 September 1966.

Notably, Ron and Russell's stepfather, Rogy Roganson, was appointed as the band's manager at that time.

The Urban Renewal Project never formally released a record and only performed at a handful of gigs, including some at Battle of the Bands events. However, one recording they made occasionally appears on compilation albums, including the original soundtrack of *The Sparks Brothers* from 2021.

The song in question, 'Computer Girl', was recorded along with three other songs on 14 January 1967 at Fidelity Recording Studios in Hollywood. It was first formally released on a CD that came with a Japanese guidebook in 2006. The compilation was put together and released by Youchi Kishino, a local artist and fan who is still active in promoting Sparks in Japan whenever they tour there.

The three other songs that were recorded on the same day but were never released were 'The Windmill', 'A Quick Thought' and 'As You Like It'. These four songs were pressed and taken home by the band on two acetates. Of these four songs, 'Computer Girl' is the least conventional, while the other three tracks are heavily influenced by the zeitgeist.

At the time, Ron played lead guitar, which is particularly noticeable during 'A Quick Thought'. Russell was the singer and he also played tambourine and harmonica. In 'A Quick Thought', the lyrics of which are based on a poem, possibly Russell's, he also plays the pan flute.

In 1968, during the height of the Vietnam War, Fred Frank was drafted. Although the remaining band members made some attempts to continue, their activities became increasingly sporadic, prompting Ron and Russell to pursue their musical endeavours independently. They placed an advertisement in a local music store stating 'guitarist wanted', which ultimately led them to meet Earle Mankey. While Mankey was a skilled guitarist, he was more interested in music recording techniques, such as overdubbing sounds and varying their speed. They were also joined by college friend Larry Dupont, who brought along a reel-to-reel tape recorder and became involved as an assistant to the band as well as their photographer.

The trio called themselves Halfnelson, named after a wrestling grip, and began recording their self-penned songs using Larry's tape recorder. They did not perform live. Around July 1969, they devised a plan to approach the music industry in an unusual manner. Even at that time, the Maels seemed to take pleasure in defying convention.

The concept was to independently record an entire album and then present it to various record companies, so that one of the companies would only need to release it. Ron played keyboards, Earle was on guitar and Russell provided vocals while playing bass guitar on most of the tracks.

Additional support was needed to complete the recordings. At that time, Mike Berns was a prominent figure in the local music scene and served as the drummer. He had also taken on the role of the band's manager, a self-appointed position that the band was not entirely comfortable with.

For one thing, he bore an uncanny resemblance to Charles Manson, which—quite understandably—did not align with the band's desired image. Additionally, his drumming technique conflicted with the band's vision. Moreover, the group believed it was unwise to have a band member serve as the manager as well, and they were eager to find someone else to assume this role.

While Mike contributed to a few songs, his true value to the band—presumably the reason they allowed him to remain—was his confidence in them, which led him to finance the recordings and pressing of the album. When Mike ultimately relinquished his ambitions of being Halfnelson's drummer (or was compelled to do so), he was replaced by John Mendelsohn, a locally known rock critic, who definitely played on the song 'Chili Farm Farney' and probably on some other tracks as well. John brought along his friend, 'Surly' Ralph Oswald, who played bass on some of the tracks, although most of the songs had already been recorded with Russell on bass.

In total, thirteen songs were recorded for the album, most of which were written by the Maels. Twelve of these songs were pressed on the album; a short instrumental outtake titled 'Spider Run' was not included.

The album was released without a formal title and featured a white label. Two persistent rumours surrounded this recording. The first was that it was titled *A Woofer in Tweeter's Clothing*, similar to Sparks' official second album. The second rumour suggested that Ron designed the cover, which depicted a surfer riding the waves in front of the Eiffel Tower under a bright moon.

This image later inspired some artists and Sparks fans to create their own interpretations of a cover that never actually existed. This misunderstanding likely stemmed from an article in the British music magazine *Sounds*, written by Kathy Orloff, who had met the band in Los Angeles. In the article, published on 17 October 1970, she mentions the title *A Woofer in Tweeter's Clothing* and describes the sleeve as depicted above. Perhaps the most logical explanation for this myth is that it was once a concept in Ron's mind, which he later discarded, at least for the time being. But it was too good a title to be completely abandoned.

In what would become a recurring theme for the Maels, once John and Ralph had rendered their services, they were no longer needed and were promptly dismissed from the band. John and Ralph went on to form their own band, Christopher Milk, and released one album, *People Will Drink Anything*, which was available only in the US on Reprise Records in 1972. John, who currently lives in London, continues to make very interesting music.

The untitled Halfnelson demo album was pressed in limited quantities. It was packaged in a large cardboard box that, as some Sparks completists may be thrilled to learn, measured approximately 35 × 60 centimetres. An 'order sheet' was attached to the box, featuring the printed phrase 'Please pay cashier' and the handwritten words 'Halfnelson Album'. The price of this gem was indicated on the cover package: $100,000.00 plus $5,000.00 in taxes. In addition to the record, the package included popcorn, photos of the band, postcards and other small items. The back of the postcards read 'Halfnelson's swell'.

Larry Dupont commented on this album:

> There were a very small number, all handmade and never 'released'. The box [not really an album cover], was built to look like an oversized diner or restaurant check of the era but it was in black and white. The entire box top looked like one of these restaurant checks complete with oversized staples we got from boxes found in dumpsters late one night.

The striking presentation was sent to various record companies—perhaps even personally delivered—but it was met with confusion, mockery, disinterest and ultimate rejection: nobody wanted to sign the band. Everyone—at least those who bothered to listen—thought the music was simply too unconventional to market commercially. This response surprised the band, as they were convinced that their album referenced iconic British groups like The Who, Pink Floyd and The Move while still maintaining a unique sound. Perhaps the Maels had not considered that these bands, while iconic to some Americans, did not resonate with the majority of music enthusiasts. They failed to recognise that not all their countrymen marched to the same beat.

Most were still mourning the slow demise of the hippie era, and those who had moved on found solace in the music of The Eagles, Steely Dan or The Allman Brothers. Aside from The Beatles and the Rolling Stones, not many Americans knew—or cared—about the 'British Scene'. The Maels' bewilderment at their failure to attract record companies became a recurring theme throughout their career. While fans adored them and some critics praised their work, the general population continued to echo the sentiments of those early record company executives: 'They're just too weird.'

Long before the poorly received album was distributed, Halfnelson were already planning for the future. They understood the importance of having a complete band for press photos, presentations and potential concerts. After all, it was only a matter of time before one of the recipients would respond enthusiastically to the album and officially release it!

During the recording sessions, the Maels came across an advertisement on a bulletin board at Ace Music in Santa Monica, posted by drummer Harley Feinstein. Ron, Russell, Earle and his wife, Elisa (née De Leon), went to visit Harley at his parents' house, during which they brought with them their instruments and a reel-to-reel player. They played some songs from the demo album for Harley and after that set up their gear and played together for a while. They performed some surf music, both Earle and Harley being into the genre.

As fate would have it, Harley's brother, Alan, had a good friend named Harold Zellman. This was the same Harold Zellman who had been part of The Urban Renewal Project a few years earlier and was therefore quite familiar to Ron and Russell. Harley had learned from Harold that he used to play in a band whose former members were now recording an actual album in a professional studio. It soon dawned on him that those ex-members were now in his parents' living room and that he might become their new drummer.

During conversations between jam sessions at that first meeting, Ron mentioned that they weren't entirely happy with the band's name Halfnelson. Harley suggested the name The Three Minute Earwash, a name he had heard from Harold and that Ron had come up with back in the days of the Urban Renewal Project. Ron recognised the name, of course, and thought it was hilarious that Harley came up with it. It helped secure his place in Halfnelson and he started visiting the studio to observe the album's completion. Earle's brother, Jim, also spent time there, though neither he nor Harley participated in the recordings.

Now a four-piece band, Halfnelson decided it was time to prepare for live concerts. They remained convinced that their album would soon be picked up by a record label, and they needed to be ready. They found a rehearsal space in North Hollywood at the Dog Bunk Bed Factory. Russell referred to it as the Doggy Factory and expressed his desire to stop playing bass guitar in order to focus entirely on vocals and move freely on stage. Thus, the search for a bass guitarist began.

After auditioning several candidates, Earle finally proposed that his younger brother, Jim, join the band. The reason he had not suggested this earlier was that Jim was actually a lead guitarist—and a much better one than Earle himself. Under the condition that Earle would continue to play guitar, he allowed his brother to join the band. Rehearsals now took on a more serious tone, with new songs being written in the meantime. Occasionally, Mike Berns managed to entice an A&R representative from a record company to attend a rehearsal, but this always resulted in disappointment. There was no interest in releasing the record. The band took this somewhat cynically, hanging all rejections from various record companies on a noticeboard in the rehearsal room as a form of misplaced pride.

Halfnelson decided to start performing live in public, with their first gig taking place at the Lindy Opera House on Wilshire Boulevard, followed by the Gregar on Beverly Boulevard, both in Los Angeles. They performed there for four consecutive nights, starting on 20 August 1970.

Additional sparse concerts included ones at the New Stoner Avenue Coffee House on 25 and 26 September, and they were booked as one of the opening acts for Alice Cooper, alongside Christopher Milk, on 20 November; however, they withdrew at the last minute. The group also performed at Palisades Charter High School, Ron and Russell's alma mater, which proved to be a great success, as well as at Bishop Amat Memorial High School in La Puente, where they were also well received.

One of the earliest local fans of *Halfnelson* was a girl named Diane Mallory-Jamieson. In a letter to the local university newspaper *UCLA Daily Bruin*, she wrote:

> It has come to our attention that, while you have been gracious enough to make note of Halfnelson's heretofore largely underground but tremendously enthusiastic Southland following, we are somewhat less than pleased to discover that, owing to what we can only assume to be some quaint personal prejudice on Mr. Mendelsohn's part, the Daily Bruin has seen fit to discount the group's splendid but hardly surprising showing in the Bruin Pop Poll. We urge to reconsider your hasty decision and recognize Halfnelson as the finest new English group since Traffic.

According to John Mendelsohn, she was also a hairstylist and occasionally worked her magic on some of the band members.

Meanwhile, Russell had a new girlfriend named Miss Christine (Christine Ann Frka, 1949–72), a member of the GTOs (Girls Together Outrageously). This group of young women frequented concerts and befriended numerous well-known and lesser-known artists, including Frank Zappa, Alice Cooper, Keith Moon, Jeff Beck and Mick Jagger. Amongst this group, Miss Pamela has gained the most recognition and has authored several books about this era. The GTOs also recorded a rather unconventional LP featuring musicians such as Frank Zappa, Jeff Beck and Rod Stewart. The album, produced by Frank Zappa, was titled *Permanent Damage* and was released in 1969.

Besides Russell, Miss Christine was also the girlfriend of Todd Rundgren, who had recently been hired as a producer and engineer for Bearsville Records, a relatively new record company founded by Albert Grossman. Miss Christine was particularly impressed by the Russell-penned song 'Roger', which appeared on the *Demo Album*. She introduced Todd to Halfnelson, and after he listened to the record, he was intrigued enough to travel to Hollywood with his friend and fellow engineer, Thaddeus James Lowe, to attend a presentation by Halfnelson. Sadly, James passed away peacefully of natural causes at the age of 82 on Thursday, 22 May 2025.

James was the singer and guitarist for the local band The Electric Prunes, who had a fairly big hit in 1966 with 'I Had Too Much To Dream (Last Night)'. Incidentally, James kept it to himself that he had been a part of the band.

The live presentation that the band gave to Todd, Miss Christine, James Lowe and his wife, Pamela, took place at The Doggy Factory and was not significantly different from previous presentations they had conducted during the sporadic visits of interested record company representatives. This was not merely a rehearsal; rather, it was a creative performance with a keen sense of presentation. The band successfully created the illusion of a real concert. They had a toy cash register where they sold so-called tickets, a recorded tape of applause and, in between songs, female friends of the band offered drinks, candies and popcorn to the bemused spectators.

Todd was impressed by the way Halfnelson presented themselves, the striking music and their unwavering belief in their own success. He convinced Albert Grossman to offer the band a contract, and Grossman agreed, trusting Todd's insights. However, there was one aspect the band had not considered: they did get a record deal, but not for the album they had recently recorded. Grossman wanted Halfnelson to create an entirely new LP, produced by Todd Rundgren with James Lowe as the engineer. He also insisted on a new manager for the band: Roy Silver, whose company, CMA Management, was managing Bill Cosby, Tiny Tim and the all-female band Fanny. Later in 1972, Halfnelson would write and record short, very amusing radio jingles for Fanny and another artist, Bobby Charles, who were also under contract with Bearsville, to promote their respective albums.

In May 1971, the recording of the album began at I.D. Sound Studios in Hollywood. Todd Rundgren stated that his intention was not to make excessive changes to the songs as presented by the band, but rather to focus on enhancing the quality and clarity of the music to make it more accessible to novice listeners.

The band members had expressed their desire to stay true to the original music, with no approval for Todd to transform their songs into slick ballads. In February 1971, Ron had already conceived an idea for the album cover. He wanted to use an old Oldsmobile advertisement from 1959 as the basis for the cover, featuring the members of the band, and received written approval for this.

There are rumours that a song written by Jim, 'I Am An Old Retired Man', was recorded for the album but ultimately not included. However, this has not been confirmed by official sources. Another potential contender for the album was a staple in their live performances, written by Russell, called 'Manchester Overcarry', inspired by a holiday in England. Russell had indeed been on holiday in England with Earle and his wife, Elisa, in December 1969 and January 1970. They visited his mother and stepfather, as well as a friend in France. Rogy and Miriam had sold the Gilded Prune in 1969 and moved to London, where Rogy had found a good job in a chain store that sold shoes and boots, mainly to American tourists.

Two songs from the Halfnelson demo album are featured on the official *Halfnelson* release: 'Roger' and 'Saccharin And The War', both written by Russell. The album was released exclusively in the United States in September 1971 but sold very few copies. Although the band continued to perform occasional concerts, this had no impact on the album's popularity or sales. Outside of Los Angeles, Halfnelson remained virtually unknown, and within the city, they were frowned upon. The long-anticipated breakthrough remained as distant as ever.

In the spring of 1972, the band members were summoned by Albert Grossman for a meeting at the Château Marmont Hotel, located at 8221 Sunset Boulevard in Los Angeles, to discuss their current situation. Grossman had concluded that the poor sales of their album were attributed to the band's name, which he deemed unappealing and overly unconventional. He requested that the group come up with a new name for the band.

Back at the Doggy Factory, Earle suggested naming the band The Poodies, but the idea was met with disapproval from the other members. The band members were fans of movies featuring W. C. Fields, and in the 1933 film *International House*, the term 'Chinese People' was used. Initially, this seemed like a fitting name for the band, but one member ultimately changed his mind, expressing doubts about its suitability.

When the band had yet to come up with a new name, they received a call from their manager, Roy Silver, requesting that they report to his impressive office in Beverly Hills. There, he informed them that he had devised an excellent name for the band: The Sparks Brothers, a nod to the immensely popular Marx Brothers.

The band thought that was a terrible name because they did not want to be portrayed as brothers, and The Sparks Brothers sounded like a country band. After much internal deliberation, they decided to use only the name Sparks. Silver agreed to the change, and it became the new name for the band.

The album was reissued under this new name in July 1972, when the cover design, once again by Ron Mael, had undergone a complete transformation. For the first time, a single was released. 'Wonder Girl', with '(No More) Mr. Nice Guys' on the B-side, was released in May of that year in the US and Canada, marking the band's first international release of their music.

The single unexpectedly gained popularity, receiving airplay from several unlikely radio stations far beyond California, and even reached number ninety-two on the Cashbox chart. It almost made it into The Billboard Hot 100, but it peaked at number 112 on the Bubbled Under chart. In the charts of *Record World*, it even reached number 89.

This success led to Sparks receiving an invitation to the popular music programme *American Bandstand*, presented by Dick Clark. On 29 July 1972, they made their television debut, performing both sides of the single. They got along very well with the host, Dick Clark appreciating the somewhat eccentric musicians.

Another television appearance followed when they were invited to the *Real Don Steele Show*, a weekly programme broadcast locally in Los Angeles and the surrounding area. An old acquaintance, Pamela Des Barres, was a regular go-go dancer on the show. Limited information is available regarding Sparks' performance; however, some black-and-white photographs serve as evidence of this event.

During the very occasional local concerts in Los Angeles, Russell was pulled across the stage by a roadie in a home-made boat, artfully converted from a pram, while singing and throwing confetti. This event took place during the song 'Slowboat'. This somewhat whimsical action did not exactly convey a dynamic and aggressive rock image, but it was perhaps understandable given the fact that nothing was logical or obvious with this peculiar band.

In June 1972, the group left California and performed for the first time in Houston, Texas, as the opening act for Cold Blood. They played at a newly opened venue, The Liberty Hall, for three consecutive nights, providing two performances each night, except for the last night. The band made the trip to Houston in several sedans, but the journey was plagued by heavy rains, thunderstorms and the breakdown of one of the cars. Despite all of the band's efforts and perseverance, they soon discovered that the venue did not necessarily accommodate the most obvious audience for their performance. Interestingly enough, they were announced in the local press as The Sparks Brothers, but the poster simply said Sparks.

Their misfortunes continued; on the first night, Russell threw his recently acquired sledgehammer into the air, only for it to land squarely on his head instead of being caught gracefully. This incident was one of the few moments the audience seemed to appreciate, mistakenly believing it was part of the act. Unfortunately, this was far from the case, and Russell was rushed to the local Saint Joseph Hospital to treat his serious injury. Ron was genuinely worried about his younger brother, although he was rather light-hearted about his concerns at the time in Edgar Wright's documentary.

Upon their return to Los Angeles, the recordings for their second official album commenced. This time, the producer was James Lowe, who had handled the engineering for the first album. Apparently, Todd Rundgren was occupied with producing another band and therefore unavailable. James also took on the engineering duties himself. Ron once again designed the album cover and Larry Dupont took the photographs.

Before starting the actual recording session for the second album, a test recording of 'Girl from Germany' was done at Wally Heider's studio in Hollywood. As the results were promising, the official recordings began a week later.

Grossman had given James Lowe some important instructions: the singer had to be heard clearly and distinctly. It was already difficult to understand his pronunciation in the songs, which in Grossman's opinion did not sound American. Given the sometimes fast-paced melodies, this factor had to be taken into account.

For the album sleeve, the band and Larry Dupont visited his workspace in the Ethnic Arts Department at UCLA. During one of the photo shoots, Harley jokingly pulled Ron's chair out from under him. When they saw the printed result, they knew they had found the perfect cover for their new album. However, the German version of the original release had the sleeve reversed and the blurry photo of Ron was moved to the back. The 1979 reissue had the cover arranged as originally intended.

At Russell's request, Larry spent a lot of time meticulously hand-painting a green and black chequered pattern on his suit into red and black, which was used for the back sleeve.

During the recording sessions, the band concluded that they should travel to England, as they believed their music and image would resonate much better there. They attempted to persuade their manager, Roy Silver, who ultimately agreed but now needed to convince the record company. The strategy Silver employed was straightforward yet effective.

He spoke to everyone at Bearsville Records as if it was already a foregone conclusion that the band would be going to England, and he asked them to arrange the trip. Meanwhile, Bearsville had been acquired by Warner Brothers, and Silver also led Moe Ostin, the head of that record company, to believe that it was a certainty that Sparks would be touring England. Remarkably, Bearsville agreed to this plan, and by the end of October 1972, the band indeed departed for London. Prior to that, from 5 to 9 October, a brief residency was scheduled for performances in New York, with Bob Gibson serving as the opening act for all these shows.

At Max's Kansas City, a nightclub and restaurant located at 213 Park Avenue South, the featured music primarily consisted of songs from their newly recorded second album, along with a new track titled 'I Like Girls', which appeared to resonate well with the audience. They also performed covers of 'Give It To Me', a single by the English band The Troggs, and 'My White Bicycle' by Tomorrow, another English group. Both songs were released as singles by their respective bands in 1967. Additionally, they frequently included a cover of 'Baby Come Back' by The Equals, a British group that achieved a number 1 hit with this song in England in 1968.

In the audience was Joseph Fleury, a devoted fan and one of the few who had purchased the original Halfnelson LP. The reception was significantly better than it was in Houston a few months earlier, largely due to a group of individuals who were part of the entourage residing at Andy Warhol's The Factory. They were always interested in any form of artistic expression that deviated from the prevailing norms, and Sparks certainly fell into that category. Others in attendance included Sylvain Sylvain of the New York Dolls and Sal Maida, a local bass player who would move to England the following year to play with Roxy Music and later with Sparks.

On Saturday afternoon, 7 October, between a series of performances at Max's Kansas City, Joseph was at the local record store, Discount Records, located on 8th West Street. To his astonishment, he unexpectedly encountered Ron and Russell, who were also browsing the store.

They eventually purchased the single 'Fire Brigade' by The Move. Joseph approached them to express how much he enjoyed their performance and the Halfnelson LP, and he quickly established a rapport with the brothers. Joseph and a friend were invited to join the band for dinner after their final gig at Max's Kansas City, where Roy Silver's assistant, Florence Gordon, was also present. In 1973, Jim Mankey would marry Flo Gordon. During this dinner, Joseph proposed the idea of establishing a fan club for the band, and they enthusiastically agreed. In December 1972, the first fanzine, *Sparks Flashes*, was published and distributed to some four-dozen fans.

In a five-page article in the American music magazine *Trouser Press*, published in November 1982, the Mael brothers discussed their first album with fan and journalist Ira Robbins:

Russell: 'The album was done at a studio on La Brea in Hollywood; it's now called Rusk Sound Studios. It's right across the street from the last remaining drive-in restaurant in Hollywood.'

Ron: '…and a motel for prostitutes. It took a long time because we weren't used to having to play on time and in tune. Todd's way of recording was totally different from Earle's way. Earle was a genius at doing home tapes. It's a different thing getting into the studio where somebody's trying to make what was thought to be a professional record. The object for us was to keep as much of that amateur quality as we could, but still have it be a record. We've tried to carry that through for 11 albums: keeping it a little slapdash so that it has some personality and doesn't sound like it's done in conference room. A lot of bands now seem to be rebelling against a certain kind of slickness; that's always been our aim. Todd was really easy to work with because he was of our age group, he was in a band—so there wasn't that barrier between the producer and band—and he screwed around a lot.'

Russell: 'He had a beautiful girlfriend—Miss Christina [sic] of the GTO's—and I screwed around a lot.'

Ron: 'I think the songs we did with Earle and the songs that are on the album sound fairly close. Todd likes a real trebly sound, and I'm not especially partial to that, but at that time just having a record was more than enough for us.'

Russell: 'Tod approached it in an amateurish way. Not that he wasn't professional, but he had fun and stuck drumsticks up his nose and stuff like that. We were the first band (outside the Nazz and Rundgren's solo work) he produced.'

Ron: 'Our first single "Wonder Girl", got into the American charts. We thought, this is easy! It took 11 albums before we had another single in the charts.'

Halfnelson—The Songs

All songs written by Ron Mael, unless otherwise stated.

'WONDER GIRL'
Duration: 2:15

The opening track of the debut album is a pleasant and open tune that makes great use of the stereo effects coupled with the double vocals. A striking bass line complements the minimalist guitar and occasionally takes the lead. The subtle piano contributions are modest but complete the track perfectly. It is not hard to see why this song was selected as the first single and even became a local hit in certain regions of the US after the album was released under the new band name. Compared to the demo album, this was a huge step towards a more accessible sound, although it still would have sounded quite strange to the average listener in 1971.

It made future Sparks bassist Sal Maida an instant fan when hearing it on the radio and was the reason that Sparks was invited to *American Bandstand*.

It is noteworthy that Russell does not explicitly pronounce the phrase 'Self-made men have daughters who just won't ball'. For reasons unknown, he distorts the word 'ball', perhaps out of a misplaced form of prudishness, although nothing is explicitly said. Russell had done this before in a song on the unreleased demo album, where he disguised the name of a local celebrity.

The song was released as a single not only in the US but also in Canada, the UK and the Netherlands, where it appeared in Sparks' very first picture sleeve.

'Wonder Girl' is one of the few songs appearing on the Bearsville albums which was also included in live concerts later on. During the first North American tour in the spring of 1975, this song was a permanent part of the live set, and it was also used during the 2022 world tour.

> Russell: 'This song [was] probably responsible for getting us signed to a record company. A number one in Montgomery, Alabama—God knows why!'
> Ron: 'Our first top 100 single in the U.S. Our last top 100 single in the U.S.'

'Fa La Fa Lee'
Duration: 2:54

Never too shy to address controversial topics, Ron wrote this mid-tempo song about an imaginary incestuous relationship between brother and sister. The cheerful tone of the song conceals the heavy train of thought, and the use of the keyboards, in which piano and organ alternate almost imperceptibly, makes it rather special. During the verses, the rhythm guitar runs parallel to the percussion, sounding like a magpie tapping on a tree.

There is little use of backing vocals, something that is one of the defining characteristics of Russell's interpretation of the songs. However, this does not make this song any less interesting.

The bass loop after the short pauses that appear twice in the song was greeted with loud cheers during the only time Sparks played the song live after the Bearsville stint, at the Sparks Spectacular in 2008.

> Ron: 'Incest at the roller-rink. Russell had a cold, so he did his voice on four tracks to compensate. It ended up sounding like four tracks of a person with a cold.'

Russell: 'She ain't heavy, she's a brother to me, one of my favourite lines, and I didn't even have anything to do with writing it. I sang the song with a cold in my nose.'

'Roger'
Written by Russell Mael
Duration: 2:30

This song is arguably the reason why Sparks, or Halfnelson at the time, was finally offered a record deal. It was the favourite song of Miss Christine, who was dating Russell at the time. She subsequently pointed out the recording to her friend Todd Rundgren, and this song in particular.

'Roger' is one of the two songs that also appeared on the Halfnelson demo album, and this version is not so very different from the one that was originally recorded. It is even suggested that the same backing tracks were used and only the vocals were rerecorded, but the two renditions differ just a bit too much to support that assumption.

The arrangements, too, are hardly different from the demo version, and the percussions seem to be played on other instruments than a regular drum kit. Also, there appears to be little or no use of the bass guitar. The somewhat manic guitar riffs that run through the song are sped-up recordings, similar to what was done earlier on the demo.

It does not happen very often with Sparks, and certainly not on the Bearsville albums, that a song is defined by a rhythm guitar and even starts with that. The chord progression is childishly simple and quite basic, and you can imagine Russell writing this on an acoustic guitar while jamming a bit.

It's quite difficult to figure out what exactly this song is about, and Russell himself has never explained it. It has never been part of their live set after the Bearsville period.

Ron: 'I don't understand this song, ask Russell.'
Russell: 'My first major composition of any stature.'

'High C'
Duration: 3:03

This song was in fact the first song they recorded for the album. The original version, as played live, was a lot heavier than what ended up on the record. For a rock band, if that's any qualification that applies to Sparks, the subject matter is quite unusual.

The relatively bombastic start of the song, which is joined by the subtle twinkles of Ron's piano, initially puts the listener on the wrong track. The break halfway through the song is unexpected and would prove to be an important ingredient for Ron's writing. The other paramount element of a typical Sparks song, the many layers in Russell's vocals, are fully present on this track. The guitar is mainly used to create short riffs or punches, while the bass alternately follows the melody line and weaves its own runs through the song. This song also makes subtle use of stereo effects, which clearly add value to the mix.

Like most tracks from the Bearsville releases, this track was not played after 1973.

> Ron: 'My favourite track off the first two albums. A simple tale of an opera singer. Not a bad form for a young songwriter.'
> Russell: 'One of the better received songs when performed live during that period. The waitresses at the Whisky A Go Go were particularly fond of this one.'

'FLETCHER HONORAMA'
Duration: 4:01

'Fletcher Honorama' embodies every aspect that made Sparks' music during the early years, including the unreleased demo album, so remarkable. This song combines mysticism with an intriguing melody wrapped in striking arrangements, complemented by Russell's clean and clear vocals, along with Ron's typical lyrics that leave listeners with many questions, even though the content of the text is still fairly obvious.

Earle's guitar riffs sound almost romantic, while Ron's organ subtly surfs in between. In the instrumental break, he transitions to the piano, beautifully emphasised by a wonderful stereo mix.

After 1973, 'Fletcher Honorama' was only played live once, during the Sparks Spectacular in 2008. This performance was special because it was the first time most people in the audience heard it live. Although it lacked the subtlety of the studio version, it was very well received at the Carling Academy in London.

> Ron: 'For some reason, this one took between eighteen and twenty takes to get. To answer those of you who think it's only a bunch of gibberish, let me say that besides the gibberish angle, we have here a tune about a celebration being thrown for an old man named Fletcher just before his death. His friends didn't want to wait until he died to get together.'
> Russell: 'The instrumental's really good.'

'Simple Ballet'
Duration: 3:50

Completely in line with its subject, this song opens with a serene, almost fairy-tale-like guitar, accompanied by a modest bass guitar and an emphatic presence of the piano. A second guitar sets the rhythm, drummer Harley mainly limiting his input to the cymbals.

Once again, a striking choice for a topic, but the song itself is a gem that falls into the same category within the album as the aforementioned 'Fletcher Honorama' and 'Slowboat'. With a hint of romance and light mysticism intertwined into an intriguing whole, it is instantly recognisable as Sparks, with a vocal delivery that you cannot imagine being sung by anyone else and still exuding the same magic.

There is a somewhat curious mix, the origin of which is unknown, but is probably a monitor mix, with nearly all instruments mixed to the back, with the exception of the guitars and Russell's backing vocals. This mix was never released as it is not suitable for that.

Unfortunately, this song was never played live again after 1973, with the exception of the Sparks Spectacular in 2008, where the subtle guitar was replaced by a distorted one, causing the song to lose some of its elegance.

> Russell: 'One of our first songs that almost sounded musical. Seven takes to get the best performance of me singing "Oh no" preceding the instrumental.'
> Ron: 'A Swiss miss.'

'Slowboat'
Duration: 3:50

Side two of the album opens with 'Slowboat'. Quietly, with a leading role for the twinkling piano, the intro leads to a pleasant melody that gradually gains a fuller sound.

The bass guitar has an appealingly smooth sound and is nicely mixed into the background, without losing its important contribution. The drums are emphatically present, determining the unchanging rhythm in this low-tempo number, while the rhythm guitar plays a minimal role, which suffices. However, the lead guitar is cleverly used during the break in the middle, where it introduces a fairy-tale-like sound, gently moving from left to right and vice versa throughout this section.

There is an actual guitar solo in the instrumental part that closes the song. During this part, Russell could have easily thrown handfuls of confetti as he was pulled across the stage by a roadie in a converted pram.

The song itself is a true tale of unattainable love, experienced by someone stubbornly clinging to their unruly target against their better judgement. 'Slowboat' has never been heard live after 1973 at regular concerts.

Despite the beautiful melody and subtle, open arrangements of the song, the simple chord structure consists of only three standard chords. This makes the song extremely suitable for beginner guitarists who want to try their hand at a Sparks song.

> Ron: 'This was written around the time of 'Bridge Over Troubled Water' and 'Let It Be'. The reason for this one not being accepted can only be attributed to a lack of backing by the record company.'
> Russell: 'Should have been a single at some point during its lifetime. Shouldn't it have?'

'Biology 2'
Written by Earle Mankey
Duration: 3:50

The Mael brothers were not the sole songwriters for the band. More importantly, they were not the only ones who, starting in 1968, shaped the sound and execution of the songs they recorded together with Earle. All three of them had a unique approach to writing and recording music, which is evident on 'Biology 2'.

Thematically, 'Biology 2' shares similarities with the song 'Tryouts For The Human Race', which the Maels would later record. Both songs explore the concept of human reproduction. However, 'Tryouts For The Human Race' is clearly more danceable, if that is preferred.

A notable aspect of 'Biology 2' is that Earle, not Russell, provides the lead vocals this time. This was likely at Earle's insistence, as he had no qualms about seeking attention on stage during concerts. The song opens by mentioning Lisa, who is Earle's wife, Elisa De Leon, a dental surgeon. The couple would later divorce.

The song features prominent guitar and bass, with minimal piano until the final minute, when percussion is subtly introduced. The conclusion of the song showcases Earle's incorporation of sound effects into his music. The end of the track shows how he has managed to integrate his passion for sound effects into his music.

'Biology 2' may not have been ideal for live performances, especially if Earle had to handle both guitar riffs and vocals. It is uncertain if it was included in the set list at all, at the time. However, it was performed during the Sparks Spectacular in 2008, with Russell handling the vocals, which was met with enthusiastic applause and loud cheers.

Russell: 'The first Sparks song I ever heard on the radio. How boring—I didn't even get to hear myself singing on the radio as Earle sang this one.'
Ron: 'Corpuscle capers. Sparked a dance craze that took the Married Students' Housing Block by storm.'

'Saccharin and the War'
Written by Russell Mael
Duration: 3:57

The second track from the Halfnelson demo album that was considered good enough to be included on the official debut album is another song by Russell, written at least two years earlier. The fact that this song made it onto the album may have something to do with Russell's desire to have some of his songs featured. Nonetheless, it fits perfectly within the overall sound of the album.

The arrangements of this final version differ somewhat from the original demo recording. The major difference is that the first version is a bit more laid-back, while the rendition on the official release sounds tighter and more professional. There is also a greater emphasis on the drums, which clearly set the tempo. Additionally, the song is about a minute-and-a-half longer, mainly due to an instrumental part added to the original.

The lyrics of the song are rather confusing. Russell claims that the song is about weight reduction and there are elements in the lyrics that support this, but many parts remain incomprehensible. The theme of the song is something that the Maels hold in high regard, as they are extremely conscious of their physical appearance to this day. This subject would later be revisited in the song 'Instant Weight Loss' on the album *Angst In My Pants*.

Ron: 'The main reason we never used a vibra-clap since 1972. I don't get this song, ask Russell.'
Russell: 'A weight reducing song. You should have heard the home demo we recorded in our living room. More character.'

'Big Bands'
Written by Russell Mael and Ron Mael
Duration: 4:15

This song originated from an early composition by Russell, who had written the basis several years previously for a school film project. It was then called 'Summer Days'. In all likelihood, Ron wrote the lyrics and provided some musical additions which eventually resulted in this song.

It is a touching first-person story about someone whose great passion is the music of big bands and who does not mind enduring some personal discomfort so long as his record collection continues to grow. Nevertheless, he occasionally muses on how it would be if he had more financial freedom, possibly through a relationship with a woman who would have more money at her disposal.

In the last part of the song, the melody line changes slightly to up-tempo, making it clear once again how much the narrator prefers to be in the warm ballrooms, rather than in his own cold house. Despite the self-inflicted poor circumstances, he can at least hold on to his collection.

The arrangements are built up from the typical conventional rock elements of guitar, drums and bass, with an important contribution from the keyboards. The sound of a cheerful piano opens the song but is overshadowed by the other instruments competing for attention. Just before the beautiful vocal line comes in, delivered with verve by Russell, the keyboards regain prominence and introduce the singing. During the verses, the guitar stays quiet, but it stands out in the interlude of the first part, which deviates strongly from the rest of the song.

Just before the two-minute mark, an extremely appealing instrumental section unfolds, transitioning into a change of tempo that serves as the introduction to the deviant second part of the song. It is noticeable that certain instruments are limited to one side of the sound spectrum, with keyboards exclusively on the left and some guitar riffs only on the right. Todd Rundgren and James Lowe deserve compliments for the way this song is mixed, which actually applies to the entire album.

Around the three-and-a-half minute mark there is another change in both the melody line and tempo, and the song concludes in style with beautiful falsetto backing vocals, accompanied by a basic drum rhythm. 'Big Bands' has not been played live since 1973 at regular concerts.

> Russell: 'The fast part stuck on the end is worth waiting for. Or just lift the needle and move it to that bit. And the breathy sigh in the instrumental is pretty good too.'
> Ron: 'A medley, or to be more blunt about it, a song composed of about six parts spliced together, that we couldn't play straight through from the start to end. A typical "set-up-that-final-rave-up-song" song.'

'(No More) Mr. Nice Guys'
Written by Jim Mankey and Ron Mael
Duration: 5:45

The closing number is special because it is the only song on the album for which Jim Mankey has a writing credit. This would also be the case on the next album, where he once again composes a song with Ron.

It is a track that most closely resembles a conventional rock song and likely originated from the riff Jim came up with. It is easy to hear why Earle had reservations about letting his brother join the band, as the riffs and solos that Jim plays probably could not have been done by Earle himself. That is why Jim plays the lead guitar on this song and also provides the bass lines.

A song with almost the same title was recorded by Alice Cooper, but it is a completely different song. However, it may have been inspired by this title as Cooper was well aware of Halfnelson/Sparks and later approached them requesting permission to use a lyric fragment from a different song.

The song is about how nice guys always seem to get the short end of the stick. The subject of the song neglects himself for the benefit of others, while adhering to conservative values and norms that he considers important. In the end, he will be fine and have a nice family, but his wife abuses his benevolence and does not take the wedding vows seriously.

The song appeared in an edited version as the B-side of their first single, 'Wonder Girl', and was mimed during their appearance on *American Bandstand*.

The instrumental section halfway through the song lasts almost a full minute and is dominated by an iconic guitar solo by Jim Mankey, which is experienced by earlier Sparks fans in the same way as Thom Rotella's guitar solo in *Introducing Sparks'* 'Goofing Off'.

It was an important part of the live set and both Jim and Earle played guitar, so there was no bass guitar during the live version. During the Sparks Spectacular in 2008, this song was played for the first time since 1973, and it was also the last time to date. The solo was performed with great enthusiasm and skill by Jim Wilson but was considerably shorter than the studio version.

Ron: 'That final rave-up song. Pre-Alice, of course. Edited and speeded up version used as the "B" side of original "Wonder Girl" single.'
Russell: 'Well, at least somebody discovered this song and made a buck or two out of it.'

2
A Woofer in Tweeter's Clothing

Release date: 26 January 1973
Produced by: Thaddeus James Lowe
Engineer: Thaddeus James Lowe
Sleeve design: Ron Mael
Photography: Larry Dupont
Recorded at: ID Studios, Hollywood
Duration: 39:56
Personnel: Ron Mael: Keyboards
Russell Mael: Vocals
Earle Mankey: Guitar
Jim Mankey: Bass guitar, guitar
Harley Feinstein: Drums

Side 1
'Girl From Germany'
'Beaver O'Lindy'
'Nothing Is Sacred'
'Here Comes Bob'
'Moon Over Kentucky'
'Whippings And Apologies'

Side 2
'Do-Re-Mi'
'Angus Desire'
'Underground'
'The Louvre'
'Batteries Not Included'

Singles from this album:
'Girl From Germany'/'Beaver O'Lindy'

Manager Roy Silver's persistent efforts finally paid off when a top executive agreed to a budget of $10,000 for the band to visit England. However, Warner Brothers failed to inform their British branch of this relatively small amount. Silver reached out to Derek Taylor, a personal friend of the family, who had previously worked as the press man for The Beatles and now served as Bearsville's UK press director, to handle the situation.

Upon their arrival in London, the group was greeted at Heathrow Airport by the Maels' mother and stepfather, Miriam and Rogy, who had moved to London a couple of years earlier. The band was initially accommodated at the Constantine Hotel in South Kensington for the first month, and then moved to the Snows Hotel on Cromwell Road for the remainder of their stay.

Before their arrival, Taylor had enlisted John Hewlett, the former bass player of John's Children, to assist them during their time in England.

However, the band was disappointed to discover that there was no official tour arranged by Warner Brothers' UK affiliate, WEA Records. While there were some sporadic performances during the first weeks, gigs were only scheduled on weekends. Their first concert in the British Isles took place at The Pheasantry on King's Road in Chelsea.

Their first concert outside the US had not been booked for London, but as the opening act for Slade at the Forest National in Brussels on 22 October. However, for unknown reasons, they did not perform and were replaced by the band Fumble. Despite this, they were still mentioned on the announcement poster.

Hewlett had started to focus on management, and the band he was currently working with was Jook. Drummer Chris Townson had also been a member of John's Children and had even briefly replaced The Who's drummer, Keith Moon, during a gig in Germany in the late Sixties. The other members of Jook were Ian Kimmet, Trevor White and Ian Hampton. Whenever they had time, the group members would attend a Sparks gig in London, and both bands got along quite well.

John Hewlett's enthusiasm and the band's signing to WEA generated interest from mainland Europe. On 9 November, the band left for Zurich to record the music programme *Hits à Go Go*, where they lip-synced 'Wonder Girl' and 'Do-Re-Mi'. The show, hosted by Dutchman Eddie Becker, was also broadcast in Germany. This footage is the only surviving record of the band in this line-up.

On 10 November, they flew from Zurich to Amsterdam, experiencing the excitement of their first international tour, albeit on a small scale. The Netherlands greeted them with heavy rain showers. They were welcomed at Schiphol Airport by journalist Constant Meijers and photographer Jarti Notohadinegoro, with whom they spent the rest of the day.

A meticulous and comprehensive report of the visit was featured in the monthly magazine *Aloha*, which later evolved into the well-known pop magazine *Oor*. What follows is a summary of the report.

Unlike Switzerland, a performance had been arranged in the Netherlands at the small club Tiffany in Scheveningen, a seaside town which was part of The Hague.

Before the performance, the band had an exhausting day ahead of them, organised by WEA's Dutch affiliate, Negram, who also released the single 'Wonder Girl' with a rush release on the same day. It was the first single by Sparks to appear in an actual photo sleeve.

First, the band gave an interview at Radio Veronica, where they laughed uncontrollably, and Ron commented that 'Beethoven would have made a terrible lead guitarist'. Leaving the DJ confused, the band continued to Naarden to conduct another interview with Radio Noordzee.

During the ride, the band members amusingly discussed their experience at the *Hits à Go Go* studio in Zurich, where they were approached by a group of girls who requested autographs. Upon arriving in Naarden, they found DJ Alfred Lagarde, who was just setting up his three-master. The band was happy to lend him a hand, and after the interview, a Christmas jingle made on the spot was broadcast.

A session in Hilversum, at the music television programme *Toppop*, was then recorded for the new single. Unfortunately, it was never broadcast. The final stop on their local promotion tour was at Radio Hilversum 3, where they were interviewed by DJ Felix Meurders. Meanwhile, several local newspapers published an article about the band on the same day.

Before freshening up at the hotel, they quickly checked the venue for the evening's concert. It turned out to be much smaller than expected, with room for a maximum of 400 spectators. Somewhat disappointed, they quickly searched for a restaurant before preparing for the performance. The tourist town was deserted in the winter months, but they eventually found a restaurant that was open, called Cosy Corner. Initially, they were refused entry due to their long hair and unconventional clothing, but they were eventually served.

Upon arrival at Tiffany, it turned out that the support band had not shown up. Ron suggested that they play the set twice, but in a different order, and that's exactly what happened.

The next morning, the *Aloha* journalists picked them up from the hotel. Ron requested a short sightseeing tour of Amsterdam. Constant Meijers directed them to the Concert Hall, where, in his opinion, they should have performed. Interestingly, the Maels would indeed give a sold-out performance there two years later with the British line-up of the band.

Back in London, the band continued to perform concerts. They opened for The Kinks in Bournemouth and supported Electric Light Orchestra in Norwich. Meanwhile, John Hewlett had not been idle, arranging a television appearance on *The Old Grey Whistle Test*, a music programme hosted by 'Whispering' Bob Harris. Surprisingly, they played 'Girl From Germany' and '(No More) Mr. Nice Guys', but the presenter was anything but complimentary about the music and image of the band. Back in the hotel lobby, the band arrived just in time to catch their performance on television while listening to the rants of another hotel guest who was not impressed by the band's performance, unaware that he was actually in their presence.

Despite Harris' negative comments, the band was offered four gigs at London's Marquee Club, every Thursday, starting from 4 December. The band performed two sets per night: one at 7:15 p.m. and another at 11:00 p.m.

The band's television performance generated a lot of interest, evident by the queue outside the venue. It was the first time this had happened, a promising sign for the band's future. The first two performances went well, and the band was looking forward to the next one.

However, before their third performance, Russell met a girl from Switzerland who suggested they go to Zermatt. Zermatt is known for skiing and winter sports, and the girl's father owned a hotel and club (Hotel Post), where she claimed they could perform. The band and crew indeed left for Zermatt, but during the first sound check, the club owner burst in and informed them that their music was too loud and unsuitable for his club. As a result, there was no performance, but they did get to enjoy a fair amount of skiing. This caused them to miss the third performance at the Marquee Club, scheduled for 21 December.

There have been discussions about Queen being the opening act at one of the Marquee shows, and they were indeed listed as a support act for the concert on 21 December. However, this would have happened while they were in Zermatt, so it is unclear whether this actually took place. It is not inconceivable that Queen also opened for one of the previous performances at the Marquee, but those announcements only mentioned 'plus guests'. Queen was specifically mentioned as a support act of Sparks in the 21 December announcement.

It seems more likely that Queen made their debut at the Marquee Club the night before, on 20 December. Several sources indicate that they were the headliner, with the opening act being a band called Fantasy. Still, it is conceivable that the bands met in or around the Marquee Club.

The fourth and final performance at the Marquee never took place. WEA found out that Bearsville had only approved a limited budget for their stay in England, which had been generously exceeded. Additionally, the fact that the band went to Zermatt instead of playing their show at the Marquee did not sit well with the record company, especially as their popularity was growing.

Sparks were rushed back to the United States, arriving in New York on 6 January 1973, before flying to the Bearsville studios in Woodstock to record the live favourite 'I Like Girls', planned to be the next single. The producer of the song was Nick Jameson, who would later play bass guitar in Foghat. However, both the band and the record company were unsatisfied with the result, and the single was never released. This recording eventually surfaced on a 1991 compilation CD called *Profile—The Ultimate Sparks Collection* on Rhino Records and was the very last recording made by the original American band.

Back in Los Angeles, the band was uncertain about their next steps. The local interest paled in comparison with that of the British audiences, and the sales of *A Woofer in Tweeter's Clothing* were not much better than those of the previous album. It was considered to release 'Do-Re-Mi' as a single in the US and 'Girl From Germany' in Europe, but ultimately, Bearsville was not convinced.

The band performed at the Whisky A Go-Go on 29 and 30 January, with Stepson as the supporting act. They were billed as 'From London', which was factually not incorrect, but this attempt to attract more concertgoers did not have the desired effect.

There were a few more performances from 14 to 19 February at the same venue, supporting Little Feat. When a planned tour with Todd Rundgren for April was cancelled, the group realised that they had reached a dead end. Both Bearsville and manager Roy Silver were unsure what to do next; ultimately, nothing was done.

With no reason to rehearse or try out new songs, the other three members began pursuing their own projects, while Ron and Russell considered a return to Britain, where they had received much more appreciation than in their home country.

Russell called drummer Harley Feinstein to ask if he would be interested in returning to England with the band. After some initial hesitations, mainly due to concerns about who would cover the trip and local expenses, Feinstein decided he was willing to take the leap.

Meanwhile, the Maels had contacted John Hewlett in England to inquire about him managing their affairs in London and securing a record deal. Hewlett believed Island Records would be the best fit for Sparks and reached out to Muff Winwood, the head of A&R and brother of musician and songwriter Steve Winwood, with whom he had performed in the Spencer Davis Group. Winwood was intrigued after hearing the two Bearsville albums. Island Records founder Chris Blackwell was often away, searching for Jamaican bands to sign, so David Betteridge was running the label in his absence.

John and Muff convinced Betteridge of Sparks' potential, but he was only interested in the Mael brothers as the band's composers, voice and image. Island agreed to cover the airfare to come to the UK and see what opportunities awaited. Sparks were able to be released from their contracts with Bearsville and Roy Silver without issue. In June 1973, Ron and Russell flew to Heathrow, where they were greeted by John Hewlett.

The following interview covering events at this time appeared in *Trouser Press*, the US music magazine, in November 1982:

Russell: '[Producer] Jim Lowe was Todd's engineer. Todd had some other commitments, and they wanted to keep us within the Bearsville family. Jim Lowe wanted to continue working with us, so he did it on his own. At least we knew the sound quality—if there was sound quality to the first album—would be as good. If anyone wants to know, Jim Lowe was the lead singer in the Electric Prunes. He has since dropped out of sight completely.'

Ron: 'This album includes our only non-original other than "I Want To Hold Your Hand", but that came much later. Once in a blue moon we would—

excuse the expression—"jam" to "Do Re Mi" in rehearsal hall. We were still a democratic band as far as song writing went.'

Russell: 'But we got over that.'

Ron: 'Yeah, we wised up fast. The only person who wasn't writing was Harley; he probably felt intimidated. There was always the question of whose songs were better. Russell wrote the music to "Girl From Germany"; I think it's the last song he ever wrote.'

Russell: 'I figured I should end my career on a high note.'

Ron: 'A lot of people misconstrued the sentiments in those lyrics; they don't read beyond "Germany". It isn't like there are a million yocks in that song. I don't like parodies because they're too easy. I'll sound like a hick, but "Whippings and Apologies" wasn't an S&M song. It was done in a naïve way – about parental restrictions on a girl and how it affects somebody else. When we played Max's Kansas City in New York and I found out what the song really meant, I was surprised.'

Russell: 'Everybody came with their rubber suits on.'

Ron: 'A real-life equivalent to the lyrics of "Here Comes Bob" happened recently in LA. A man was arrested for being a freeway bumper: bashing into the rears of women's cars, then getting out and raping them.'

Russell: 'Bashing into other cars in order to meet girls is a real LA idea. Everybody's got a car in LA and you tend to be real isolated, never meet anybody. It's not like New York, where you can bump into somebody on the street.'

Ron: 'That song's arrangement for string quartet was by a guy who toured with the Temptations.'

A Woofer in Tweeter's Clothing—The Songs

All songs written by Ron Mael, unless otherwise stated.

'Girl From Germany'
Written by Russell Mael and Ron Mael
Duration: 3:26

Of all the songs on this album, 'Girl From Germany' is probably the most accessible. It has a traditional structure of verses and choruses along with a beautiful middle eight where the chords remain the same, but the arrangements and tempo are altered. The chords, which are quite basic, were written by Russell. The double rhythm guitars, split over two channels, create a nice stereo effect, something that producer and engineer James Lowe also emphasised on the previous album.

The song's subject matter reflects Ron Mael's wry sense of humour; it tells the story of a boy who wants to introduce his new girlfriend to his Jewish parents but faces resistance because she is from Germany, which is hard for them to accept.

'Girl From Germany' was considered to be the follow-up single to 'Wonder Girl', but it never materialised. A test pressing was made on an acetate, where you can hear Russell counting to four before the song starts, a detail that was omitted on the album.

After the sudden success of 'This Town Ain't Big Enough For Both Of Us' in Europe, the single was eventually released by Bearsville/Warner Brothers on 28 June 1974, with the hope of capitalising on its popularity. The same occurred in France and Germany, where the single was presented in an attractive photo sleeve. In Belgium, the imported British single was housed in a cheap sleeve, and even in New Zealand, Warner Brothers had enough confidence to release the song as a single. However, it did not chart in any of the mentioned countries.

This probably had more to do with the fact that the public was barely aware of the existence of this single. Bearsville limited its promotion to a one-time tiny advertisement in a few music magazines, and radio stations hardly paid any attention to it. In France and Germany, promotion was virtually non-existent.

During live performances, 'Girl From Germany' was a regular part of the concerts in 1974 and 1975, both in Europe and North America. However, on the second tour in 1975, it was no longer included in the set list, being replaced by songs from the recently released album *Indiscreet*.

On 27 November 1999, at Shepherd's Bush Empire in London, the audience was pleasantly surprised by a short live version of the song, featuring only Ron's keyboards and the simple accompaniment of Tammy Glover on drums. This recording can be found on Sparks' first official DVD, *Live in London*. Following that, the song was only played once during the Sparks Spectacular in 2008.

Russell: 'The best of the more conventional song type songs. Lyrically the best of the more lyric type lyric songs. I wrote the music, Ron the lyrics.'
Ron: 'I like this one a lot. It was our favourite pick for a follow-up single to "Wonder Girl". In order to avoid the risk of a failure, no follow-up was released, thereby relieving us of a lot of anxious moments. Whew!'
Russell: 'You might be interested to know that we've recorded one song that's already been banned in Germany. It's called "The Girl from Germany". I guess they think it's an anti-German song.'
Ron: 'It's also been banned because it's a pro-German song.'

'BEAVER O'LINDY'
Written by Ron Mael, Russell Mael, Earle Mankey, Jim Mankey and Harley Feinstein
Duration: 3:44

The only song from the Bearsville albums credited to the entire band. It is unclear what the contributions of the other band members were, but it could be that they composed the chorus together. In that part, you can probably admire all band members' vocal efforts.

The song starts off with a calm and somewhat drab, yet appealing, waltz-like intro, with only Russell's vocals accompanied by two different organ sounds. This initial calmness can mislead the listener, as after a minute, all hell breaks loose with a pounding snare drum leading to the chorus sung by the entire band accompanied by loud guitars and bass.

During the recordings, an accordion was required, and James remembered his former bandmate's brother, 14-year-old Kip Tulin, who was an accomplished player. He was brought in and did the job.

According to Joseph Fleury, the song caught the attention of Alice Cooper. In *Goldmine* magazine, Joseph said this about it:

> Alice Cooper rang up to ask if he could borrow the 'girl in your/boy in your bed' lyric. We said no, so he pinched 'Nice Guy' instead.

The lyrics' meaning has been interpreted in various ways over the years, as is often the case. The most common interpretation is that it is about a young teenager and his masturbation sessions, inspired by a photo of a pin-up. Some parts of the text do indeed align with that idea. However, Ron provides a completely different description that is less recognisable in the lyrics.

Nevertheless, there wasn't enough controversy to prevent it from being released as the single's B-side.

Up until recently, the song had only been performed once after 1974, at the Sparks Spectacular in 2008. However, during the 2023 tour, it suddenly became a fixed part of the live set.

> Ron: 'A tune about a mythical rock singer named "Beaver O'Lindy". So fragmented that it holds together.'
> Russell: 'I wrote the music to the choruses (the B-E-A-V-E-R etc. part). Ron wrote all the other bits. We didn't know what we were doing with this one.'

'Nothing Is Sacred'
Duration: 5:11

The longest track on the album is about humanity achieving immortality with the help of medical and scientific advances. Similar to the previous song, the build-up is calm and minimalistic, with Russell accompanied only by a slow soothing drum rhythm.

As the guitar and bass join in, the latter sets the baseline for the song with an infectious melody that complements the vocal line. In the first part of the song, Ron's piano plays a modest role, but right before the instrumental section, there is a magical moment where only the two brothers introduce this part. After that, the piano becomes a more emphatic part of the arrangements. Russell's vocals, with their high pitches, are typical of his singing style, and he doesn't use any backing vocals this time.

The arrangements are open and there is minimal use of double layers, making it easy to define each instrument. Just like in the previous song, the vocal qualities of several band members are briefly showcased here.

Unfortunately, this gem has not been played live since 1973 during regular concerts.

> Ron: 'We were recording this song. As we got near the end, we all simultaneously forgot to stop and double-time ensued. Caramba!'
> Russell: 'A lot of people hate the singing in this song.'

'Here Comes Bob'
Written by Ron Mael and Russell Mael
Duration: 2:09

A rather light-hearted and frivolous song dominated by instruments not played by the band itself, 'Here Comes Bob' tells the tale of a man with a peculiar approach to interacting with the opposite sex. He chooses the least subtle route, hitting them with his car in hopes of starting a relationship with the unfortunate driver.

When it was decided to use a string quartet, four expensive middle-aged session musicians were brought in to record an arrangement by George Vogel, an associate of James Lowe. Earle, Jim and Harley were not required for this recording.

This song has rarely been performed live. Of course, it was included in the Sparks Spectacular in 2008, and made an unexpected appearance in March 2003 during a concert at the Royal Festival Hall as well as at two concerts in Stockholm a few days later. The live version was just over a minute long, with Russell accompanied only by Ron's piano and without any string arrangements.

> Russell: 'First use of outside instruments on a Sparks song. It still doesn't sound like a real song.'
> Ron: 'Our only excursion into the land of supplemental instruments on the first two albums. The tale of the best way to meet people in Los Angeles, that is, smash your fender into their fender, "Dents? I'd love to."'

'MOON OVER KENTUCKY'
Written by Jim Mankey and Ron Mael
Duration: 4:08

The song's serene yet somewhat ominous intro is a hopeful prelude to things to come. This is another collaboration between Ron and Jim, but it's difficult to indicate exactly how the roles were divided.

The song opens with a beautiful combination of Russell's unmistakable falsetto screams, Ron's fairy-tale-like piano and Jim's bass guitar. The staccato-like guitar that follows sets the rhythm, leading into the entrance of the drums and a shift in the guitar's sound to a distorted format. The staccato rhythm is then accompanied by similar piano strokes. The guitar subsequently transitions into an individual melody line, delicately dancing between the arrangements. The arrangements in the second verse mirror those of the first.

The middle eight is centred around Russell's yodel-like screams; pure, clear and perfectly integrated into the composition of the song. This section is reintroduced after the next verse and repeated, supplemented by the riffs of a biting guitar. Just when it seems like the song is heading towards a fade-out ending, Ron's soft but unmistakable organ joins in. Following a brief moment of only the organ and Russell's vocals, Ron takes over solo and concludes the song with a dignified chord progression, which wouldn't have been out of place in a mediaeval church.

The captivating vocals are both beautiful and eerie. It makes you wonder how many other artists can combine so many emotions and atmospheres in such a compelling way in a song that's just over four minutes long.

Opinions differ regarding the meaning of this song, but it seems to be about an adolescent who is ready to start a life of his own and wants to break free from his dominant mother, despite the uncertainty of what lies ahead.

This closing track on side one was not played live after 1973. However, it was covered live by Morrissey four times in concert between 2009 and 2016, three of which were performed in London.

> Ron: 'I wrote the intro theme after seeing *Death in Venice* the previous day, which proves nothing at all.'
> Russell: 'The echo on the voice of this one more than compensates for the shallow lyrical content.'

'DO-RE-MI'
Written by Oscar Hammerstein II and Richard Rodgers
Duration: 3:38

Ron and Russell's fascination with the film *The Sound of Music* was evident not only in certain lyrical fragments, but also in complete songs that could have seamlessly fitted into the film. This particular song, the first cover they recorded and released, may seem like an unexpected choice for a band who claim to have been inspired by The Who, The Move and The Kinks.

The song fades-in with a piano and bass guitar interplay, accompanied by Russell's vocals, which are sung in falsetto. The drums provides a subtle rhythmic backdrop until they become more prominent. Throughout the song, the bass guitar remains the main accompanying instrument, while the guitar is barely audible until later when distortion is added. A second vocal line joins Russell's falsetto, and as the song progresses, the instruments become more pronounced, giving it a rock song structure. The drums shine in this section.

A lengthy instrumental portion allows the piano to stand out before the song concludes with a glockenspiel fade out.

Despite this, there was serious consideration given to releasing this song as a single. During a television appearance in Zurich, Switzerland, they mimed to this song along with 'Wonder Girl'. If they had decided to release it as a single, the intention was to rerecord it and give it a slightly harder edge. However, this plan never came to fruition.

Throughout the Bearsville period, the song was a regular part of their live set and was well-received by audiences for its familiarity. Even during their first concert in London in 1994, after nineteen years, this track was included in the set and transitioned into the song 'Angst In My Pants'. This transition can be heard, for example, on the official release of the DVD *Live In London*, recorded on 27 November 1999. Nearly ten years later, at the Sparks Spectacular, the song was played in its original arrangement and instrumentation, though only once.

> Ron: 'This developed from one of our infrequent jam sessions. A crowd pleaser, but hard on the pocket book since it was written by a couple of other guys.'
> Russell: 'While everyone was tuning up, I started making like Julie Andrews. The best live tune because the song resembled something that everyone had heard. Scary when the beat got off in the middle.'

'ANGUS DESIRE'
Written by Ron Mael and Russell Mael
Duration: 3:25

A beautiful ballad with typical Sparks characteristics, calm in construction and again with minimalist accompaniment of organ and bass guitar, with a modest role for the guitar and drums. A subtle second vocal line emphasises the stereo effect and adds to the somewhat mystical atmosphere of the song.

The song begins with Russell's serene vocals, accompanied by a simple bass guitar, that may actually be coming from the keyboards, due to a certain vibration in the notes. Then, a recognisable organ joins in, complemented by minimal but extremely effective guitar runs. There is also a faint use of an acoustic guitar in the background.

The following section is a bit busier, especially with the addition of a loud snare drum, indicating a fairly basic rhythm. The organ has taken on a more prominent role, and the bass guitar is clearly distinguishable in the mix this time.

Around the two-minute mark, the instruments fade out, leaving only Russell's vocals accompanied by an acoustic guitar. Shortly after, Ron's piano joins in.

The ensuing piece, lasting only about eight seconds, captures the quintessential sound of Sparks in an unparalleled way. It features multiple vocal layers and an organ subtly woven between the notes.

Intense debate has surrounded the meaning of this number. On the official Sparks website forums, one interpretation suggested it referred to bestiality involving a cow, with a striking 48 per cent of participants expressing agreement. However, a more plausible explanation is that it refers to drawing nude models in an art class, as Russell once noted. Since the Bearsville period, this song has not been played live at regular concerts.

> Russell: 'One of the best titles in the history of Western music. Sounded awful on the basic track—especially that break thingy near the end. We've never sounded good on basic tracks.'
> Ron: 'Title inspired by Dean Detrick Jr. Blame him, not us.'

'UNDERGROUND'
Written by Earle Mankey
Duration: 2:59

Another contribution from Earle Mankey, just like on the first album. The song is much more musically accessible than 'Biology 2', but the lyrics lean towards a desire for adventure, mysticism and romance. The arrangements are quite traditional, featuring a nice fade-in and a prominent bass line. Noteworthy is the use of castanets and the piano, which moves from left to right and back again.

The song begins with a fade-in of bass, guitar and drums, with Russell joining in with double vocals. The structure is led by the bass guitar, while the electric guitar plays regular riffs that dance around the melody line. Only after the first verse does the organ join, transitioning later into cheerful, fast piano runs that frame the entire piece.

Two minutes into the song, a beautiful vocal line, supported by additional vocals, elevates the song to a higher level. Strange-sounding riffs play alongside the other instruments. The song concludes with a repetition of the first part, including the fade-in and delightful double vocals.

Ron: 'Mankey-mania hits side two!!'
Russell: 'Earle's first smash since "Biology 2". I think I prefer songs about microscopic organisms.'

'THE LOUVRE'
Duration: 5:04

A combination of harpsichord and organ, supplemented by a bass guitar, opens this song, showcasing unmistakable European influences. One can imagine that this would have been well-received at a Louis XVI matinee at Versailles.

This leads to Russell's serene singing in French. Modest and almost intimate guitar flourishes complete the special atmosphere, followed by a transition into the underlining of the five chords, presented by the guitar with an almost industrial sound. The song is constructed using more chords than are typically employed.

The second verse has the same arrangement as the first, but after a small change in the chord scheme, the drums unexpectedly come in hard, changing the tone of the song. The third verse is almost identical to the first two, except for a subtle variation in the spooky guitar riffs. An instrumental interlude, in which Russell eventually interjects with limited 'la la la, la la las', adds a typical French chanson-like vibe to the song.

This forms the final section, where the verse is sung in English and the arrangements are much firmer. The drums play an important role and frame the other instruments perfectly with short rolls. It ends with a longer roll and the final combination of the C-F final chords.

This is the first Sparks song sung partially in French, and Russell performs it well. Later, an intensive course at the Berlitz School of Languages would ensure that his knowledge of French improved significantly. The original lyrics, written entirely in English, were translated by Josée Becker, likely a fellow student or friend of the Mael brothers.

As the title suggests, the song is about the Louvre Museum in Paris. However, it is narrated by one of the marble statues, who is frustrated by his lack of choice, as he must always remain within the museum walls.

Like many songs on Sparks' first two official LPs, this song is characterised by an almost indefinable sense of mystery and a fairy-tale-like atmosphere. This mood is maintained until the lyrics switch to English, and the musical arrangement shifts toward a more traditional rock style. The song was not performed live at regular concerts after 1973.

Ron: 'Russell recorded the vocals on this totally in French, then totally in English. After countless debates, that threatened to delay the release of the Woofer LP several decades, all centering around which language worked best, a compromise was reached. All's well that ends well.'

Russell: 'If you can't make out the French it ain't your fault cause I didn't know any French when I sang it either.'

'Batteries Not Included'
Duration: 0:47

Even with a playing time of less than a minute, Ron Mael is perfectly capable of basing a song on an everyday occurrence and in doing so, creating a smile for its listeners.

Consisting solely of Ron's piano and Russell's voice, enhanced by multiple vocal layers at the end, the track almost feels like the intro to the last track of the album, even though they are completely unrelated in construction and lyrical content.

Ron: 'A typical "set-up-that-final-rave-up-song". Only shorter.'
Russell: 'Really proud of this one.'

'Whippings And Apologies'
Duration: 5:05

The loudest and perhaps most compelling song concludes this album. Despite Ron's claim that no bass was used, the first notes do seem to come from a bass guitar. The lead guitar that joins in resembles a violin. With the addition of drums and rhythm guitar, the whole thing becomes an organised chaos, only held together by the somewhat hysterical vocals.

Despite the length of the song, the lyrics are quite limited and leave some room for different interpretations, which undoubtedly have happened. The brothers themselves claim that it is about disciplinary means in an average family situation, and nothing seems to contradict this.

It was a song that was not always appreciated by the public, but at the time it was performed after the Bearsville period, it was received with extraordinary enthusiasm by the audience in London in 2008. Surprisingly, it suddenly appeared during the 2025 tour. With two guitars and a bass, it was probably the loudest song in the set and was received with great recognition.

Russell: 'Always misconstrued to be about some perverse going on, when in fact it was about spankings at home. Maybe that's why we were well received at Max's Kansas City in New York.'
Ron: 'Recorded loud and without bass. The bottom, if one exists, is the left hand of the keyboards. Two chords always make the best chord progressions.'

Note: On the CD versions of this album, the last three songs are slightly speeded up. This happened when the initial CD releases combined the first two LPs on one disc. Without the acceleration, they would not fit on one CD. Those who are used to the LP versions may find this change quite jarring and may prefer to obtain a digital version directly from the original vinyl album.

3

Kimono My House

Release date: 1 May 1974
Produced by: Muff Winwood
Engineer: Richard Digby-Smith, Tony Platt
Sleeve design: Nicholas De Ville
Photography: Karl Stoecker
Recorded at: Island Basing Street, London; Ramport Studios, London
Duration: 36:19
Personnel: Ron Mael: Keyboards
Russell Mael: Vocals
Adrian Fisher: Guitar
Martin Gordon: Bass guitar
Norman Diamond: Drums

Side 1
'This Town Ain't Big Enough For Both Of Us'
'Amateur Hour'
'Falling In Love With Myself Again'
'Here In Heaven'
'Thank God It's Not Christmas'

Side 2
'Hasta Mañana, Monsieur'
'Talent Is An Asset'
'Complaints'
'In My Family'
'Equator'

Singles from this album:
'This Town Ain't Big Enough For Both Of Us'/'Barbecutie'
'Amateur Hour'/'Lost And Found'
'Talent Is An Asset'/'Lost And Found'

On 8 June 1973, Ron and Russell Mael arrived at Heathrow Airport and settled in Purley, south London, at the apartment of new manager John Hewlett. They were excited and hopeful about securing a record deal with Island Records.

However, there was one small issue: they had no new songs! Even though titles of a few new tracks had been mentioned at the Whisky earlier that year, the brothers did not feel these would meet the requirements. Consequently, they began writing new songs, which they recorded on 19 June at Island Studios.

Some of these tracks would eventually be recorded with a full band for formal release, ('Alabamy Right', 'Marry Me' and 'Barbecutie'), but the others did not progress beyond the demo stage and were ultimately released in their original form on the fortieth-anniversary edition of *Kimono My House* in 2014 and on CD with the combined fiftieth-anniversary release of *Kimono My House* and *Propaganda* in November 2024, with an additional disc of bonus tracks.

After their arrival in London, Ron and Russell attempted to persuade Island Records to bring the remaining members of the American band to England, as evidenced by a postcard they sent to producer James Lowe on 22 June 22:

> Hello—Russell and I are over here. Island Records seems interested, but so far only in the 2 of us. We'll try to convince them to take all 5, but if not we'll probably get 3 English guys and try again. The 2 of us record demos of some new stuff at Island. Hope everything is o.k. there. Temporarily we'll be at 73 Northwood Ave, Purley, Surrey, England. Ron + Russell of Da Sparks.

Their sincere attempt to reunite the entire band under the Island Records label unfortunately fell short. Both Muff and John were impressed by the songs' potential but believed they needed to be properly recorded with a complete band of British musicians.

In July 1973, ads were placed in leading music paper *Melody Maker* for a guitarist, bass player and drummer. Around the same time, John Hewlett was also managing another British band, Jook, with singer Ian Kimmet, guitarist Trevor White, bass player Ian Hampton and drummer Chris Townson, who had previously played with John in John's Children. There was a brief consideration of having Jook drop their singer and join the Maels as the new Sparks, but the Jook members were not interested, having high hopes for their own band. They were familiar with Sparks, having seen their London concerts six months prior on John's recommendation.

One of the first responses to their ads came from Martin Gordon, a young bass player who auditioned on 20 August 1973, accompanied by his friend, drummer Bob Sturt. Additionally, Sal Maida, a New Yorker living in England at the time, applied, but his American nationality disqualified him, since they were specifically looking for British musicians. Sal would later join Sparks in 1976 for the *Big Beat* album.

Bob Sturt did not meet the Maels' criteria, but they did express interest in Gordon, who inquired about their specific needs. In response, Ron allegedly said, 'A Lennon for my McCartney'. As an aspiring songwriter, this was music to Martin's ears.

A few days later, John Hewlett called Martin to invite him to another audition at the Friern Barnet Cricket Club on 28 August. There, he joined temporary stand-ins Chris Townson and Trevor White for another session, performing 'Wonder Girl', 'Girl From Germany' and 'I Like Girls'.

On 22 and 23 September, Gordon was invited to participate in another demo recording, but he did not play. A demo recording session was then arranged at Island Studios on Basing Street, with Roxy Music's bass player and producer John Porter, Canadian guitarist Paul Rudolph, and drummer Chris Townson. However, they were never truly seen as the 'new' Sparks. During this session, they recorded versions of 'I Like Girls', 'Barbecutie', 'In My Family' and 'Marry Me'.

According to Rudolph, however, other musicians were involved in these recordings, with John Porter only there to oversee and produce the recordings. He claims that Mick Taylor, then with the Rolling Stones, played guitar, and Mike Kellie of Spooky Tooth played drums. While this information has not been confirmed by anyone else, it cannot be ruled out. Taylor was likely in England on 22 September because the Rolling Stones were playing in Birmingham on 19 September. However, on the 23rd he was in Vienna for a gig. It is also intriguing that he would have participated in a two-day session with a virtually unknown band between concerts with his own band.

Regardless, these recordings have never been released, and it is highly doubtful whether they are still lying in a drawer somewhere.

After the session, Ron handed Martin £10, a significant sum of money at the time, and told him it would cover his expenses for the next time he came down. If proof was needed, it was at this moment that Martin realised he was in the band.

Now they needed a guitarist and a drummer. An audition for a guitarist was scheduled for 6 October at the Tunnel Rehearsal Studio on Great Suffolk Street, located on the south side of the Thames. They listened to Adrian Fisher perform, and due to his appearance aligning perfectly with the band's image, he was selected as the new guitarist.

Meanwhile, Chris Blackwell had approved the signing of Sparks to his Island label, prompting the band to place another advertisement: 'Major Recording Label artists Sparks require drummer. No beards.' On 13 October, another audition was arranged. As soon as the Mael brothers heard Norman 'Dinky' Diamond, they realised they had found their drummer. Sparks was once again a genuine band.

They began rehearsals in a wooden-floored dance studio in Clapham, where the new songs were played. Dutch journalist Constant Meijers, who accompanied the band during their brief visit to the Netherlands in November 1972, noticed the advertisements for new band members. Through John Porter, he obtained the Maels' telephone number and arranged a meeting at their rehearsal space in London in early November 1973.

During this meeting, he engaged in an enthusiastic conversation with Ron and Russell as they were preparing to record their new album. They had requested that Island Records reach out to Roy Wood (of The Move, ELO and Wizzard) to produce the album and were currently awaiting his response to begin the process. Interestingly, Russell expressed his excitement about the forthcoming single 'Barbecutie'. Furthermore, the tracks 'She's Getting Funnier' and 'About To Burst' were highlighted as potential inclusions for the upcoming album.

Roy Wood was unavailable for the job, and Muff Winwood suggested that he handle the production himself; the Maels agreed. Between November 1973 and February 1974, the actual recording of the album took place at Island Studios on Basing Street and Ramport Studios in London, the latter of which was owned by The Who.

For the album cover, Ron considered using an old photograph of two Japanese geisha-like women holding a picture of Winston Churchill, expressing their discontent. His intention was to replace Churchill's image with the cover of Sparks' previous album, *A Woofer in Tweeter's Clothing*, but that concept never materialised.

Instead, the cover was designed by Nicholas De Ville, with two members of the Japanese Red Buddha Theatre—Michi Hirota and Kuniko Okamura—being invited for the photo session that resulted in the front sleeve. Hirota would later provide the Japanese vocals for David Bowie's 'It's No Game'. The photographer, Karl Stoecker, was responsible for several of Roxy Music's album covers.

During the recording of the album, tensions began to emerge between the Maels and Gordon, who played his Rickenbacker bass guitar on all the tracks. However, he was instructed to use Ian Hampton's Fender on 'Amateur Hour', a directive with which he reluctantly complied, much to his chagrin. To convey his feelings about this situation, he played the instrument while pretending to read a newspaper. The Maels were neither impressed nor charmed by his demeanour.

And there was more. Martin Gordon stated: 'One day, I made the enormous, grievous mistake of suggesting that I had a song which I felt was appropriate for what we were doing. I think you could've heard a pin drop.' The song, 'Cover Girl', would later appear on the album he recorded with Jet (1975), after his adventure with Sparks had come to an end.

Despite this, he still played a significant role in the band's image. When Martin suggested visiting the hairdresser, Ron decided to accompany him and returned with the close-cropped haircut he still sports today. Combined with his now-trimmed moustache, his appearance elicited both amusement and some unease within Island Records. Initially, Ron could be seen as reminiscent of Charlie Chaplin, but his new look also evoked a completely different character from more recent history. Goodbye Charlie, hello Adolf!

Towards the end of the recording sessions, it was suggested that a second keyboardist be added for live performances, leading to another advertisement. Peter Oxendale auditioned at the Furniture Cave on King's

Road on 16 February 1974. He was initially accepted and participated in rehearsals for about a week, but was ultimately not hired.

To the Maels' surprise, Island Records decided to release 'This Town Ain't Big Enough For Both Of Us' as the first single on 22 March 1974, backed by 'Barbecutie'.

Meanwhile, John Hewlett reached out to Larry Dupont, whom he had met during Sparks' first visit to the UK at the end of 1972. He needed an assistant and thought Larry would be the perfect candidate. However, Larry graciously declined.

At the suggestion of Ron and Russell, Joseph Fleury—who had established a Sparks fan club in New York—was the next person Hewlett approached. Joseph was more than happy to take the flight to the UK to act as the assistant manager to Hewlett.

On 23 April, Sparks appeared in the studios of Island Records, where they were scheduled to record a session for *Top of the Pops* to be broadcast on 25 April. However, their performance was unexpectedly cancelled. They were replaced at the last minute by The Rubettes, whose single 'Sugar Baby Love' eventually reached number 1 in the British charts.

Thanks to a visit by Constant Meijers from the music newspaper *Oor*, we have a detailed eyewitness account of this unfortunate event:

> An atmosphere of controlled excitement and slight nervousness was palpable as we entered London's Island Studios on Basin Street, on Wednesday morning, April 24.
>
> Two modern yet extremely well-dressed young men stood out in the room. One had his hair slicked back tightly and greasy, accentuating his contoured cheekbones as he leaned casually against the white wall. These men were Ron and Russell Mael, better known as Sparks. This Wednesday was going to be memorable for the Maels and the world. After a long period of little excitement, they were going to perform for the first time, on Top of the Pops. Their single 'This Town Ain't Big Enough For Both Of Us' was on the verge of a breakthrough, and this TV spot would bring the song to millions of people.
>
> We greeted each other warmly, and I handed them my usual business gift: a packet of real Dutch chocolate hail. Ron and Russell happily accepted the gift, and Russell read the uplifting slogan at the bottom of the packet with a genuine American accent. 'Fine dat lekkurr oek gayzoend kan ziene,' ('It's nice that tasty can also be healthy') he recited vividly, showing off his education at the Berlitz School of Languages in L.A.
>
> A grey-haired Englishman, dressed in an immaculate charcoal grey chalk suit, who had been in the background, approached upon hearing Russell's recital and asked where he was from. 'Los Angeles,' he answered unsuspectingly.
>
> 'Oh,' was all Robin Day, the boss of Top of the Pops said as he was present to supervise the recording of the backing track, and then he was gone.

'Did I say something wrong?' Russell asked his brother. A few minutes later, I saw Robin Day busily making phone calls while Muff Winwood took the Maels aside. Personal secretary Joseph was dragged away with a pale face, and a meeting started upstairs that lasted forever.

The tension that had been built up to an unbearable level was broken as suddenly as it had been created, when a blustering Muff Winwood stormed downstairs and exclaimed: 'It is not fucking happening! Pack up again!'

Pale as a sheet, we found Ron and Russell upstairs many minutes later, and the only thing I could think was that this town wasn't big enough for either of them. Cynical laughter became my role, and in the meantime, manager John Hewlett started what turned out to be a marathon of telephone calls. He had called dozens of agencies and authorities. 'Why?' was all he wanted to know. Everything was in order, right? Even work permits!

However, things aren't that easy in the extremely formal Albion. Being a member of the musicians' union is, of course, not enough if you are a singer and make movements. Then you fall under the regulations of the actors' union, and Russell wasn't a member! At one point, Muff thought that it would work out after all and requested everyone back. At three o'clock, however, the curtain finally fell. There were no more possibilities. Perhaps next week...

Two weeks later, on 9 May, the band finally appeared on *Top of the Pops*, and their performance struck unsuspecting British television viewers like a nuclear bomb. The following day, it became the talk of workplaces and playgrounds across the UK.

Meanwhile, the Maels had grown weary of Martin Gordon and wanted him gone. Martin watched the broadcast at Peter Oxendale's apartment:

> We had a party. I think we saw it on a small black and white portable on the other side of the room, but I was probably too pissed to see it clearly.

The following day, Martin continued his celebration. After an exceptionally enjoyable night out, he was awakened from his drunken stupor at 4 a.m. by Joseph Fleury, the new assistant manager, who simply stated: 'It's Joseph. They no longer want you in the group.'

Martin spoke to John Hewlett the next morning and he was informed that it was true and final. Later, Martin formed his own bands, first Jet and later Radio Stars. He has been living in Berlin for many years and remains active as a musician, having released many excellent solo projects.

Ian Hampton took over his position in Sparks, and Trevor White was added as a second guitarist. This time they were interested in joining Sparks, Jook having been dropped by their record label, RCA.

Meanwhile, 'This Town Ain't Big Enough For Both Of Us' stormed the charts, only being halted at number 2 by 'Sugar Baby Love' by The Rubettes, the band that had previously replaced them on *Top of the Pops*.

On 1 May 1974, the album by the newly revived Sparks was finally released. The title was a variation of 'Come On-A My House', a 1951 hit single by American singer Rosemary Clooney that held the top position for six weeks. Suddenly, Sparks emerged as the new sensation, featuring prominently in magazines and on television shows all across Europe.

On 24 May, they recorded another segment for *Top of the Pops*, this time featuring Ian Hampton in place of Martin Gordon, but without Trevor White. The original broadcast with Martin Gordon has become a rarity, as it appears to have been lost forever. Hewlett and Fleury attempted to secure Sparks as a support act for David Bowie's American West Coast tour, but they were informed that Bowie did not require a support act.

The first British tour started on 20 June at The Winter Gardens in Cleethorpes and concluded at the Rainbow Theatre in London on 7 July. It was a sold-out tour; however, music publications were divided regarding the quality of the live sound compared to that of the album.

Although they did not hire an additional keyboard player, the live band had been strengthened by guitarist Trevor White, who joined Adrian Fisher. Ian Hampton had also joined as a regular member. Unfortunately, there are no known recordings of this brief tour, and even photos from the performances are quite scarce.

Meanwhile, WEA, the record company that managed Sparks in 1972, saw an opportunity to recoup some of the money they invested in the band and released 'Girl From Germany' as a single on 28 June, accompanied by 'Beaver O'Lindy', but it failed to make any impact.

Initially, the second single from Island Records was intended to be 'Something For The Girl With Everything', a completely new song not included on the LP, but this plan was abandoned.

Subsequently, Island Records released 'Amateur Hour', with the outtake 'Lost and Found' on the B-side. Although it did not achieve the same level of success as the first single, it still reached number 7 on the British charts, confirming the ongoing interest in Sparks. The album itself climbed to number 4 on the British album charts. Ron and Russell had finally made it.

In the summer of 1974, former drummer Harley Feinstein was both surprised and delighted to receive a large envelope from Russell. Inside, he found a comprehensive collection of clippings and publications from the British press, detailing the sudden success of the 'new' Sparks. Feinstein fully understood their decision to relocate and was genuinely pleased with the achievements of Ron and Russell.

Still, this must have seemed a little sobering to him, especially considering that on 9 May 1974, an ad was placed in the local college newspaper *UCLA Daily Bruin*, under the 'Help Wanted' category:

SPARKS (Halfnelson) reforming, singer needed for recording. Harley - 828 ****, Earle, 391 **** (nights).

Little did they know that the Sparks name had become a sensation in England and across mainland Europe.

When Harley was asked about the ad, he was surprised that it had actually been placed. He had briefly spoken to Earle about it earlier but had no idea that Earle had actually taken action. Needless to say, no second band called Sparks was formed.

Kimono My House—The Songs

All songs written by Ron Mael, unless otherwise stated.

'THIS TOWN AIN'T BIG ENOUGH FOR BOTH OF US'
Duration: 3:00

The opening track of the third album marking the breakthrough of the Mael brothers with new band members is a song that defies description. Sparks' music, regardless of who is playing the instruments, is always challenging to define.

Ron penned this song in Clapham in late 1973, initially titled 'Too Hot To Handle'. The brothers were hesitant about it being the first single, but Island Records saw things differently.

Despite initial issues due to the American brothers lacking the necessary paperwork to work in the UK, the song made its way on to *Top of the Pops*. At the time, television offerings for bands and singers were limited and a huge part of the British population tuned in to this weekly music programme, the nation then only having three channels.

The band's music, combined with their unique image, made a huge impact in the UK, with everyone talking about the song the next day. The song showcased an unparalleled blend of power and originality, leaving the viewer in awe.

The stark contrast between the two brothers and the rest of the band, who seemed to support the Maels calmly and without attracting attention, was striking. Russell, on the other hand, was full of energy and enthusiasm, while Ron seemed as though he had been forced on stage, as if losing a bet.

Ron's stoic presence at the keyboards drew comparisons to a certain historical figure, though he claimed only a slight influence from that figure's piano techniques.

People who had previously heard the song on the radio were left feeling confused. Most listeners were convinced that the singer was a woman, as Russell's vocals have often been described as androgynous. Additionally, many struggled to comprehend the lyrics. While the lyrics did not rely on typical pop song clichés, the title itself was, of course, a textbook example of a clichéd expression frequently used in American westerns.

Once the lyrics were finally available in writing, they still didn't make much sense. Ron has never explained in detail what the song is about, but one interpretation suggests that it depicts the fears and insecurities of a young man who must talk himself into courage each time he goes on a new date. Furthermore, he is determined to bring this date to a successful conclusion, as indicated by the line, 'And it ain't me who's gonna leave'. Although there will undoubtedly be other interpretations of the lyrics, the aforementioned analysis seems to be a reasonable assumption.

The song begins with a gentle fade-in of Ron's piano, accompanied by Russell's signature vocals, which rise and fall in pitch like a kite dancing in short bursts of wind. When the full band's instrumentation finally joins in, it confirms that you are experiencing a type of song unlike any you have encountered before.

For those familiar with Sparks' first two albums, the shift in their musical style was unexpected. They adopted a more traditional structure, following the classic format of verse, chorus, verse, middle eight and finale. The music featured driving guitars, a conventional drum accompaniment, an aggressive bass line and even a gunshot sound effect sourced from the Island Records sound archives. This tighter approach made their music more accessible, leaving listeners feeling as though a whirlwind had swept through their lives, leaving them dazed yet energised. After a mere three minutes, the song concluded, leaving listeners bewildered, excited and craving for more.

Muff Winwood provided a fresh interpretation of the music, infusing it with a traditional essence while simultaneously creating a sound that was distinctly different from what was prevalent on the radio at the time. The band's visual identity also developed, rendering them impossible to overlook. Although their music and image may not have appealed to everyone, dismissing them was simply not an option.

The song peaked at number 2 on the UK national charts and became a top ten hit in the Netherlands, Belgium, Germany and Switzerland. It reached number 15 in France. In all these countries, the single was issued with a picture sleeve, while the B-side, 'Barbecutie', did not appear on the album, as initially suggested by Russell. In the UK, there was no picture sleeve.

A music video directed by Rosie Samwell-Smith was filmed but rarely aired. In this video, Martin Gordon, then still a member of the band, is given the opportunity to fire a shotgun at Russell. Instead, the band frequently performed the song in television studios, miming to the track.

The single was released in sixteen countries, including unexpected locations such as Singapore, South Africa and Yugoslavia. Nearly fifty years later, it remains Sparks' most defining song, securing their place in music history.

The original recording of the song included an additional verse that was omitted from the final mix. This verse occasionally appeared in live performances and was ultimately included in the album *Plagiarism*, decades later.

The song has been covered numerous times, with notable versions by Siouxsie and the Banshees and British Whale. The latter's cover reached number 6 on the UK charts and included a music video featuring Ron and Russell as presenters in a darts tournament.

Since its release, the song has been a staple in Sparks' concerts, missing from only a few performances in California during the early 1980s. To this day, it is still regarded as one of the highlights of a Sparks performance.

> Ron: '"This Town Ain't Big Enough For Both of Us" was written in A, and by God it'll be sung in A. I just feel that if you're coming up with most of the music, then you have an idea where it's going to go. And no singer is gonna get in my way.'
>
> Russell: 'When he wrote "This Town Ain't Big Enough For Both of Us", Ron could only play it in that key. It was so much work to transpose the song and one of us had to budge, so I made the adjustment to fit in. My voice ain't a "rock" voice. It's not soulful, in the traditional rock way; It's not about "guts". It's untrained, unschooled, I never questioned why I was singing high. It just happened, dictated by the songs. Ron has always written Sparks' lyrics and never transposed them into a rock key for me to sing. He always packed each line with words and I had to sing them as they were.'
>
> Ron: 'Basically, most situations and most people are—you have to admit—a bit on the boring side, like all of us. So the way that a person is able to cope with this, in all these situations is to kinda make more out of things than are actually there. So what is actually happening in this song, is Russell, the singer, is living just tedious, everyday situations and then kind of magnifying them into a kind of movie sort of situation, at different times, just to kind of make everything interesting for himself.'
>
> Russell: 'He always reverts back to the situation. 'This Town Ain't Big Enough For Both Of Us', is sort of a rant illustration of his little tiny predicaments that he has in visions… an American pilot bombing Hiroshima, and then he reverts back to his little situation, 'This Town Ain't Big Enough For Both Of Us', which sort of sums up each of his little dream-like fantasies that he has.'
>
> Ron: 'Actually, the truth of it is, that those were the only words that would fit that longer gap in the song.'
>
> Russell: 'Actually, it's not about any of that at all.'

'Amateur Hour'
Duration: 3:24

The instrumental introduction and structure of this song confirm the dynamics that the British band members and producer infused into the sound of the new Sparks. Adrian Fisher's crisp guitar, featuring a tone not present on previous albums, immediately sets the mood, while the other instruments build upon that foundation. Martin Gordon's bass guitar, assertive in just the right way for the song, enhances the overall sound. Although we can only speculate how it would have sounded on his own Rickenbacker, the decision to temporarily use Ian Hampton's Fender appears to be a wise choice.

Dinky Diamond is clearly trained as a traditional rock drummer, filling every available space with precision. While there is minimal use of multiple vocal tracks, the reverb—especially in the chorus—is distinctly noticeable.

The lyrics are quite straightforward and address an adolescent's tentative steps on the journey of his first sexual encounters, highlighting how his lack of experience contributes to his insecurity. The lyrics suggest that seeking guidance from a professional is advisable, as it allows one to quickly acquire the necessary skills.

This song was chosen as the follow-up single to 'This Town Ain't Big Enough For Both Of Us'. It was released in Western Europe, Australia and New Zealand, and also marked Sparks' first single in Japan. In Europe, the song achieved minor success, peaking at number 7 in England. However, outside of Europe, it disappeared without a trace.

Unfortunately, no television recordings were ever made for *Top of the Pops* due to massive strikes that occurred in the UK during the months of its release.

During concerts, this song has consistently been a staple of the live set. However, during the 2022 tour, it was only performed at the initial concerts before being removed from the set list. The 2023 tour did not feature this song at all, and neither did it appear on the 2025 tour.

Ron: 'Amateur Hour wants to say that there are still plenty of people in the world that wants to be amateurs and who feel good about that. You might have noticed that everyone is a professional nowadays.'
Constant Meijer: 'What are you?'
Russell: 'Can you come back next week?'
Russell: 'Singles have a lifespan of about four minutes in England. Thus, while "This Town" was losing steam, "Amateur Hour" was released as the follow-up. It was satisfying that a song that was so different in nature from our initial success with "This Town" could also be successful with the British and European public.'

'FALLING IN LOVE WITH MYSELF AGAIN'
Duration: 2:59

It doesn't happen very often, but occasionally Ron writes a song in three-four time, which is typical of a waltz. This track falls into that category. The song opens with loud drums, and for the first time on this album, Ron incorporates organ sounds instead of the usual clear piano. This choice creates a slightly dramatic, somewhat cinematic atmosphere, with a distinct nod to the baroque style.

As is often the case, the middle eight section of the song diverges wonderfully from the rest. Russell's vocals are complemented by a playful and cheerful bass line, which eventually evolves into a duel between the lead guitar and bass. The percussion briefly joins in as well. The vocals in this song showcase Russell's distinctive high tones, but once again, no backing vocals are employed.

The lyrics exhibit a clever wit in their simplicity and embody the typical irony associated with the genre. The main character chooses to concentrate exclusively on himself. It remains ambiguous whether this decision stems from pure narcissism or from disappointment in his past interactions with others. This theme will resurface multiple times throughout the extensive career of the Mael brothers.

Live, this song was regularly performed during the tours of 1974 and 1975. Interestingly, it was also played at their 'comeback concert' in London in 1994. Furthermore, it was included in the 1995 tour and was performed again during the Revenge of Two Hands One Mouth tour in 2013. The last live performance of this song occurred in 2015 during special concerts with the Heritage Orchestra to commemorate the fortieth anniversary of *Kimono My House*.

> Ron: 'This is a three-four number, for all of you waltz-type persons, and it's a beer drinking song for people who don't drink beer. It's about the idea of people usually becoming close with people of the, if you'll excuse the expression, opposite sex, that are very close to being like themselves in all ways.'
> Ron: '"Falling In Love With Myself Again" is about the tendency to fall in love with people that resembles you a lot. Who seem to be an idealised form of oneself.'
> Constant Meijers: 'How often have you fallen in love with yourself?'
> Ron: 'Ehm, frankly, I never liked myself. I'm not my type.'

'HERE IN HEAVEN'
Duration: 2:40

Bursting forth at the unsuspecting listener and somewhat confrontational in the most positive sense, this track opens abruptly without an introduction or build-up. It features a cheerful melody accompanied by light arrangements that offer a unique perspective on a failed suicide pact. The classic narrative of boy meets girl unfolds as they fall in love, encounter obstacles and ultimately make a pact to end their lives together. However, at the eleventh hour, the girl experiences a change of heart, leaving the boy to confront his demise alone. This scenario, though tragic, is presented as a common occurrence, and this time it is sung from heaven, where the boy bitterly reflects on his disappointing circumstances.

The solid bass line provides a strong foundation, while the drums serve more as filler than as a rhythmic anchor. The guitar riffs emphasise the protagonist's desperation during the middle eight section, while Ron's piano remains relatively subdued within the arrangement.

As anticipated with a subject of this nature, it provides abundant opportunities for lyrical creativity, resulting in numerous puns, irony and a reference to Romeo and Juliet.

Like the previous track, this song was a staple of the tours in 1974 and 1975. It made a surprise return during the second set of the performances in Stockholm in 2004 for the live DVD.

Additionally, it was performed during the Revenge of Two Hands One Mouth tour in 2013. The last live performance occurred in 2015 during special concerts with the Heritage Orchestra, commemorating the fortieth anniversary of *Kimono My House*.

Russell: 'It's a suicide pact song. That all it is, it's a suicide pact song.'
Ron: 'I liked the title a lot so I wrote some lyrics to it. A boy and a girl decide to commit suicide together. He jumps, she changes her mind at the very last moment. From heaven he's looking to her and sings to her how he regrets that she's not up there with him.'

'THANK GOD IT'S NOT CHRISTMAS'
Duration: 5:00

The closing song on side one opens with a captivating melody played by the solo guitar, accompanied by a sixteenth-note rhythm on the hi-hat cymbals. The piano soon joins in, followed by a playful bass line that enriches the overall sound. This introduction is repeated, with the drums becoming more prominent and adhering to a solid rock pattern. Only then does Russell's vocal line enter.

In a rare moment within a Sparks song, there are also brief guitar solos. However, the primary focus is on the section where everything abruptly halts after just under four minutes, leaving only Ron's piano audible. This part serves as a genuine moment of respite in the song. Following this, all the instruments enthusiastically rejoin. Surprisingly, the song concludes with the sound of a Japanese gong.

The song is quite straightforward and seems to depict an individual who revels in going out and fully embracing life. He dreads Christmas because he must spend time with his wife, which prevents him from indulging in the nightlife he typically enjoys.

The song was not included in the live set after 1974, except when the *Kimono My House* album was performed in its entirety. During the brief concerts recorded for *Don Kirshner's Rock Concert* and *The Midnight Special*, the song can be seen performed live, as footage is still available. By that time, Ian Hampton and Trevor White had replaced the original musicians.

> Ron: 'This one's difficult to explain without getting involved with some Moody Blues philosophy. Look, every day you can find an excuse to escape from others. At Christmas time everything is closed and you have no choice. However...'

'Hasta Mañana, Monsieur'
Written by Ron Mael and Russell Mael
Duration: 3:33

The first song on the album that we encounter which was not solely written by Ron. In fact, many may be surprised to learn that the lyrics, which closely resemble Ron Mael's typical style, were actually penned by Russell. One of the most memorable lines from a Sparks song is the fragment, 'You mentioned Kant, and I was shocked. You know, where I come from, none of the girls have such foul tongues.' This brilliant pun is quintessentially Ron Mael, until it is revealed that it was actually written by his younger brother.

The song opens with a gentle fade-in of the keyboards, creating a brief yet captivating and somewhat melancholic atmosphere reminiscent of a funfair. This introduction lasts only thirteen seconds before the sudden arrival of the other instruments completely alters the tone.

Throughout this instrumental progression, the piano and bass guitar take centre stage. When the vocals enter, a beautiful interplay between the guitar and bass guitar unfolds, featuring playful riffs that swirl around the vocal line. The piano maintains a prominent presence, contributing a sense of lightness to the song that embodies a distinctive characteristic of Sparks.

A brief yet perfectly suited guitar solo by Adrian Fisher serves as a break, which has been adapted in various ways during live performances over the decades. In early concerts, Ron's piano took over this segment; later, the focus shifted to short, sharp, jabbing chords on the guitar. Eventually, the intermezzo was preserved as closely to the original as possible.

It is the second Sparks song to feature castanets. Russell also utilised castanets during his performance at the Meltdown Festival in London in 2004, where the entire album was performed. He repeated this during the presentation of this song at the Sparks Spectacular in 2008 and at Royce Hall in 2009. Castanets were a regular part of the live set during the 2018 tour.

The album's title is derived from a fragment of this song, and its subject matter revolves around the narrator's struggles to communicate with a girl of foreign origin. In his attempts to be as clear as possible, he employs terms he is familiar with from the two languages in which he has some proficiency.

During the Bearsville band's final concerts in February 1973, three new songs were added to the set list, although Ron later claimed that Russell only mentioned the songs during those performances. One of these songs was titled 'Pardon My French', and it has been suggested that this was an early version of the song that would eventually become 'Hasta Mañana, Monsieur'. While this has never been officially confirmed, the similarities in the titles and the timeline make it a possibility that cannot be dismissed.

> Russell: 'Dedicated to the Berlitz School of Languages and an effort to combine two languages within one song. It's about problems in communication. In fact a song to practice two foreign languages.'
> Ron: 'Living and working on "that" side of the world (England) saw a rapid continentalisation of our lives… a guy's confusion over how to communicate with a girl who speaks a foreign tongue, yet not knowing exactly which tongue that might be. Kind of like being a cashier at Harrods.'

'TALENT IS AN ASSET'
Duration: 3:14

There are not many songs dedicated to the life of Albert Einstein. This cheerful melody narrates the story of young Albert's close relatives who recognise his potential early on and are determined to keep him focussed and free from distractions.

The song opens with an upbeat drumbeat, complemented by handclaps and the bright, twinkling notes of a piano, along with subtle xylophone sounds in the background. The bass guitar establishes its own rhythm, while the guitar contributes a delightful staccato that is initially overshadowed by the bass line.

In the chorus, Russell demonstrates his vocal abilities by intertwining two independent vocal lines, which can make it challenging to follow the lyrics. This distinctive vocal technique is a signature sound for Sparks and is more pronounced during live performances.

The song concludes with a fade-out of multiple vocal layers, cautioning the listener about what actions to avoid in the presence of young Albert. The urgency to allow him the space to fully develop into the genius he is destined to become is emphasised.

Interestingly, this song was selected as the second single over 'Amateur Hour' in the USA, Canada and New Zealand; however, it did not chart in any of these countries.

From 1974 to 1981, the song was a permanent staple in their live performances, including shows in Los Angeles, France and Belgium. After 1982, it was only performed live as part of the entire album. During the recording of the *Live in Stockholm* DVD, a performance featuring only guitarist Dean Menta and Russell was presented to the audience, marking a rare occasion without Ron's participation.

'COMPLAINTS'
Duration: 2:45

The title of the song is quite revealing. It addresses an individual who tends to complain about everything and possesses a rather pessimistic outlook on life.

During the chorus, the tempo increases, and handclapping—a prominent feature of the previous song—is reintroduced.

The instruments in this song are well-balanced. Aside from the occasional guitar riff, there are no jarring outbursts. However, there is a proper introduction to the song. The vocal line is straightforward and, similar to the previous song, employs double vocals in certain sections.

'Complaints' has only been performed during a regular concert once. This occurred at the Coventry Theatre on 10 November 1974. It is unclear why it was played there and not elsewhere. Aside from that singular performance, the song has only been performed when the album as a whole was presented, starting at the 2004 Meltdown Festival.

> Ron: 'Just three minutes of complaints. In stereo.'
> Constant Meijers: 'The first stereophonic headache?'
> Ron: 'Exactly.'

'IN MY FAMILY'
Written by Ron Mael and Russell Mael
Duration: 3:11

Another song on this album co-written by both brothers. The subject of this song is clearly articulated by Ron Mael, and there are unlikely to be many dissenting interpretations amongst listeners. The song features the ironic lyric fragment 'Gonna hang myself from my family tree', which is regarded as one of the standout lines in Sparks' lyrics.

Instrumentally, the song is quite straightforward, featuring a prominent lead guitar complemented by Russell's slightly yodelling backing vocals, which add an extra dimension to the piece. The piano skilfully weaves in and out of the arrangement without drawing much attention, except in the final section, where the guitar and piano engage in a duel, while the bass makes a half-hearted attempt to join in.

Ron: 'That song is about someone who feels cheated because he's ended up in a family where he doesn't feel at home.'

'Equator'
Duration: 4:38

If there is one song that serves as a significant divider amongst Sparks enthusiasts, it is 'Equator', the final track on their third album. Russell's falsetto truly shines in this piece, particularly in the concluding section, where he demonstrates his vocal prowess and conveys a sense of ecstasy for many listeners, although it may be somewhat overwhelming for others.

The song begins with a standard guitar riff lasting eight beats, but as soon as the saxophone joins in, it adopts a more jazzy interpretation. The saxophone is played on a Mellotron, providing the song with a significant transformation.

The lyrics are as witty as they are absurd. The narrator recounts a potential romantic encounter with someone he has arranged to meet on 10 March at 3:00 p.m. on the Equator. Unfortunately, his journey proves futile, as his date never arrives.

Curiously enough, the term 'Happy Equator Day' has become a tradition amongst some Sparks fans, who congratulate each other on 10 March. Presumably, it was not Ron's intention to initiate this custom when he composed the song, but it likely does no harm either.

Surprisingly, the song was never included in the live sets of 1974 or 1975. However, during the 1976 *Big Beat* tour it was performed at every concert. Russell delivered the vocals more like a narrator than by strictly adhering to the lyrics, while Ron's piano provided the foundation for the verses, playing a significantly smaller role than the other instruments.

Despite the controversy, this song can undoubtedly be regarded as a worthy and standout closer to the LP, a tradition evident in many Sparks records. 'Equator' certainly deserves a place on this list.

Russell: 'The old story of a girl that tells her boyfriend that she would wait for him at the equator, which the boy takes seriously. He cannot find her, while they did agree to meet around the bend! Just a sad boy-girl song. Nothing more, nothing less.'

4

Propaganda

Release date: 11 November 1974
Produced by: Muff Winwood
Engineer: Richard Digby-Smith, Robin Black
Sleeve design: Monty Coles
Photography: Monty Coles
Recorded at: AIR Studios, London
Duration: 33:41
Personnel: Ron Mael: Keyboards
                  Russell Mael: Vocals
                  Adrian Fisher: Guitar
                  Trevor White: Guitar
                  Ian Hampton: Bass guitar
                  Norman Diamond: Drums

Side 1
'Propaganda'
'At Home, At Work, At Play'
'B.C.'
'Thank But No Thanks'
'Don't Leave Me Alone With Her'

Side 2
'Never Turn Your Back On Mother Earth'
'Something For The Girl With Everything'
'Achoo'
'Who Don't Like Kids'
'Bon Voyage'

Singles from this album:
'Never Turn Your Back On Mother Earth'/'Alabamy Right'
'Something For The Girl With Everything'/'Marry Me'
'Achoo'/'Something For The Girl With Everything'
'Propaganda'/'At Home, At Work, At Play'/'Marry Me'

In the summer of 1974, Ron and Russell finally achieved what they had been striving for since their early recordings with the Urban Renewal Project in 1967: recognition, fame and stardom. This was particularly true in Britain and several other countries across the continent, where it was impossible to open a music magazine without encountering interviews, reviews or pin-up posters of the brothers. Within just a year of their arrival in London, they had joined the ranks of successful and renowned pop stars in their beloved British Isles.

A Top Ten album and two Top Ten singles, followed by a successful tour in Britain, resulted in a very pleased record company, and plans for a follow-up album began to take shape. After the tour concluded, Sparks entered AIR Studios in London to record the follow-up album in August and September 1974. AIR Studios was established by Beatles producer George Martin in 1970.

They were now a sextet. Ron and Russell were joined by Dinky Diamond, Adrian Fisher and Ian Hampton, who replaced Martin Gordon, along with Trevor White, who had been part of the British tour and remained on board. This decision was likely influenced by the Maels' uncertainty regarding Adrian Fisher's future position. It wasn't that they considered Adrian a poor guitarist; quite the contrary—Fisher was an exceptional player, arguably more skilled than necessary. However, he never truly felt comfortable or fully committed to the music Sparks were creating. Adrian was a trained blues guitarist, and that style of influence did not align with the sound the Maels sought for their recordings.

Besides, he tended to be somewhat reluctant when asked to participate, and, much like Martin Gordon, possessed a strong will of his own. He had a habit of placing his cigarette butt on one of his guitar strings while playing and occasionally held a cigarette in photographs. This behaviour did not align with the Maels' vision, as they believed it should not be part of the image they wanted to project. Additionally, he sometimes failed to show up for photo sessions, and in the photograph on the inner sleeve of *Kimono My House*, he deliberately turned his back to the camera.

Russell Mael commented on Adrian Fisher in an article published in the June 1975 issue of *Trans-Oceanic Trouser Press*:

> He (Fisher) wasn't too concerned with being in Sparks. He's a really good guitarist, but he's from "de blues skool." You can't fool people into trying to be excited about what you're doing.

Nonetheless, he remained involved in the recording sessions for the new album, which was to be named *Propaganda*, after the opening track. The pressure was intense, particularly for Ron, as there were only three months between the release of *Kimono My House* and the plan for a follow-up album. He needed to produce a complete album's worth of new songs. Russell co-wrote three of the tracks.

In the aforementioned article in *Trouser Press*, the older Mael reflects on that album:

> That album was incredibly hard because there was a lot of pressure. "Kimono" was incredibly popular in England, and we were under the microscope. Anything we did was going to be judged. We went into the studio with a lot of songs, but a bit scared. We kept thinking about The Beatles and their constant rise. We tried to make "Propaganda" a little more complex than "Kimono My House."

An example of Adrian Fisher's somewhat mischievous and insubordinate attitude towards the Maels manifested in the studio. One night, he observed Russell storming out of the studio. Believing that Russell was heading to an adjoining office, the singer instead chose a soundproofed storeroom that could not be opened from the inside. The guitarist was aware of Russell's location but neglected to inform anyone. An hour-and-a-half later, Russell was discovered, quite upset.

One song from the new album, 'Something For The Girl With Everything', had already been recorded just before the first British tour in June and July 1974. An acetate was brought to the Hull gig and handed over to the DJ at the venue. News about this song leaked, leading the English press and fans to anticipate it as the new single instead of 'Amateur Hour'.

For the first time, Sparks had two guitarists present during the recordings. However, most of Adrian's solos were either mixed down or excluded entirely. Shortly after the recordings were completed, the band parted ways with Adrian, who received a fee for his contributions to the new album, despite the fact that his recordings were significantly reduced in the final release. Additionally, Adrian was not featured on the album sleeve, the picture for which was taken by Australian photographer Monty Coles.

Initially, Coles suggested that the Maels jump out of an airplane with parachutes so he could capture sensational shots of them plummeting towards the English countryside. However, the brothers were convinced they would prefer the second option he offered: being tied up in a speedboat.

In another shot, tied up in the trunk of a car, the rest of the band, excluding Adrian, are also featured. Ron and Russell were contemplating finding a replacement for Adrian, especially as they approached their second British tour, their first concerts on the continent and, perhaps most importantly, their first visit to their home country. They had not returned since their precarious departure in June of the previous year.

Several candidates were considered for the position. Ian North, a member of the New York-based band Milk 'n Cookies, which had recently come under the management of John Hewlett, was one of them. However, the Maels quickly dismissed this suggestion. North was a talented songwriter in his own right, and they were keen to avoid a situation similar to their previous experience with

Martin Gordon. Another candidate was Ian Kimmet from Jook, a band that had just lost their guitarist and bassist to Sparks. Unfortunately, he politely declined the offer, as he did not resonate with the music Sparks was producing.

Ron and Russell had pinned their hopes on Brian May of Queen. Although May appreciated the band and their music, he envisioned a more promising future with Queen. He wasn't entirely mistaken in that assessment. In September 1974, they also considered guitarist Binky Philips, but he was not accepted after the audition.

Ultimately, it was decided that Fisher would not be replaced when the band travelled to the Maels' home country, where Sparks' status was markedly different from that in the UK and the European continent. Neither of the singles 'This Town Ain't Big Enough For Both Of Us' nor 'Talent Is An Asset' had charted, and their previous album had only reached number 101 on the Billboard charts.

In September 1974, instead of organising a traditional tour of the USA, the band performed live for various television programmes. For many Americans who were unaware of the previous Bearsville albums, these broadcasts on *Don Kirshner's Rock Show*, *ABC in Concert* and *The Midnight Special* served as their first introduction to Sparks, leading to a modest growth in their American fan base. During the *ABC in Concert* recording, they were introduced to the audience by one of their old heroes, Keith Moon of The Who, who was accompanied by Ringo Starr. By this time, Sparks must have felt like they were truly part of the music scene.

They also performed live for radio station KMET-FM in Los Angeles on 11 October. A few months later, these recordings were released on a bootleg album titled *One and a Half-Nelson—The Instant Darlings Recorded Live*, under the TAKLR label. Interestingly, the album did not include the final song of the performance, 'Amateur Hour', but instead featured B-sides from the Island singles. In 2015, the recordings were reissued on CD, this time including the missing song and additional banter from Russell between tracks.

In the meantime, 'Never Turn Your Back On Mother Earth', a track from the new album, was released in the UK and several European countries. It was accompanied by a complete recording of one of the demos that the Maels had written in the summer of 1973 to present to Muff Winwood, titled 'Alabamy Right'.

'Never Turn Your Back On Mother Earth' was the first of the Island singles not to reach the Top 10 in the UK, peaking at number 13. The album itself did not perform as well as *Kimono My House*, reaching a peak position of number 9 on the UK Albums Chart. Despite this, Sparks remained relevant and embarked on their second British tour with only five members. The tour began in York on 2 November and concluded on the 28th of the same month. Most, if not all, concerts were sold out, and the press responded more favourably to the live sound compared to the previous tour, even with only one guitarist instead of two.

For the first time since the Bearsville band performed in the Netherlands, Sparks toured the continent, with a series of concerts in Paris, Hamburg, Stockholm, Lund, Göteborg, Copenhagen, Amsterdam, Rotterdam, Zurich, Munich and Brussels, extending into December. The tour concluded with a Christmas performance at the Town Hall in Leeds on 22 December. All concerts on the continent were well received and nearly sold out.

In their home country, the album reached number 63 on the Billboard Top 200. This position in the United States was significantly higher than that of its predecessor, indicating that the national television broadcasts from the previous month had attracted a new group of fans.

While in Paris, the Maels were approached by a representative of renowned film director Jacques Tati, who wanted them to star in his new movie *Confusion*. The future looked bright for Ron and Russell as they eagerly anticipated 1975.

Propaganda—The Songs

All songs written by Ron Mael, unless otherwise stated.

'PROPAGANDA'
Duration: 0:23

The album's opening track is an exceptionally brief yet striking and powerful piece that features only layers of vocals, devoid of any instrumental accompaniment. Ron clearly articulated the song's subject matter. A longer rerecording, with the assistance of external vocalists, was produced for the album *Plagiarism*, over two decades later.

During the second European tour at the end of 1974 and the North American tour in the spring of 1975, concerts began with this song. However, it differed slightly from the album version, as it was accompanied by a drum rhythm that transitioned into the song 'Talent Is An Asset'.

The song made a comeback at several concerts in Los Angeles, France and Belgium in late 1981, and was also performed at the comeback concert in London in 1994. It continued to be played at concerts in 1997, 2008 and 2009, becoming a regular feature during both the 2017 and 2018 tours. A memorable performance took place during a broadcast on Mark Lamarr's *God's Jukebox* on BBC Radio 2 on 4 October 2008.

> Ron: 'The title song "Propaganda" is an acapella tune with Russell's voice overdubbed 30 times. It's being sung by a boyfriend of a kind of Tokyo-Rose figure, saying don't listen to her propaganda. I don't want any competition.'

Ron: 'The song "Propaganda" was originally an acoustic guitar thing: we just kept recording voices. It was a lot easier to do things with the vocals than to figure out extra guitar parts. I think that vocal style was really influential to some big English bands that have since done pretentious albums.'

'AT HOME, AT WORK, AT PLAY'
Duration: 3:01

Almost immediately, the opening track transitions into 'At Home, At Work, At Play', making it challenging to distinguish between the two songs. The arrangement of this upbeat track is robust and dynamic, showcasing Russell's remarkable ability to articulate dense lyrical passages with exceptional speed and clarity within tightly constrained timeframes.

Double vocals are utilised effectively, and the instruments blend together seamlessly, with no single instrument overpowering the others. When combined with the first track, it creates a solid block of music that may initially be overwhelming, but in a positive way.

The subject matter of the song is straightforward, focusing on an individual who is struggling to spend time with their partner, who is constantly occupied with other activities. The lyrics emphasise the importance of effective planning to create time for one another.

The combination of 'Propaganda'/'At Home, At Work, At Play' was released as a single in France, instead of 'Something For The Girl With Everything', which was the second single released in other regions. Unfortunately, it did not chart.

Interestingly, this song was not performed live in the 1970s; it was first introduced at concerts in 1981. Over the following years, it was consistently paired with 'Propaganda' and remained a regular part of the set list during the 2017 and 2018 tours.

Ron: 'An up-tempo song, so quite fast, which is also the most characteristic [aspect] of this song. It has something to do with a trip and all kinds of details about a girl who is busy each night. The only way to find some space in her schedule is to visit her in daytime when she's at home, at work or at play. Daylight lovers!'

'REINFORCEMENTS'
Written by Ron Mael and Russell Mael
Duration: 3:46

'Reinforcements' opens with piano accompanied by a military drumbeat. The song tells the story of a soldier who anxiously questions the whereabouts of the reinforcements necessary to secure a successful outcome in battle. Alternatively, the song can be interpreted as a metaphorical quarrel between a couple, where the man, losing the argument, likens his predicament to a war scenario, seeking external support to validate his position.

It is a song written by both brothers, but the specific contributions of each brother are not known.

The remaining instruments join in halfway through the verse, and only during the chorus is there a modest rhythm guitar. The quiet spaces and the swelling guitars are beautifully balanced in the second part of the song, where the dramatic essence of the subject is effectively captured. This builds to a climax, after which a sense of peace returns, almost as if some form of acceptance has taken place. There is minimal use of double vocals; however, when they do appear, it is subtle and quite functional. In the final section, Trevor White and Ian Hampton harmonise, and the piece concludes with a tone that suggests a glimmer of hope.

The song was performed live only during the European tour in 1974 and the North American concerts in the spring of 1975. After that, the song was exclusively performed at the Sparks Spectacular in 2008, until 2025, when it was a solid part of the world tour and very well received by the audience.

'B.C.'
Duration: 2:07

Another family dispute, this time from the husband's perspective, is portrayed by Aaron, the narrator. He is desperately trying to convince his wife, Betty, to return after she left with their son, Charlie. As a result, the once perfect harmony of the family has crumbled, and the desired ABC combination is no longer present.

In this song, the piano takes a dominant role, while the other instruments mainly support the chords with short strokes. The vocals feature typical combinations of lead and background, with the background vocals adding falsetto accompaniment. Additionally, Ian Hampton's bass guitar shines with beautiful runs throughout the song. The end of the track is highlighted by a subtle second voice that sings the same lyrics but an octave higher.

The song features a 'start-stop' structure, where it appears to reset with each verse. The use of double vocals is executed excellently, building towards a climax in each verse, only to abruptly stop and begin again.

During live performances, Russell enthusiastically announces between verses that more is yet to come.

This song was a staple in nearly all tours during the 1970s. It was absent in the 1980s and 1990s, but resurfaced in 2003. Additionally, it was performed during the Two Hands One Mouth tour and became a regular feature of the 2018 world tour.

Ron: 'This is a song that constantly stops and restarts again. An alphabet-song in which you'll find an A, a B and a C and where, at a certain moment, when the A seems to be missing, the B and C sing "Come back".'

'Thanks But No Thanks'
Written by Ron Mael and Russell Mael
Duration: 4:04

Another song that utilises a cliché expression is the second track on the album co-written by Ron and Russell. The song begins with just the brothers on vocals and organ, creating a mystical atmosphere reminiscent of the Bearsville albums.

The rhythm is propelled by a military-style snare drum in a four-quarter time signature, accompanied by a subtle blend of guitar and a faint bass loop that becomes more prominent with focus. Hand claps enhance the texture, and although there are some guitar riffs, they remain somewhat obscured. The backing vocals are utilised effectively, adding a sense of mystique to the overall sound. Occasionally, an acoustic guitar is incorporated, though it is nearly imperceptible.

The song's subject is a young child contemplating their doubts about following parental instructions to avoid trusting strangers and interacting with unfamiliar individuals.

Fragments of the song were later used in an adapted version for the film *Annette* (2021).

Aside from a performance during the Sparks Spectacular on 20 May 2008, this song has never been performed live.

Ron: 'This song is about a little boy who is getting candies from all kinds of people and who's confusing this with affection. People who have, in fact totally different intentions. He's getting angry at his parents who tell him to keep on walking and not to accept anything from strangers. He thinks his parents are pretty cruel and that they should show some more understanding for those people. Hence "Thanks but no thanks".'

'Don't Leave Me Alone With Her'
Duration: 2:55

Side one concludes with an upbeat song that showcases prominent solo guitar work and includes a tambourine in the chorus. While the bass guitar remains subtle during the verses, it delivers beautiful melodic lines in the chorus.

The serene break culminates in one of the vocalist's longer screeches, leading into a dynamic yet controlled final section where Russell concludes the song with his signature falsetto.

The meaning of the lyrics is clearly and unambiguously articulated by the Maels themselves, eliminating the need for further speculation.

Remarkably, this song made its live debut during a concert at the Royal Albert Hall in London on 19 October 2002, where it turned out to be a one-time performance. It became evident how quickly the lyrics needed to be sung, and at times, Russell appeared to struggle with this.

However, the final result was more than worth it. Although it was included in the presentation of *Propaganda* during the Sparks Spectacular in 2008, it has not been performed live since then.

Ron: 'Someone at a party is continuously singing in the hope that people will stay, so that he's not left alone with a girl whom he finds far too aggressive for his liking. He's trying to convince all the people present in all kinds of ways.'

Russell: 'I try to avoid clichés musically, or to use clichés in ways that haven't been used before, which makes things more interesting. It's the same with romantic situations. Love songs are generally either happy or sad, but there are so many ways to talk about relationships and put them in a new concept. "Don't Leave Me Alone With Her" takes the opposite tack to most guys' wishes.'

'NEVER TURN YOUR BACK ON MOTHER EARTH'
Duration: 2:24

The opening track of side two has become a classic, featured in the live set on virtually every tour since its release, with the exception of the 1976 tour and the 1980s. This song was also performed during the world tour of 2022, but it was not included in the presentation in 2023 or 2025.

As the album's lead single, it represented a remarkable shift in style from the singles released prior to that point, captivating both friends and critics alike. The first verse is dominated by the vocals and the harpsichord-like sound of the keyboards. It is not until the second verse that the rest of the band joins in, with strings also produced by the keyboards.

The middle eight enhances the song's serenity, and in the second part there is space for a subtle guitar solo, which is a rarity amongst the other tracks on this album.

Regarding the content of the lyrics, in this era of heightened awareness about the environment, it is considered one of the earliest appeals to exercise caution towards our planet. However, the true meaning is somewhat more ominous, serving as a warning about the retribution that nature can exact when it is disturbed, revealing that it is not as benevolent as commonly believed.

The song has been covered and officially released by numerous professional musicians, with notable versions by Depeche Mode, Martin Gore, Billy Mackenzie, Mary Hopkin and Neko Case. The original version reached a peak position of number 13 on the UK charts.

Ron: 'Side two starts with the single in which the evil side of nature is being questioned. A view in which nature is personified, just like with primitive people, and nature is thought of as an evil spirit that is quite revengeful. The music to this song was first written, after which I tried to find suitable lyrics to it.

'In this case the two are kind of working against each other. The intention of this song is, contrary to the traditional set up, not traditional at all. While writing it, I didn't even think about the fact that this title can also be considered as a statement that mother nature shouldn't be neglected. I must have been pretty dumb not having realised that then. As it is now, the song is at least also suitable for Andy Williams.

'It was one of the few ballads we'd ever recorded, so we wanted to try to make it sound really impressive. I guess that use of a lot of reverb was a way to make it so that it wasn't just a singer-songwriter kind of thing and it had the power of an aggressive song.

'It means that if you turn your back on Mother Earth, Mother Earth might just come your way and clobber you, retaliate.'

'SOMETHING FOR THE GIRL WITH EVERYTHING'
Duration: 2:13

With the second track from side two, which was also released as the second single in most countries, we return to a fast-paced, short, high-tempo song that pushes Russell's vocal speed to its limits.

The song feels like a whirlwind, ending before you even realise it. It was one of the first songs written for *Propaganda*, having already been mentioned in the English press in July 1974 as the successor to 'This Town Ain't Big Enough For Both of Us'. There was an acetate of the song that was given to a DJ at a concert during the first British tour in June.

In the first thirty seconds, the song builds up without the guitar, with the keyboards and drums taking on prominent roles. The piano's entry appears somewhat chaotic at times, yet it is cleverly arranged. The guitar is introduced during the instrumental section, halfway through the song, featuring a repeated and somewhat aggressive rendition of a simple riff.

Ron has done an excellent job of explaining the meaning behind the lyrical content. Throughout nearly every tour up to 2006, this song was featured in the live performances. However, it was last performed live in 2012 during the inaugural concert of the *Two Hand One Mouth* tour. This appearance was likely a trial, as it did not become a regular part of the live set for this tour, nor was it included in the official live CD of the same name.

> Ron: 'A fast song with a lot of vocal changes. It's about a boy who is being black mailed by a girl with the purpose to keep things from the past secret. He keeps giving her presents so in the end she's the girl who's got everything.'

'Achoo'
Duration: 3:25

According to Alex Kapranos, 'Achoo' was one of the songs that Franz Ferdinand attempted to play during their first rehearsals but ultimately abandoned due to its complexity. However, during live concerts of FFS (a supergroup combining the talents of Franz Ferdinand and Sparks) in 2015, the song was occasionally performed, and it finally sounded as they had originally hoped, thanks to the assistance of the Mael brothers.

The opening notes showcase a beautiful and harmonious interplay between a prominent piano, an atmospheric bass guitar and a modest yet subtle rhythm guitar. The bass guitar plays a crucial role throughout the song, not only supporting the vocal line but also following its own distinctive path.

After just two minutes, the stage is set for the spectacular conclusion of the song, which features several vocal layers that consist of sneezes. Adrian Fisher's original guitar solo was removed the very next day; however, during a performance with the band Alpha Mael in 2008, Trevor White and Ian Hampton made a guest appearance, with Trevor playing the lengthy original guitar solo as he recalled Adrian performing it.

'Achoo' was selected as the only single from the album in the United States, where it was released with an attractive photo sleeve. It was not a resounding success but it did reach number 102 on the Record World charts and number 112 on the Cashbox chart.

> Ron: 'The end of this song consists of 10,000 sneezes. A health song with a sneeze-solo instead of a guitar solo.'
>
> Trevor White, in *Goldmine* magazine, July 1995: 'They wiped nearly all of his (Adrian Fisher's) guitar parts off the new album, so that all that was left was my rhythm parts. A typical example was Achoo, which ended with this really great track, really characteristic long solo from Adrian. And they wiped it off and put on all these horrid multi tracked sneezes. I don't know if they were

trying to be irritating, but those sneezes were the ultimate in, I don't know what! They figured that everyone had heard a guitar solo, but they hadn't heard us all sneezing.'

'Who Don't Like Kids'
Duration: 3:28

Like several other songs on this album, this one also follows a four-quarter pattern. The piano and guitar riffs alternate, with the latter creating the outro of the song in an endless loop, intermittently interrupted by a children's choir composed of pupils from a nearby primary school. No background vocals are included.

This subject is not often explored by the Maels, likely because they are not familiar with the experience of having and raising children. Consequently, it is unclear whether the lyrics serve as a genuine ode to children or if the narrator adopts a more ironic perspective, struggling to envision children as a welcome addition to a relationship.

Like much of the Sparks' oeuvre, this song has never been performed live at regular concerts.

> Ron: 'On this song we recruited a group of children from the elementary school at Portobello Road, which was nearby, to sing a chorus. The story shows the other side of having children. A child is not only valuable for someone else but should also have the feeling that there is something positive and stimulating going on for him.'

'Bon Voyage'
Written by Ron Mael and Russell Mael
Duration: 4:42

The final song of the three written by Ron and Russell serves as a fitting conclusion to the album. Sparks frequently conclude their albums with a standout track, and in this instance, both the theme and the composition are truly exceptional.

Sung from the perspective of an animal abandoned on the doomed land just before the flood, this piece captures the creature's resentment as it watches other animals board Noah's Ark via the gangplank. While this topic may not be typical, it fits seamlessly into the world of the Maels, where the mundane is transformed into the extraordinary and the remarkable is rendered commonplace.

Lyrically, this song is a true gem and a perfect example of the exceptional talents of the brothers. While it is unclear who is responsible for the lyrical content, Russell has demonstrated on several occasions his ability to craft sharp, humorous and catchy lyrics.

Stately and somewhat grandiose arrangements, devoid of overproduction, feature a melody that would not seem out of place if performed by a church choir on a drizzly Sunday morning, accompanied solely by an organ. This touching interpretation evokes both a smile and a subtle hint of pity, despite the improbability of the entire scene.

A regular feature of the European tour in late 1974 and the North American tour in the spring of 1975, it was absent from the set list until the 2006 tour and the two concerts in Moscow in 2007, after which it fell silent once more. It was not included again in the live set until the 2023 world tour.

> Ron: 'The last song is called "Bon Voyage" and is being sung by an animal that is left behind by Noah's Ark. He's watching them leave and wishes them a good journey but in his heart he wished to sneak on board.'
> Constant Meijers: 'A song about the outsider, the left-behind, the escapist, people who cannot leave their youth behind?'
> Ron Mael: 'Oh boy ... Immediately prepared for a sociological interpretation, aren't you?'

5
Indiscreet

Release date: October 1975
Produced by: Tony Visconti
Engineer: Tony Visconti
Photography: Richard Creamer; Gered Mankowitz (back)
Recorded at: Ramport Studios, London; AIR Studios, London; Tony Visconti's home studio
Duration: 41:32
Personnel: Ron Mael: Keyboards
Russell Mael: Vocals
Trevor White: Guitar
Ian Hampton: Bass guitar
Norman Diamond: Drums

Side 1
'Hospitality On Parade'
'Happy Hunting Ground'
'Without Using Hands'
'Get In The Swing'
'Under The Table With Her'
'How Are You Getting Home?'

Side 2
'Pineapple'
'Tits'
'It Ain't 1918'
'The Lady Is Lingering'
'In The Future'
'Looks, Looks, Looks'
'Miss The Start, Miss The End'

Singles from this album:
'Get In The Swing'/'Profile'
'Looks, Looks, Looks'/'Pineapple'
'Looks, Looks, Looks'/'The Wedding Of Jacqueline Kennedy To Russell Mael'

At the dawn of 1975, Sparks were inescapable in the UK and much of continental Europe. Their presence was felt everywhere: on the radio, television, in music magazines and even in regular newspaper articles.

They were at the pinnacle of their success, and nearly everyone—with the exception of a few reclusive individuals—knew precisely who they were and what the brothers looked like.

Although their second album for Island did not perform as well as their first, and their subsequent singles did not chart as high as their Island debut single, there was no denying that Sparks remained at the heart of pop music.

This decline in record sales, occurring in less than six months since their sudden rise, may have prompted Ron and Russell to pursue a new approach for their upcoming album, along with a different producer.

It is possible that now, having established their status, they were free to pursue the music they truly wished to create. They had previously relied on someone like Muff Winwood to make their music more accessible, but now they were ready to experiment with different styles.

Muff Winwood himself suggested collaborating with Tony Visconti, an American residing in the UK, who was married to Welsh singer Mary Hopkin. Hopkin achieved success in the late 1960s and early 1970s with her debut single 'Those Were The Days', produced by Paul McCartney, which reached number 1 in 1968. After marrying Visconti in 1971, she took a break from the music industry but later contributed modestly to the upcoming Sparks album and recorded a cover of 'Never Turn Your Back On Mother Earth', eventually released in 2007 on her album *Valentine*.

Before collaborating with Tony Visconti, Sparks travelled to the Netherlands, where they received a Gold Record for *Kimono My House*, acknowledging 25,000 copies sold, at the offices of record company Ariola in Hilversum.

The following day, 14 February, Sparks appeared on the popular television programme *De Van Speijk Show*, where they mimed to five tracks from their albums *Kimono My House* and *Propaganda*. Prior to that, they had appeared on Germany's *Musikladen*, playing five songs live, which was broadcast on 1 January 1975 and released on video-CD in 1995.

Upon their return, they met with Tony Visconti and immediately hit it off. The Maels were convinced that Tony was the right person to elevate their music to the level they were seeking. He had, of course, been a significant factor in the success of Marc Bolan's T. Rex and several albums by David Bowie in the early Seventies, and Ron and Russell were convinced that he could achieve remarkable results with Sparks as well.

On 17 March 1975, Sparks entered Visconti's tiny home studio in Shepherd's Bush to record 'Get In The Swing' and 'Pineapple'. 'Profile', an outtake recorded in February 1974 with the *Kimono My House* band, was also retrieved from the vault. Martin Gordon's bass parts were rerecorded by Ian Hampton, while Trevor White contributed guitar parts.

It was released as the B-side of the first single, 'Get In The Swing'. The working title for the new album was *A Great Day For Auto Racing*. In between the recordings for the new album, the band returned to the American continent for a second visit, during which an actual tour had been arranged. They left England on 2 April and played their first Canadian concert at Massey Hall in Toronto on 6 April. Another Canadian performance took place in Montreal on 9 April, before they fully focused on the Maels' home country.

Their first proper gig in the U.S. took place in Buffalo, New York, and this time the audience was well-prepared. After the initial confusion during the television recordings of their previous visit, fans now knew exactly who they were coming to see, and the earlier hesitation had transformed into enthusiastic support for the band. Including the two performances in Canada, the band visited seventeen cities, including their hometown, where they played a sold-out concert at the Palace Theatre on 19 April, followed by an even more electrifying show at the Santa Monica Civic Auditorium on 3 May.

The after-gig party was held at a pie shop, while the after-gig celebration in New York, following their performance at the Academy of Music on 9 May, took place at the local Burger King on 59th Street. Russell arrived wearing the tightest white tennis outfit imaginable.

Despite being in the midst of recording their new album, only tracks from *Kimono My House* and *Propaganda* were performed during the tour, along with Bearsville singles 'Wonder Girl' and 'Girl From Germany'.

While in the United States, photographs for the new album cover were taken. Richard Creamer captured the front cover and inside sleeve images, while Gered Mankowitz photographed the back cover. Both photographers expressed slight disappointment that they could not shoot the entire cover. Alternative photos for the back cover were also taken, featuring Russell sitting on a horse with the rest of the band dressed as LAPD officers.

Russell reflects on the back cover:

> It's a rather sad story really. It's taken at a photo studio in LA, with Gered Mankowitz. We suggested using a fake backdrop from a movie supply house. So we went through their books and saw that one and said: 'we've gotta have that'. Then they brought in this horse. It was sedated so it would just kinda sit there and not cause a fuss during the photo shoot. Of course no one would know just by looking at it.

When the tour concluded, Ian, Trevor and Dinky returned to London, while Ron and Russell remained in Los Angeles. They rented a fully furnished three-storey house in the Hollywood Hills, complete with swimming pool and fitness facilities. During their stay, they composed the remaining songs for the new album, including the track 'Quote, Unquote', which ultimately was unused.

Armed with a bag full of new songs, the Maels flew back to England and arrived at Heathrow Airport on 21 July. Recording sessions took place at Ramport Studios, where parts of *Kimono My House* had been recorded, and at AIR Studios, where *Propaganda* had been produced.

During their time in Hollywood, Island Records UK released the first single from the new album: 'Get In The Swing', with 'Profile' on the B-side. The single was released on 11 July 1975, but only reached number 27 in the British charts. Despite appearances on *Top Of The Pops* on 24 and 31 July, and the airing of a recorded video on *Shang-a-Lang*, a children's music show hosted by the Bay City Rollers, on 12 August, the single was not a major hit.

Ron provided demos for most songs, and the Maels granted Tony full control over the arrangements and additional instrumentation. Tony frequently consulted with Ron and Russell to ensure they were in agreement with the direction he was taking the songs, which they enthusiastically supported. They felt that Tony understood precisely where they wanted to take their new sound.

However, the other band members were less enthusiastic about the new direction. In some cases, they didn't even participate in a song, which made them feel that Sparks were deviating from the conventional pop music that had brought them success. During the recording of 'Looks, Looks, Looks', Ron did not play his keyboard, as Tony had discovered a retired pianist who possessed the right sound and style for that particular track.

Apart from the thirteen tracks that ultimately appeared on *Indiscreet*, the band recorded an additional six tracks for the album, most of which were not released at the time. These included 'Intrusion' (later renamed 'Confusion' for the anticipated film by Jacques Tati), 'Looks Aren't Everything', 'Tearing The Place Apart' and 'Gone With The Wind', which was written by Russell. The only song released at the time was 'The Wedding Of Jacqueline Kennedy To Russell Mael', intended as the B-side to the second single 'Looks, Looks, Looks', but rejected by Island Records in the UK for being deemed offensive. Russell also wrote this song, and it did appear on the US release of the single, with Mary Hopkin providing the vocals for the modest role of Jacqueline Kennedy.

Meanwhile, the *Confusion* movie project was still in progress. The Maels and Tati were introduced by Peter Zumsteg, the Island promotion and marketing representative for continental Europe.

Before and during the album recording, Ron and Russell held several meetings in Paris with Tati to further discuss the movie project. However, nothing materialised, as Tati was continually seeking funding and refining the script. The project was officially cancelled when he passed away in 1982. The Maels still regard this as one of the biggest disappointments of their career, as it marked the end of their potential acting debut.

The second single from the album was released on 26 September in the UK and several European countries. Once again, they made a remarkable choice by opting for the combination 'Looks, Looks, Looks'/'Pineapple'. The A-side wasn't exactly a conventional selection. After Island refused to support it with the non-album track 'The Wedding Of Jacqueline Kennedy To Russell Mael', they could have chosen any of the other outtakes recorded for the album.

Instead, they broke tradition by releasing a combination of songs that were already included on the album. This single performed slightly better than its predecessor, reaching number 26 on the UK Singles Chart. The album itself was released in the first half of October, and unlike the previous two albums, it did not make it into the top ten, only reaching number 17 on the charts for four weeks.

Outside of the UK, the album didn't fare much better. It reached #18 on the Dutch charts and an impressive number 6 in the Swedish album charts, better than anywhere else in the world. In the US, *Propaganda* had been their first top 100 album, at number 63, but *Indiscreet* only made it to number 169.

Despite this, extensive tours in both North America and Europe had been planned. The European tour began on 2 October in Helsinki, Finland, where they had not performed before, and concluded on 9 November with a legendary performance at the Fairfield Halls in Croydon. A video recording, directed by Tony Visconti, was partially broadcast on UK television.

The North American tour lasted exactly one month, beginning in Philadelphia on 14 November and concluding in San Diego.

Meanwhile, Ron and Russell were ready for another change. After living in the UK for two-and-a-half years, they decided it was time to return to California. They missed the Californian climate and wanted to concentrate on their home country, yet with a completely new direction.

After the US tour concluded, the band members were informed that their services were no longer required, and the Maels would remain in the US to seek new musicians. Disillusioned and disappointed, Trevor and Dinky returned home immediately, while Ian stayed for a while longer before eventually heading back to England as well.

In 1981, former manager John Hewlett (vocals) formed The Four Squares, which included Trevor White (bass), Dinky Diamond (drums), Adrian Fisher (guitar) and Chuck Wagon (keyboards, guitar), also known as Bob Davis from the Los Angeles band The Dickies. They recorded nine demo tracks at Bearsville Studios with the approval of Albert Grossman.

Tragically, Davis reportedly shot himself after a Dickies concert and passed away the following morning. In 1983, two of those recordings were released on the record label New World; 'The Gates of Hell', with B-side 'The Debt'.

For Ron and Russell, the final month of 1975 appeared drastically different from the previous year, and they found themselves starting anew. They needed to form a new band, secure a new producer and devise a strategy to conquer their home country.

Indiscreet—The Songs

All songs written by Ron Mael, unless otherwise stated.

'HOSPITALITY ON PARADE'
Duration: 3:58

The sound of this record is transformed significantly through the collaboration with new producer Tony Visconti, which becomes evident in the opening notes of the first track. The mid-tempo, catchy melody bears a vague resemblance to a slowed-down demo of Scaffold's 'Lily the Pink', with a vocal performance that is noticeably deeper than those found in most tracks from the previous albums.

The music primarily features a dominant organ that produces two distinct sounds: one closely resembling a monotonous hum, while the powerful and distinctive piano provides a cheerful counterbalance. The well-known falsetto is utilised solely in the backing vocals. Handclaps are incorporated to establish the rhythm before the drums join in with the other instruments.

This phenomenon occurs after approximately two-and-a-half minutes. The input consists of short bursts following a consistent 'one, two, one, two, three' rhythm that remains unchanged and continues until the song fades out. There are no solos or bass runs that diverge from the melody.

As for the meaning of the lyrics, there are various interpretations, as is often the case with Sparks. Some believe they reference the American War of Independence and the subsequent developments in the country. Others argue that the lyrics primarily offer a critical perspective on contemporary society, where it often appears that people are willing to help others, but only when some form of self-interest is involved.

Four versions of tracks from *Indiscreet* have been leaked unofficially over time, differing more or less from the final album versions. 'Hospitality On Parade' is one of them; however, aside from Russell's countdown at the beginning, this version is not significantly different from the official release.

The song was a regular feature of the live set during the European tour in late 1975, after which it vanished for many years until it reappeared in concerts in 2000, 2004 and 2006. It was also included in the Two Hands One Mouth project and is available on the official live CD. Additionally, it was a staple of the live set during the world tour in 2017.

'HAPPY HUNTING GROUND'
Duration: 3:44

After the relatively calm opener, the fast-paced rock song featuring the full band is quickly revisited. 'Happy Hunting Ground' would not have felt out of place on the previous album and serves as a preview of the diverse styles employed on *Indiscreet*. In hindsight, this album, which consists of thirteen songs, contains only two other tracks that can be classified as rock.

The overall sound of this song is primarily crafted by the other band members, while the piano plays a subtle role, accentuating specific sections. Russell's falsetto is beautifully highlighted during the break and the ad infinitum ending, with no double vocals employed elsewhere.

Deciphering the meaning of the song is not an easy task. Some believe that it reflects the challenges individuals encounter when attempting to connect with the opposite sex after graduating from university. The circumstances they face are often different from what they are accustomed to, leading to a longing for the simpler days of dating.

Another mix of this song has also been leaked, and in this version the guitars are slightly different. However, the arrangements from the official version are maintained.

The song was a regular feature of the European and North American tour in late 1975 but did not resurface until the concerts in 2006. Since its performance at the Sparks Spectacular, it has not been played live again.

> Russell: 'We could have released "Happy Hunting Ground" as a single and it wouldn't have done bad 'cos it's a rock song. It would have been a lot safer but we really felt that if we got those songs ("Looks, Looks, Looks" and "Get In The Swing") played on the radio it would be an amazing feat.'

'Without Using Hands'
Duration: 3:19

It is quite challenging to interpret the deeper meaning of the lyrics in this song, and there may not even be one at all. Three scenarios unfold in the Ritz Hotel in Paris, illustrating how one can accomplish certain actions without the use of hands. While these represent choices, the song concludes with a bomb explosion that results in the hotel manager losing his hands, eliminating that option entirely.

It appears to be a mildly cynical yet predominantly humorous story without any deeper meaning, a narrative that could easily be attributed to Ron Mael.

A prominent piano and a supporting bass line are the primary instruments featured in this song. Occasionally, an organ is added, along with sparse use of percussion and guitar.

The style of the song is difficult to categorise. With slight modifications to the arrangements, it could easily fit into one of the Bearsville albums; however, it would have been a mismatch on *Indiscreet*'s two predecessors. In all fairness, this observation applies to most of the songs on this album.

During regular concerts, 'Without Using Hands' was only performed live in the European and North American tours at the end of 1975.

> Ron: 'I see that song in a filmic kind of way—three stories and they kind of intertwine. It's a kind of three-part song with three verses. It's just a general atmospheric situation set around the Ritz Hotel, saying that in the evening the love making will be done, without using hands. The second verse involves American tourists showing slides of Paris and there's a bit of an upheaval because their two kids are fighting and then the comment comes—by some anonymous voice—that the only way children are punished today is without using hands. And in the third verse an explosion takes place in the lobby of the Ritz Hotel but it all ends up happy except the manager had his hands burned in the explosion and he's going to have to spend the rest of his life without using hands.'

'GET IN THE SWING'
Duration: 4:00

The first single selected for promoting the album was an unusual choice, given that there are more commercially viable songs on the album. It was a bold decision that, unfortunately, did not yield the desired results. The single peaked at number 27 on the British singles chart, reflecting a decline in interest in their music just a year after the initial success with their first single on Island Records.

The song is a vibrant blend of various musical styles that convey a cheerful yet somewhat chaotic atmosphere.

Russell has drawn comparisons between this song work and Queen's 'Bohemian Rhapsody', wondering whether the concept of this track may have served as inspiration. While both songs blend various stylistic elements, the individual components of 'Bohemian Rhapsody' are more accessible and engaging than those of 'Get In The Swing'.

The song begins with a gradual fade-in of a lively marching band, accompanied by cheerful onlookers. Brass instruments play a significant role in the arrangements, diverging from the conventional setup of guitar, drums and bass guitar.

In this song, the guitar initially seems to take a backseat. While there is ample room for the drums and bass, the guitars are used sparingly until about two minutes in. A delicate violin unexpectedly emerges during the middle eight, highlighting a variety of instruments throughout the song.

The single, featuring the previously recorded track 'Profile' as its B-side, was released in most Western European countries, as well as in Australia,

New Zealand and Japan. Aside from the UK, it only achieved modest success in Belgium, where it peaked at number 38 on the local charts.

Despite its intricate arrangements, the song was performed live during the 1975 tour, showcasing a polished rendition with minimal instrumental accompaniment. It was also frequently performed in the 1990s and included in the second set during the 2014 and 2015 concerts with the Heritage Orchestra. The song continued to be a staple of the live set during the 2022 tour.

> Ron: 'It's a song about trying to find something to get involved in. There are three parts to it. The first part is about a young lad at home who is wondering what to do. His friends come by and he decides to leave home and get involved. The second part is in a slightly more scientific vein, comparing the lifestyle of people with that of salmon. In the third part we get into a religious bag, I guess. It's about the kid being got at by religion and mysticism and eventually saying "No, I ain't got time for you".'
>
> Russell: 'I think it was one of the most important singles in a long time, in the same way we feel that the album is one of the most significant albums in the Seventies.'

'UNDER THE TABLE WITH HER'
Duration: 2:19

The influence of movie classics on Sparks' music is evident in this short yet impressive song. Having previously recorded a cover version of 'Do-Re-Mi', they now had a song that could seamlessly fit into the soundtrack of *The Sound of Music*. Particularly, Russell's sublime use of double vocals in the line 'People all around the world…' is very reminiscent of vocal styles used in that film.

When Ron presented the song to Tony Visconti, he felt it needed a 'Schubert string quartet'. The result was a refreshing piece of chamber music, where the other band members played no role, including Ron himself, whose role was limited to the formal uttering of 'Dinner for twelve, thank you', two minutes into the song. Apart from the strings, Russell's vocal abilities shine.

The song appears to be about two kids hiding under a table during a dinner party, seeking comfort in their seclusion. Some have suggested it could be about two pets (dogs), banished under the table during the feast while humans enjoy a lavish meal.

In addition to being on the album, it was released as the B-side of the UK promo-only version of the single 'I Want To Hold Your Hand' in March 1976. The regular single had 'England' on the flip side.

During live performances, Ron plays a crucial role as all string arrangements come from his keyboard. However, during the initial live presentation on 21 May 2008, an authentic string quartet was hired for the occasion. The song was also featured on the Two Hands One Mouth tour in 2012 and was a regular part of the 2022 world tour, with backing vocals provided, in a modest form, by the other band members.

Russell: 'I sang that live with the strings, which was a whole new experience.'

'How Are You Getting Home?'
Duration: 2:56

Fans of the more traditional Sparks sound, if that exists, were probably somewhat relieved to hear that the first side of the album ended with a conventional rock song. It resembles the style of the previous two albums more than most of the songs on side one do, as well as side two, for that matter.

The guitar and bass guitar play an important role in this up-tempo song, with the piano mainly providing a supporting role. The arrangements are quite predictable, but amidst the patchwork of various styles on the album, a conventional approach to one of the songs is fairly refreshing.

Regarding the content of the lyrics, the meaning is as basic as the arrangements. The narrator is the prototype of a seducer and hopes, with his slightly aggressive approach, to entice one of the ladies from the party into his car, for obvious reasons.

The song was featured in French director Leos Carax's 2012 film *Holy Motors*.

It was part of the live set during the European and North American tours in late 1975, only to vanish from the set until 2013, when it was included in the Revenge of Two Hands One Mouth tour, performed without the accompaniment of other musicians, except for Ron's keyboards.

'Pineapple'
Written by Russell Mael
Duration: 2:42

One of the rare occasions where a song appears on an album written solely by Russell, which had not occurred since the debut album. Interestingly, he contributed another two songs for the recordings of *Indiscreet*, one being the previously mentioned 'The Wedding Of Jacqueline Kennedy To Russell Mael'. It is quite remarkable that the other song, 'Gone With The Wind', did not make it to the album, as it was just as strong as 'Pineapple'. Russell begins with an extensive acapella intro for the song, providing background vocals himself.

The instruments join in after about fifteen seconds, with a dominant piano, minimal rhythm guitar and occasional tuba-like bass. Backing vocals are a mix of Russell and Trevor White.

The song's meaning is quite unambiguous and seems to be nothing more or less than a paean to the pineapple, enumerating all the benefits of this fruit with great enthusiasm.

The upbeat and slightly quirky opening hints at the more unconventional style to come. Apart from the presentation at the Sparks Spectacular, 'Pineapple' was only performed at concerts in 2006 and 2007. One of these concerts was recorded for the *DeeVeeDee*, preserving a live version for eternity. This rendition is similar to the album version, with the tuba replaced by a bass guitar.

> Russell: 'That's in a much lighter vein. It definitely isn't "Tits". It's about a director of a Pineapple corporation who's making a speech in front of some prospective investors and telling them what a worthy investment the pineapple is. It's a song in praise of the pineapple! After all these years, to my knowledge no one else has come up with a better song extolling the virtues of the tropical fruit.'
>
> Ron: 'A long neglected subject.'

'TITS'
Duration: 4:56

A somewhat ominous, slow drumbeat accompanied by a bass guitar opens the song, followed by keyboards that take it in a completely different direction. The guitar joins in, but its contribution remains limited to occasional riffs.

At times, the song resembles a traditional rock song, but the arrangements in other parts do not fit at all, setting the song in a different category.

The story is both comical and tragic, telling of a man and his wife who are no longer sexually active after having a child. He also suspects that his wife is cheating on him. The narrator finds solace in drinking and confides in his friend, slowly realising that Harry might actually be the one his wife is having an affair with.

Russell perfectly captures the mood and subject matter of the song, using his voice to express complaints, despair, anger and acceptance, to illustrate the different stages of this tale of woe.

To prevent the cover art from being censored in certain retail chains, the song was presented as 'T*ts' on the back cover. However, the original title was mentioned on the label and on the enclosed lyric sheet.

'Tits' was also one of the tracks that had a different mix that made it onto the collectors' circuit. While there were no particularly notable changes from the official version, this unreleased mix was over forty seconds longer, mainly due to the much longer outro of the track. Russell prefaces it with 'Tits, take two'.

During concerts at the end of 1975, the song was a permanent part of the set list. It was only played again during the one-off presentation of the entire album in 2008.

> Russell: 'I think there will be a lot of tee-heeing on the surface but actually it's a deep song lyrically, [although] maybe it's frivolous calling it "tits". I think deep down it's the most poignant song on the album.'
> Ron: 'I see it as a song that maybe Frank Sinatra could be singing in a bar or something where he's with a drinking partner. It's definitely not a teenage song. It's all about one guy who's having marital problems and the symbol of a good or bad state of marriage to him are tits! When the marriage is good, his wife's tits are a playground: and when it's going bad it's purely functional.'
> Russell: 'We were sure the English store chain WH Smith would ban "Tits". They would ban something with the word "drat" in the title. So we called it "T*ts"—real hard to figure out.'

'IT AIN'T 1918'
Duration: 2:05

The arrangement of this song is somewhat similar to 'Here Comes Bob' from *A Woofer in Tweeter's Clothing*, mainly due to the fiddles. The chord structure and subject are completely different, but one could draw a comparison. The melody sounds rather cheerful and wouldn't be out of place at an annual corn harvesting festival in Nebraska.

Once again, the guitar plays a negligible role in the song, which is centred around the fiddles and piano, with the bass guitar providing support.

During the 1975 tours, the song was included in the set list, with Ron's keyboards replacing the fiddles. The drums took on a more prominent role in the live version and there was more space for the guitar, as there were no string instruments available.

At the Sparks Spectacular, the only other time this song was performed live, a fiddle player was on stage and the arrangements were focussed on him and the bass guitar, with Ron's keyboards barely noticeable. During the build-up to the final line, Russell sang the last word extra-long in his characteristic falsetto, which was greeted with loud cheers.

The final song slipped out of the studio with a different mix that is noticeably distinct from the official version, as the fiddles have been replaced by a xylophone. This may have been an initial attempt, with the decision later made to incorporate fiddles instead. While the mix is open and intriguing, it is understandable why fiddles were ultimately chosen.

Russell: 'Musically, it's a Sparks hoe-down. Lyrically it's about a guy who lives in a dream world about the way things were in the past—in particular 1918—and he wants everything to stay that way.'

Ron: 'In the end there's this lady who's a kind of a patron and she buys Johnny, the character in the song, a new house and new clothes and he gets upset. The people get really upset and say: "It isn't 1918 for us or for you and if we can't enjoy living in 1918, then you can't either." And their gifts of the present-day luxuries are a way of getting him into the present 'cause they'd like to be living in the past.'

'The Lady Is Lingering'
Duration: 3:40

The band's traditional instruments are fully present in this mid-tempo ballad, which is devoid of additional outside musicians, something that is the exception rather than the rule on this versatile album.

The song opens with the full band, with the guitar and bass leading the vocal line of the chorus while the piano characteristically plays a fresh countermelody with short strokes. The vocal line makes beautiful use of falsetto outbursts, and in the second verse, a second vocal layer is used beautifully, accompanied by the piano and bass, to the rhythm of a mid-tempo drumbeat. In the repetition of the chorus an unobtrusive organ blends in, which also supports the middle eight, this time with minimal contribution from the piano. The song finally ends in a fade-out.

Subtle stereo effects and thoughtful backing vocals are standout features in the production of this song. It tells the story of a man on a date with the perfect woman, realising how lucky he is and feeling unworthy of her interest. He fears ruining the moment with a wrong word, always on edge that it could end at any moment.

This song has never been performed live during regular concerts.

Ron: 'A really romantic song, and you can't say that too many of the Sparks things have been really romantic in an overt kind of way. It's romantic in a rock kind of way. I just see it as a rock love song.'

'In The Future'
Duration: 2:13

'In The Future' is the fastest and shortest song on the album. The tempo and speed at which the lyrics are sung can be compared to earlier songs like 'Something For The Girl With Everything' or 'At Home, At Work, At Play'.

Similar to the previous song, only traditional instruments are used, with the piano playing a prominent role. At certain moments a second line seems to be played on a harpsichord. The other instruments act more as fillers than a baseline, and with some goodwill, this could also be labelled as a rock song.

The vocals are mainly in falsetto and the whole vibe of the song indeed exudes a futuristic atmosphere.

It is not inconceivable that there is a deeper meaning behind the lyrics of this song, but it is difficult to fathom. At first glance, it seems to be mainly about someone who is not satisfied with what life has bestowed on him and is convinced that it will all become more appealing in the future. He seems to want to convince others of his beliefs as well.

Besides the obvious rendition of the song at the Sparks Spectacular, where it was performed for the last time, it was a regular part of the second tour in 1975 and was also played in concerts in 2006 and 2007.

'Looks, Looks, Looks'
Duration: 2:32

The previous song abruptly cuts off and seamlessly transitions into 'Looks, Looks, Looks', the second single from this album.

If there were any doubts about the wide range of styles that the Mael brothers wanted to showcase on this album, this recording puts an abrupt end to that. 'Get In The Swing' was already a peculiar choice for the first single, but with 'Looks, Looks, Looks' as its successor, it was clear that Ron and Russell no longer wanted to be told which songs to use to promote the album.

The song, on which no band member—not even Ron—played, was a huge departure from the hits with which the band had conquered a large part of Europe the previous year. All instruments were played by the Ted Heath Orchestra, an original ensemble that had been around for decades.

The arrangements were written entirely in the style of big band swing and could have been released as a single forty years earlier, at 78rpm, admittedly.

'Looks, Looks, Looks' was released as a single on 4 October, with 'Pineapple' on the B-side. In the United States, the outtake 'The Wedding of Jacqueline Kennedy to Russell Mael' was used as the flip side. In the UK, it peaked at number 26, one position higher than its predecessor, but in most other countries it went unnoticed.

The lyrics are quite witty and criticise the superficial nature of society's obsession with physical appearance. They can be seen as a complaint about people who rely solely on their looks for success and recognition. If you don't have that, you can only look.

Ron: 'On "Looks, Looks, Looks", I was saying that all that matters are looks. I'm ambivalent on that 'cos sometimes I think that is the case. Usually not 'cos it's too simple. But you run into instances where you say "God, that's all that matters, the way things look."

Russell: 'We didn't set out to be deliberately different with the single. The song lent itself to a big band arrangement, so we tried it out. And with this one, the arrangement worked. We're really pleased with it.'

Tony Visconti: 'We did it with a 1930s band arrangement, and it was an absolute delight to record. We did it at the Who's studios, Ramport, and we got all the old faces in from the Ted Heath Band. I did some research by listening to all my old records from the 1930s, listening closely to the harmonies, and the way you have to write for saxophones, and for the things I wasn't sure about. I rang up a friend of mine, Bruce Lynch, who's a brilliant arranger, and with a little help from him, I wrote the arrangement.'

'Miss The Start, Miss The End'
Duration: 2:42

The song begins serenely with a warm piano, bass guitar and a guitar with a phaser effect. The vocals are subdued, and only after more than a minute can a supporting drumbeat be heard. Halfway through the song, two backing vocal lines from Russell are subtly introduced. During the rendition of the final chorus, an additional backing vocal adds a sense of closure to the song, resulting in a moving feeling.

The clever contradiction between the melancholic verses and the upbeat chorus, reminiscent of an 'all together now' anthem, is another fine example of Ron Mael's genius. This is complemented by the usual profound lyrics.

Surprisingly, the song was not originally intended to be included on the album, but due to the insistence of Tony Visconti, Island Records eventually agreed.

The song appears to be a protest against people who arrive late for and leave early from shows. However, it becomes clear that these individuals find happiness in each other's company and do not necessarily need to experience the complete performances.

In the documentary *Never Turn Your Back on Sparks*, directed by Pini Schatz and released in 2014, a professional opera singer is challenged with this song. She initially struggles with the vocal lines and various key changes, but eventually succeeds. This demonstrates how Russell is challenged by Ron's uncompromising song writing.

Unfortunately, this song has never been performed during regular concerts.

6

Big Beat

Release date: October 1976
Produced by: Rupert Holmes
Engineer: Godfrey Diamond
Sleeve design: Tom Steele
Photography: Richard Avedon
Recorded at: Mediasound Studios, New York
Duration: 35:30
Personnel: Ron Mael: Keyboards
Russell Mael: Vocals
Jeffrey Salen: Guitar
Sal Maida: Bass guitar
Hilly Boy Michaels: Drums

Side 1
'Big Boy'
'I Want To Be Like Everybody Else'
'Nothing To Do'
'I Bought The Mississippi River'
'Fill-Er-Up'
'Everybody's Stupid'

Side 2
'Throw Her Away (And Get A New One)'
'Confusion'
'Screwed Up'
'White Women'
'I Like Girls'

Singles from this album:
'Big Boy'/'Fill-Er-Up'
'I Like Girls'/'England'
'Confusion'/'I Bought The Mississippi River'

At the end of 1975, Ron and Russell Mael found themselves back at the drawing board. After experiencing a decline in record sales and a commercially failed album, they made the decision to part ways with their British band and were now considering their next move. Back in Los Angeles, they aimed to make a breakthrough in their home country and had signed a recording deal with CBS Records for the US and Canada, while still being handled by Island Records for the rest of the world.

One of the first things CBS demanded was to bring in a new producer. They enlisted Rupert Holmes, whose initial task was to record a duet between Russell and Marianne Faithfull. The song chosen was the Beatles' hit 'I Want To Hold Your Hand', although there are sources suggesting that the Sonny and Cher classic 'I Got You, Babe' was also considered. The latter, however, has never been officially confirmed.

The fate of the song for Sparks was not entirely favourable. The official story was that Faithfull felt that it was too reminiscent of the era in which she had played a significant role, prompting Ron to write a new song for the duet titled 'Room For Two'.

Unfortunately, CBS declined this new song, leading to the decision to move forward with 'I Want To Hold Your Hand' as a solo project for Russell. The recordings took place at Studio A of the Mediasound Recording Studios in New York City. Additionally, they recorded another version of 'I Like Girls', intended to serve as the B-side of the new single.

Both CBS and the Maels wanted to have a big orchestral arrangement for both songs, which is why Holmes had been brought in. He had previously produced the British band Sailor and Barbra Streisand, and would have a smash hit single himself in 1979 with 'Escape' (The Piña Colada Song).

British Sparks fan Leslie Hanagan had an email correspondence with Rupert Holmes to find out more about these recordings, and Rupert informed him of the following:

> When we cut 'I Want To Hold Your Hand' we also cut 'I Like Girls', intended as the B-side using the same lavish instrumentation, lots of brass and strings, which included Vincent Bell's famous, self-created set of effects pedals. We recorded and mixed both cuts at Studio A at Mediasound Recording Studios (where we later also recorded *Big Beat* with much different and smaller instrumentation).
>
> I liked doing both projects with Sparks, who were easy to work with and who had clear ideas on what they wanted both projects to sound and feel like. For 'I Want To Hold Your Hand', Russell said he wanted it to be lavish, a bit over the top. I asked if he wanted it to be Hollywood-lavish or Broadway-lavish, he considered and said, 'Broadway.' So that's what I tried to give them.
>
> For *Big Beat*, they wanted the sound spare and tough. That's what we tried to achieve. Two major talents to this day.

The musicians who played on the recordings of these two songs, in addition to Ron and Russell, were: Allan Schwartzberg (drums), Wilbur Bascomb (bass), Vincent Bell (guitar), Margaret Ross (harp) and a collection of backing singers, including Martha Thomas, Vivian Cherry, Tasha Thomas and Cissy Houston, Whitney's mother.

'I Want To Hold Your Hand' was released in March 1976, as a Sparks project, not as a Russell Mael solo project. It was released by Island in the UK, France, Australia, New Zealand, Japan and the Philippines, but without the intended B-side. Ron and Russell had recorded a new song, 'England', produced by ex-band member Earle Mankey. 'England' reflected on the years the Maels spent in the UK and was stylistically different from the A-side.

The single 'I Want To Hold Your Hand', was released in the UK on March 19, but was withdrawn shortly after due to EMI re-releasing 24 Beatles singles the same month. Island felt the Sparks single would be overshadowed.

The original recording of 'I Like Girls' produced by Rupert Holmes was released on the CD-compilation *In The Swing* in 1993. Or was it? Leslie Hanagan sent that recording to Rupert Holmes, who claimed it was not the original. He believed it was a slimmed-down version of the recording. Holmes wrote to Leslie:

> So, it's possible that no one has ever heard the truly orchestral mix of 'I Like Girls'. I'll have to see if my friend and producing partner still has a copy. It's quite grand in scale. I'll let you know if I have any luck finding the original 'Wagnerian' mix of 'I Like Girls'.

There was a 10-inch acetate pressed of 'I Want To Hold Your Hand'/'I Like Girls' in the US, which probably contains the original version of the latter. This was dated as early as 17 November 1975, which is strange because, at that time, they were still in the middle of a tour with the British band.

Russell also gave his take on those recordings:

> I was going to do a lush, orchestrated duet version of 'I Want To Hold Your Hand' with Marianne Faithfull. Rupert Holmes did the score for the song, yet Marianne dropped out of the project at the last minute, leaving Rupert and ourselves with a score and no one to sing it. I ended up singing the song, yet it seemed so incongruous even for Sparks, that it never appeared on an LP. A single of the song was released as Sparks in a few assorted foreign countries.
>
> We continued working with Rupert, even though 'Big Beat' was going to be a more stripped down LP with more guitars and fewer of Ron's keyboards.

After the session with Rupert Holmes, the Maels had their sights set on New York City, where a lot of exciting things were happening. Just like in the UK, the punk wave had arrived and Ron, Russell and manager John Hewlett were eager to explore it. They reached out to bass player Sal Maida, who had previously auditioned for them in 1973 for the *Kimono My House* band. He was turned

Ron and Russell at *The Big T.N.T. Show*, 1965.

Halfnelson: Harley Feinstein, Jim Mankey, Earle Mankey, Russell Mael, Ron Mael. (*Promotion shot, Bearsville Records, 1971*)

Marquee Club, London, December 1972: Ron Mael, Jim Mankey, Russell Mael, Harley Feinstein.

Sparks—food first, music second

"Too many groups we know are into music."

By ANDREW TYLER

SPARKS are heavily into food ... Kit Kats, matzos, Jet gum, peppermint Aero and burgers, definiteiy burgers. The L.A. Times knows. They've published some of their choicest recipes and Albert Grossman knows, or will do any day now, because right alongside his Bear snackhouse in Woodstock (Dylanburgers, Runtburgers, Winchester Plate) they plan to erect The Silver Sparks, and it might just serve the finest burgers in the whole of Woodstock County.

A very peculiar situation since Grossman just happens to have the gronp lassoed to his Bearsville label, Sparks' manager Roy Silver thinks it's a good idea, but then he and Albert fell ont some time ago over who was to take charge of Bobby Dylan's career. Albert came out tops but now Mr. Silver reckons he has a new Bob Dylan or maybe five of them.

Silver, it's worth noting, specialises in the wantonly bizarre. Tiny Tim, Mamas and Papas and Bill Cosby were some of his earlier brainstarms, and who would have given half a chance to a black comedian or a twittering middle-aged banjo player?

LATENT INSANITY

Sparks are from Los Angeles and are causing an almighty furore, mainly because nobody knows what to make of them. They could easily be early Mothers. They have that same air of latent insanity but then they're pretty and taneful enough to stand in line with David (wait for it) Cassidy.

A few weeks ago on a trip to Switzerland they were signing autographs on hands and foreheads while Gary Glitter and Lynsey De Paul, who should have been signing autographs on hands and foreheads, were standing around smiling uneasily.

"It was pretty embarrassing, really," says Ron Mael. Ron plays piano and for a long time thought he looked just like Alvin Lee until Charlie Chaplin saw him on Dick Clarke's *American Bandstand* and wrote to him saying he was impressed with his Chaplinesque manner.

Ron's brother Russell handles most of the vocals and their father, a film producer, is married to Doris Day. There are two more brothers in the line-up —Jim (guitar, bass) and Earle (guitar) Mankey. Their father was one of the famous Mankey twins—Earle and Merle—who tap-danced on roller skates while playing guitar and banjo.

Harley Feinstein plays drums and his father is also in showbiz. He once did a linoleum job for Zsa Zsa Gabor.

Earle, Ron and Russell got together in 1967 and recorded all sorts of wierd stuff for a couple of years not being particularly interested in playing live gigs.

Harley joined them two years later and then late '69 Earle remembered he had a kid brother called Iim and he was invited along.

"Round about this time," says Earle. "we sent a tape to Todd Rundgren and his girlfriend really liked us. This was his post-Nazz, pre-millionaire stage. We wanted to stay in our doggy Iactory and practice but Todd got us out."

It meant a live gig so they rented a delicatessen in Hollywood called *Gregar*. "They ran ont of pastrami and no one came. But we recorded the whole thing. When we listened to the tapes, it was ridiculous. We were so nervous we were playing at 90 m.p.h. like a bunch of speed freaks doing a Broadway musical."

Cndeterred, Todd Rundgren hired a studio and produced their first album, released in America in July and called "Sparks." It sat about on record store shelves for a while until Roy Silver did a bit of shoving. Now the single "Wonder Girl" is aumber one in Council Blofis, Iowa and Montgomery, Alabama and both single and album have just been released over here.

SECOND ALBUM

And there's a second album, recorded at Wally Heider's very famous Hollywood studio and due around January or February. It's called "A Woofer In Tweeter's Clothing".

"Earle's studio is finally up to date," says Ron, "and we might just produce the third one there.

"Everybody over here thinks it's happening in Hollywood and over there it's the other way 'round. We used to sit around dreaming of being in Britain and writing songs. Now we're here, we write nothing. We spend all our time driving aronnd buying chocolate bars and asking Albert for more money.

"But when we go back they'll be this hig mystique, yon see. Everyone will say 'gee where've you guys been . . . yon been ill or something? Gee what a lot of mystique you guys have'."

But they won't be going back just yet. A series of dates have been set up across Britain and the Continent thrpugh November and December.

One American reviewer has already described Sparks as "the greatest Euglish band to come out of America since the Nazz" . . . but first things first. Ron says their main goal is to set up a hall-bake shop selling pastries and cream cakes and they've got to get to work on the menu for the Silver Sparks. They're thinking in terms of Kinkburgers, Moody Blue Malts and Rod Stew.

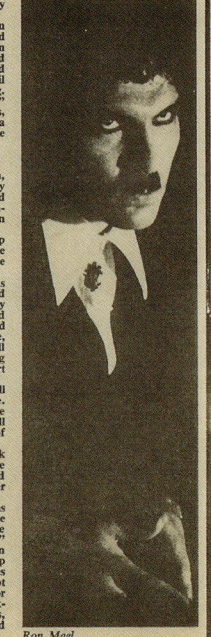

Disc & Music Magazine, UK, 11 November 1972.

Ron Mael, November 1972, UK.

The *Kimono My House* band, 1974; *Muziek Express Magazine*, Netherlands: Adrian Fisher, Ron Mael, Dinky Diamond, Russell Mael, Martin Gordon.

Ron and Russell receiving a Gold Record for *Kimono My House*, Hilversum, Netherlands, 2 February 1975, with host Willem Ruis.

Tower Theatre, Philadelphia, 18 May 1975. (*Photo by Ken Montgomery*)

Ron and Russell at the Louvre, Paris, February 1976; *Best Magazine*, France.

Sparks, 1975; *Zip Magazine*, Sweden: Ian Hampton, Russell Mael, Dinky Diamond, Trevor White, Ron Mael.

The *Big Beat* touring band, 1976: Hilly Boy Michaels, Luke Zamperini, David Swanson, Jim McAllister, Ron Mael, Russell Mael.

Ron and Russell Mael; *Muziek Express Magazine*, Netherlands, 1977.

Ron Mael, Giorgio Moroder, Russell Mael. (*Promotion shot, Virgin Records, 1979*)

Ron and Russell Mael, UK, 1979.

Rock Planet, Utrecht, Netherlands, 1979. (*Photo by Bart van den Hoogen*)

Promotion poster, 1980, Virgin Records.

Ron and Russell Mael, London, May 1981. (*Promotion shot, Wi-Fi Records*)

Ron and Russell Mael, RTBF Studios, Brussels, 21 March 1981.

Ruud Swart and Ron Mael, Halle Polyvalent, Arlon, Belgium, 19 November 1981.

Ron Mael, Halle des Gérard Champs, Verviers, Belgium, 20 November 1981. (*Photo by Ruud Swart*)

Russell and Ron Mael, Halle des Gérard Champs, Verviers, Belgium, 20 November 1981. (*Photo by Ruud Swart*)

Sparks, 1983: Leslie Bohem, Bob Haag, Ron Mael, Russell Mael, David Kendrick, Jim Goodwin.

Ron and Russel Mael outside K-ROQ Radio, Los Angeles, 5 May 1982. (*Photo by Pody Hansbrough*)

Russell Mael, Magic Mountain, Valencia, California, 23 April 1983. (*Photo by Henry Mowry*)

Ron Mael, Magic Mountain, Valencia, California, 23 April 1983. (*Photo by Henry Mowry*)

SPARKS

Russell and Ron Mael. (*Promotion shot, Curb Records, 1985*)

Russell Mael, Beach Scene Festival, Los Angeles, 31 August 1986.

Russel and Ron Mael, K-ROQ Radio, Los Angeles, April 1986.

Ron and Russell Mael, Tower Records, Hollywood, 1986. (*Photo by Pody Hansbrough*)

Russell and Ron Mael with Russell's 1956 Ford Thunderbird, Los Angeles, 1988.

Ron and Russell Mael. (*Promotion shot, Rhino Records, 1988*)

down at that time because they were only accepting British musicians, but this time, the circumstances were different.

After spending a few weeks in New York, the idea of a new album produced by Rupert Holmes was nearly forgotten. The Maels had now decided they wanted Mick Ronson, the guitarist who had made significant contributions to David Bowie's career in the early 1970s.

Hewlett scheduled a meeting with Ronson, and in the early summer of 1976, Ron, Russell, Joseph Fleury and Sal Maida visited Ronson's flat on the Lower West Side to get acquainted and discuss a potential collaboration. At that time, Ronson was living with his wife, Suzi, and Hilly Michaels, a drummer who often played with Ronson and was likely to join his new band.

Hilly had been a devoted Sparks fan since he first heard 'Wonder Girl' on the radio back in 1972 and had always dreamed of being a part of the band. Ronson hadn't informed his roommate about the appointment with the Maels, so when he found out they were coming to the loft he was ecstatic.

After exchanging pleasantries and engaging in additional conversation, it was suggested that they head to the rehearsal room to try out some of the new songs Ron had brought with him. This marked the first full band rehearsal of the songs and laid the groundwork for the direction the Maels would take for their next album.

The rehearsal lasted just over an hour and included all the songs that would feature on the new album, with the exception of 'I Bought The Mississippi River'. The session was recorded on a small mono cassette player and is highly sought after, not only by Sparks fans but also by collectors of Mick Ronson recordings. However, the quality of the recordings is rather poor.

Following the promising rehearsals, Ron and Russell asked Ronson to join Sparks as a permanent member and produce the new album. He would also be part of the upcoming tour, following the album's release. Mick, however, was hesitant due to other offers and plans to start his own band. Ultimately, he declined the offer, as he did not want to commit to one band indefinitely. Ron and Russell then had to find another guitarist to take his place. Fortunately, they had no trouble convincing Hilly Michaels to join them as the drummer. New auditions were held, and at one point Cheap Trick guitarist Rick Nielsen and bassist Tom Petersson stopped by for a chat.

There was mutual interest in having Rick as the new Sparks guitarist, but when he expressed a desire to contribute songs as well, the Maels politely declined the offer and the opportunity was passed up.

Feeling frustrated with the situation, Ron and Russell contemplated abandoning the project, returning to Los Angeles and finding local musicians there. Sal Maida then suggested reaching out to Jeffrey Salen, who at the time was playing for a band called Tuff Darts. Jeffrey was interested in playing on the album but made it clear that he did not want to join the tour, as he wanted to focus on his own band. Sadly, he passed away from a heart attack in 2008.

In the same month, Morrissey, who was visiting his relatives on the East Coast, spotted Russell outside CBGB's in New York and persuaded him to have his photo taken with him under the club's iconic awning.

With the recording band now complete, Ron and Russell sought out producer Rupert Holmes once again. He came to see them rehearse and was quite surprised by the musical direction the band had taken. It was evident that the new album would be quite straight forward rock, very guitar-oriented, not the lush, orchestrated music he was accustomed to producing.

Nonetheless, he accepted the job and in August 1976 the band began recording the album, which would be titled *Big Beat*.

Rupert Holmes commented to Leslie Hanagan about those recordings:

> The album *Big Beat* was a rush job. The boys wanted the album to come out by a certain release date, they had photographed the cover before the album was recorded, and I was obliged to do something I'd never done before: list the songs and decide the sequence before we recorded the songs, so that the album sleeve could be printed while we were making the record! Amazing. It was decided to save on time and budget and make use of 'I Like Girls' on *Big Beat*, so I did a new mix in which I tried to make the song compatible with the other cuts on the album, hiding a lot of the orchestra as best I could, although the brass came through. I also had to make the drum sound of Alan Schwartzberg (a popular session drummer on the 'I Want To Hold Your Hand' session) sound like Hilly Michaels (who was less of a session musician and more of a live band musician).

Obviously, the other *Big Beat* musicians were not on the 'I Like Girls' recording, except for Ron on piano. A decade later, Ron reflected on this period:

> *Big Beat* was a stiff, sales-wise. It shook our confidence, because we had just signed with Columbia and moved back to the States. We thought it would be the same as when we moved to England and signed with Island.
>
> When that didn't happen it was a little maddening. So much of a record has to do with the circumstances around it, and there was no atmosphere around *Big Beat*. That was really a miserable period for us. I don't know if it's for musical reasons or what, but I don't especially like that album. The demos we did with Mick Ronson were so much better than the finished thing. While Rupert might be really good for someone like Barbra Streisand, I don't think he's a rock 'n' roll producer.

The general consensus, shared by the other members of Sparks and Joseph Fleury, was that Holmes was not the right choice for the album. Meanwhile, John Hewlett remained in London and declined to join the band in the US. Instead, he appointed another assistant, Bill Siddons, to assist Joseph in managing the band.

In a local music paper in Illinois, Ron commented on the lyrical content of the album:

> Unfortunately, those are feelings that come from within me. I try sometimes to not have the songs so personal maybe but then they come out that way anyway. Deep down I'm really a romantic at heart but I can't transfer that to a song without cracking up saying what a piece of garbage that is.

The cover of the album was rather unique. The photos, taken by the renowned portrait photographer Richard Avedon, were shot in black and white, showcasing his distinct style and working method. They portrayed a powerful image of a shirtless Russell, flanked by a somewhat stern-looking Ron in a profile pose. On the back cover was a similar photo, but the inner sleeve displayed a photo in which the brothers appeared less self-assured, with Russell looking uncertain and Ron seeming somewhat resigned. Whether consciously or not, the photo likely reflected the mood the brothers were experiencing.

With the album now completed, they needed to assemble the touring band. Jeffrey Salen was not available, and Sal Maida expressed a desire to remain in New York to focus on his band Milk 'n' Cookies. Hilly Michaels was enthusiastic about staying on board, and they recruited Jimmy McAllister as a replacement for Jeff. While McAllister may not have been as skilled a guitarist as Mick Ronson or Jeff Salen, the Maels believed he would excel as a rhythm guitarist.

The four of them relocated to Los Angeles, with Michaels and McAllister staying at the Sunset Marquis hotel, as they began their search for a lead guitarist. After several auditions, they selected Luke Zamperini, the son of Louis Zamperini, an Olympic athlete and Second World War veteran who had been captured by the Japanese in 1943. His story was the basis for the film *Unbroken*, directed by Angelina Jolie. They also found David Swanson as bass guitarist for the upcoming tour.

During the intensive rehearsal sessions, they played two takes of a previously unknown song, possibly called 'Christmas Time For Two Of Us'. However, they didn't include that in their set list and no known studio recording of it exists.

The tour started on 6 November 1976 in Santa Barbara. Pretty soon it became clear that David Swanson wasn't the bass player they had hoped he would be. Stressed by Hilly Michaels' concerns, Bill Siddons called Sal Maida in New York to convince him to join the band again. After some consideration, he did, and he was installed at the Tropicana Motel in Los Angeles.

A remarkable article appeared in the *American Cash Box* on 5 March 1977:

> $3 Million Asked In Pop/Sparks Suit
> Los Angeles—A suit against Ron Mael and the group Sparks, seeking $3 million in damages on six counts, has been filed in the Superior Court of the State of California by David Swanson and Roger Prescott, musicians in the group

Pop! and Allan Rinde, Pop!'s producer. The suit, which was filed Feb. 3, also names Sparks members Russell Mael, Luke Zamperini, Hilly Boy Michaels, Sal Maida, and (John) Does one through 15, as well as Sparks manager Bill Siddons, as defendants.

The action stems from alleged statements made by the defendants on the Rodney Bingenheimer radio show on station KROQ, Pasadena. The suit charges that 'on or about November 21, 1976' Ron Mael used the following language concerning plaintiff Swanson: 'He had a drug problem, drug overdose'. Swanson was formerly a member of Sparks. According to Rinde, Ron Mael and the rest of Sparks have not yet been served with summonses.

Whatever was said or not said during the radio interview in question, Swanson was clearly unhappy about being forced to leave Sparks. No further information has come to light regarding the charges, so it's safe to assume that nothing came from it.

Sal Maiden's first gig after rejoining Sparks was unexpected; it was for the film *Rollercoaster*. Sparks wasn't the first choice of director James Goldstone. Both The Bay City Rollers and Kiss were asked prior to him turning to Sparks, both bands having declined the offer.

Russell commented on that performance caught on film:

Yes, you did see Sparks performing 'Big Boy' and 'Fill-Er-Up' in the film Rollercoaster during your last aeroplane trip. And no, we didn't know that the film was going to turn out like that. Rollercoaster proves that you have to be continually careful about what you do. You never know what's going to last and what's going to fall by the wayside—and man, does that last!

In *Rollercoaster*, Russell appeared in a flashy red shirt with a 'wifebeater' vest underneath, the latter which he would expose during the performance in the movie and would also wear often on tour.

The circumstances of the tour left a lot to be desired. Their new road manager, Jim Seiter, turned out to be difficult to work with. He used to be part of The Byrds gang in the Sixties, and had now ended up as a bus driver of bands he'd barely heard of.

Seiter was bitter, frustrated and showed little interest in the band. He was impolite and grumpy and wasn't all that concerned about the musicians, often just tossing the room keys to the band members upon arrival at hotels before leaving. Ron and Russell handled the situation politely and with diplomacy, but it was far from ideal.

Things took a turn for the worse when it was decided to combine the tour with the Patti Smith Group, who had just released their album *Radio Ethiopia*. There was tension between the bands, and it was agreed that the headline would be determined by each band's popularity in individual cities.

In Montreal, Canada, a large crowd of Sparks fans was making so much noise before the show started that Smith, who had agreed to open that evening, wouldn't even come out of her dressing room and go out on stage. However, on 12 December, at the Masonic Auditorium in Detroit, a devoted audience of Smith fans greeted Sparks' arrival on stage with a hail of abuse that swiftly escalated to flying bottles.

During the tour, Ron decided to smash his piano stool to pieces during the closing song 'Big Boy'. In Chicago, he was so into it that he leapt off-stage to finish destroying the remainder of the stool. However, while jumping off the stage, he badly injured his leg. Suddenly, the police moved in, assuming he was a frantic fan and nearly took him away until the rest of the band yelled that he was part of the band.

At New York's Bottom Line gig, Ron lost his balance again and landed on a table where all the Columbia VIPs were seated. He left a mess behind, launching food and drinks throughout the venue.

Meanwhile, Island Records had released 'Big Boy', backed by 'Fill-Er-Up', as a single in a selection of countries worldwide, but it failed to make any impact. The same fate befell the next single, 'I Like Girls', which had the same B-side as the previously-released 'I Want To Hold Your Hand': 'England'.

CBS didn't even release a single from the album in the US or Canada. The album didn't make any entries in any charts worldwide, except for Sweden, where it topped at number 24. Outside the USA and Canada, no live performances were given.

There were some considerations to release a live album, specifically the gig that was recorded at the Cleveland Agora Ballroom, but Ron and Russell thought that performance not good enough to immortalise on vinyl. Nevertheless, an acetate of the performance was pressed.

Meanwhile, *Big Beat* was the final album released by Island Records. They also issued the *Best Of Sparks* in Scandinavia, the Netherlands, France and Germany. The album featured a sleeve that referenced the *Kimono My House* album. Around the same time, the original 'This Town Ain't Big Enough For Both Of Us'/'Looks, Looks, Looks' was rereleased in the UK, but it didn't chart. In 1979, the *Best Of Sparks* was also released in the UK.

Looking back, it is evident that the Maels attempted to capitalise on the punk rock phenomenon. Despite Ron's efforts to write harsh, macho lyrics and return to a standard rock format, it did not resonate well. 'Friggin' In The Riggin' it was not.

In October 1977, during a visit to the Netherlands, the brothers shared their thoughts on *Big Beat* with a local music magazine.

Ron: 'When we returned to America, we discovered a plethora of these heavy rocking guitar bands that greatly influenced the Big Beat album. Bands like Aerosmith and Ted Nugent were extremely popular at the time, so we felt that was the direction Sparks should take, if we wanted to stand out. We decided to incorporate our usual lyrical content with that guitar sound. Looking back, we realise that was a mistake on our part. Additionally, we were facing other issues with our record company at the time, which were too frustrating to delve in to. Overall, it was a challenging period for us.'

Russell: 'That album should have been less stylised, but in fact, the opposite happened. It sounds like we were conscious of making a rock album, but that wasn't the case. We attempted to create a guitar record, but it didn't work out as planned—it sounded different.'

Ron: 'No, it wasn't a commercial decision to do that; it was based on a fear that no one in America would listen to what we were doing, that was the mistake. Not that we made a record like that, but that we didn't have the confidence in ourselves, in the direction we needed to go, to continue as we were doing before.'

Russell: 'I think it was just us getting cold feet. We doubted what we had done up until now and thought that our previous work was too focused on a smaller group of people, like an in crowd kind of music. With *Big Beat* we tried to break away from that and attract more listeners. However, real Sparks fans turned away from us because of that record and non-Sparks fans weren't too crazy about it either because it was just too weak. So it failed on two different fronts.'

Big Beat—The Songs

All songs written by Ron Mael.

'BIG BOY'
Duration: 3:17

From the very first notes of the opening track, it is clear that this album does not follow the same style as its predecessor. This was not 'Under The Table With Her'. The guitar and drums take centre stage in this fairly conventional midtempo rock song, with the piano serving as a background element. Guitar solos are featured, backing vocals adding depth beyond Russell's voice.

While the guitars are distorted, they are softened with a slightly warmer sound. This results in a less raw sound, deviating from the hard rock or punk vibe that may have been intended.

The song's meaning is not particularly deep, focussing on the glorification of patriarchy and the objectification of women. This theme is prevalent throughout the album, presented with a tongue-in-cheek approach, that was emphasised during the album's 2008 presentation. Ron even cautioned against taking some lyrics too literally.

The song seems to depict the anticipated arrival of a stereotypical macho figure who intimidates men and captivates women. References to David and Goliath, and an oversized genital, are included, but the song does not delve much deeper than that.

'Big Boy' was released as the lead single in the UK, France, Germany, Japan and Brazil, but did not chart in any of those countries. It was not released in North America.

Live, it was a regular part of the 1976 tour and was also performed during the 2013 Revenge of Two Hands One Mouth gigs with only Ron's piano accompaniment.

> Russell: I think we all know a particular instance where there's a—a guy who you could—you could refer to as the 'Big Boy.' Whatever walk of life you're from. If it's school, you know, it's that one guy that just has such a command of the English language that he can just pull any girl—I mean *any* girl—on campus. I mean, the guy—the guy can score on the football field. I mean, he's a lot bigger than you are. And the guy's a lot wealthier than you are. Lives on the better side of the town. His family are the really influential people in the community, and your dad just works, like, at a shoe shop or something. And the guy just always seems to be able to one-up you, whatever it is. I mean—you don't really even have to see the guy. You can just kind of feel his presence. Whenever you think you're into something good, you go, 'Oh, God, here comes that guy. He's gonna pound the crap out of me or something.' And you just kind of feel the earth sort of trembling around you when he's—when he's around. And it gets real still, except for this pulsating sort of sound.

'I Want To Be Like Everybody Else'
Duration: 2:53

A standard riff in E major, interspersed with an E7 and borrowed from Chuck Berry, opens this up-tempo song. The guitar sound is thin, which becomes even more evident when the drums and bass join in. The presence of the piano is also rather difficult to distinguish in this song. Every live performance of songs from this album had much more emphasis on the piano. Although the instrument was not used more emphatically, it was simply heard much more clearly in the live mix.

There are no surprises in the further course of the song and the arrangements remain unchanged, except for a witty stereo effect of the guitar that hops from left to right in short bursts halfway through the song.

The lyrics seem to be about an individual struggling to keep up with the people around him. This is not intentional, he does not realise when a trend is current and his timing is therefore less than perfect. Not an extraordinary song due to the basic chord progression, arrangements and text content, but certainly quite pleasant to listen to.

During the 1976 North American tour, this song was practically always played, but was never included in any set list after that.

'Nothing To Do'
Duration: 3:05

The first song on the album where the piano can be heard quite clearly is also one of the catchiest melodies. It follows a fairly traditional chord progression, centred around E major, A and D, with only a small addition in the chorus with an F# and a B minor. The lyrics are not profound and the title actually reveals all there is to know about the storyline.

Unlike the previous album, all songs on this album are produced and arranged in virtually the same way. As a result, the listener is rarely surprised and this song is no exception in that regard. However, it features a very pleasant melody and was regularly performed during the 1976 tour, often used as an opener.

The song was also played during concerts in 2004, which led to its inclusion on the *Live in Stockholm* DVD. The performance, featuring just guitar, piano and drums (no bass guitar), is barely inferior to the album version.

> Russell: 'Joey Ramone has told us that he wanted to do a version of this song, yet has never been able to convince the other Ramones. I hope he's successful one day. The LP cover was shot in 15 minutes by Richard Avedon at his NY assembly-line style photo studio. In by 9, out by 5.'

'I Bought The Mississippi River'
Duration: 2:27

It is quite nice and refreshing to hear a song start again with the distinctive sound of Ron's piano. Like most songs on this album, the chord structure is fairly basic, as are the riffs played by the guitar. The overall sound of this album is rather more down-to-earth than most other songs from Ron's writing desk, but that was the whole point of this album. There are very few unexpected melody changes or remarkable middle eight sections, but the tunes are easily accessible and pleasant.

This fourth track is no exception. It has a basic verse-chorus-verse construction and the mandatory guitar solo, something that is generally quite rare on a

Sparks record. Russell's vocals are slightly lower than he usually sings, which is characteristic of this album.

The subject of the song is quite recognisable as one written by Ron, and at one of the performances during the 1976 tour, Russell explained it again for those who had missed it. It has never been played live during regular performances.

> Russell: 'There's this guy, an independently wealthy fellow. The guy had so much money, didn't know what to do with all of it and this guy had some fetish for anything to do with water and all. One particular thing he liked about water was rivers, so he bought himself a little river. And you'd think that would be the end of his problems and he'd be happy about that but it turned out it was just the start of it.'

'Fill-Er-Up'
Duration: 2:17

A Fifties rock 'n' roll vibe on speed is up next. Again, there are hardly any noticeable piano inputs, just frantic drumbeats, guitar riffs, solos and an enthusiastic bass guitar that cheerfully bounces through the song. Sometimes it supports the other instruments and at other times it runs its own course.

Russell frolics through the song, singing the words hastily, as if he's afraid he's going to miss his train. The lyrics appear to be very clear and unambiguous, about adding petrol to a car and seeing what mileage can be made with that input. Some have suggested that the lyrics are a metaphor for the reward a woman will give you when you invest enough in her. Given the rather misogynistic approach of this album, there could be some truth in that interpretation.

This song was not always played during the 1976 North American tour, but it did appear at a few concerts. It has never been included in any other tour or regular concert.

'Everybody's Stupid'
Duration: 3:35

The closing track of side one begins with a rather thin guitar that is soon overpowered by the other instruments, especially the drums, which seem to be favoured by producer Rupert Holmes on most of the tracks. It is a mid-tempo standard tune with a staccato-like guitar riff and slightly poisonous, juvenile lyrical content.

In keeping with the tone of most songs on the album, it is light-hearted and casual, and certainly pleasant to listen to. There is no undefinable atmosphere or deeper meaning in the lyrics, which are often trademarks of a Ron Mael song, but that is intentional. This album, and this song, were created with a specific purpose in mind—to piggy-back on a certain wave of music, a departure from Sparks' previous albums.

Like most songs from *Big Beat*, it was only played at some concerts during the 1976 tour.

> Russell: 'Probably an autobiographical tune about its author, and this guy over here being its author, on the keyboards, my big brother. He wrote this song with his own two little hands, it's a song called "Everybody's Stupid".'

'THROW HER AWAY (AND GET A NEW ONE)'
Duration: 3:38

We must assume that the lyrical content of this song is as ironic as irony can get. Ron's lyrics can often be interpreted in multiple ways but the message in this song does not seem to have a hidden layer. It could have been the advice of a man in his midlife crisis but when it was written, Ron was only 30 years old. At the Sparks Spectacular, he made sure to point out that his lyrics weren't always to be taken seriously. However, when played occasionally during the 1976 tour, there was apparently no need to soften the meaning of the lyrics, probably because the level of absurdity in this one doesn't need a defence.

Guitar riffs and accompanying drumbeats open this song, followed by the bass joining in. The bass plays a prominent role throughout this song and is given the freedom to create beautiful runs, while also getting some extra space in the mix.

The vocals are modestly supported, with only a few moments featuring a second layer. In the break, we hear a short but adequate guitar solo. The heavy drums and thriving bass guitar dominate, with some space in the mix for the piano, especially during the chorus and the instrumental part in the second section of the song.

Interestingly, on most editions of the original vinyl release, the song fades out. However, on the Dutch, German, Australian and Irish pressings of the album, the song suddenly stops and transitions into the next one. Some CD reissues have included this abrupt break as well.

> Ron: 'Warning. Do not take all the songs completely literally.'

'CONFUSION'
Duration: 3:21

'Confusion' was a song originally written and recorded for the *Indiscreet* album. Originally titled 'Intrusion', the lyrics were rewritten when French director Jacques

Tati asked the Mael brothers to appear in his forthcoming film *Confusion*, which, unfortunately, never took place. Long-time Sparks fan and friend of the Maels, Tomáš Prášek, managed to get hold of a rare file containing the notes about the film project a few years ago. He then gave it to Ron and Russell.

The original recording was later released as a bonus track on the 2006 21st Century Edition CD.

The version on *Big Beat* has a slightly more 'swing' quality to it than the original, and it is noticeable that the variation in the chords is somewhat more advanced than most other songs on this album. This is another indication that Ron had a different approach and purpose in writing the songs for this record. It also has a 'softer' production than most other songs on the album, partly due to the fact that the guitars are not distorted. Additionally, there's more use of backing vocals on this track.

The song was released as a single in France, with 'I Bought The Mississippi River' on the B-side. However, it was withdrawn almost immediately, for unknown reasons. Perhaps the local record company had acted a little too hastily and then changed their minds, realising that the timing might be better, if the Jacques Tati film was coming out in the near future. Either way, this remains speculation. The fact is that this single is one of the most sought-after by avid Sparks collectors.

The song has only been performed live during the Sparks Spectacular.

Russell: 'In the middle Seventies, we were gonna do a film with him (Jacques Tati). Ron and I were gonna be these US television directors from a television company in the States that come out to this rural town in France, to help bail out a really feeble understaffed, under-equipped, under technology-ish film TV studio there. And we were gonna show them all [this] American know-how and all that sort of thing and Tati was going to be the bubbly director of that film studio. And that song was gonna be from that film. Unfortunately, he died. But it's another regret.'

'Screwed Up'
Duration: 4:16

Short bursts of distorted guitar are almost immediately accompanied by a solid drumbeat and bass, which is initially inconspicuous, opening the song. The piano remains quite inaudible but becomes much clearer in the chorus. The guitar also adds nice riffs during the verse. The chord progression is basic, centred around the C-chord, with a cleverly inserted E7 and A-minor, making the melody line more interesting.

After about two-and-a-half minutes, an instrumental break is presented in which the guitar is given more space for an actual solo. Following this, only the vocals and piano can be heard for a short while before the accompanying instruments burst out again in full force. Pleasant guitar riffs are added again during the fade out, completing the song and tying it back to the overall theme of the album.

The production of this song is more open and varied than most other songs on the album. There is more space for the piano, the drums are not as dominant and the guitar provides appealing little riffs in a sound that is not too harsh. There is even a guitar solo in which Jeffrey Salen has a chance to show his virtuosity.

The first verse provides a brief history lesson per decade, ending with a nod to Bob Dylan. The rest of the song mainly displays discontent, possibly in comparison to the situation as it was before.

Similar to the previous song, this one has never been played live at regular gigs.

'WHITE WOMEN'
Duration: 3:20

At the time this song was released, it did not cause a stir or scandal. People who heard it just thought it was funny, satirical and over the top, which of course it was. When played in 2008 at the Sparks Spectacular, Ron made sure the audience would understand that he was only kidding when he wrote it. If played today, he might not even be able to get away with that.

From the first sentence, it is clear that the song is very tongue-in-cheek. Assuming the Biblical Eve was white, or did exist at all, was the first clue that this song was meant to be funny. And it is.

Musically, this mid-tempo track has some appealing arrangements. It has reversed cymbals presented in a basic but nice stereo effect, and the guitar adds some subtle staccato rhythms to it. There are not that many songs in which Russell makes an effort to scream, but he certainly tries to show his dedication to the cause on this track.

The song was a regular feature during the 1976 tour. Apart from that, it has never been heard during regular concerts.

> Ron: 'Warning. Especially for the next song. Do not take all of our songs literally.'
> Russell: 'The Rolling Stones and people had songs praising the brown people and the black people all over the world with tunes like "Brown Sugar". Well, here's our answer to them, it's a little song off of *Big Beat*, it's called "White Women".'

'I LIKE GIRLS'
Duration: 2:53

Four years after the original Bearsville band recorded it, and after several demo recordings in England, this song was finally officially released. It was recorded in the same session Sparks did with Rupert Holmes, months before meeting Mick Ronson. None of the musicians on *Big Beat* were involved in the initial recording, which was used as the basis for the album version. Originally, it was intended to be released as the B-side of the single 'I Want To Hold Your Hand'.

This version differs considerably from the first recording, done in January 1973. The *Big Beat* version is the only song on the album that has a brass section involved; it is clearly present from the very first notes, dominating every other instrument except for the drums, which were added later.

The full sound, arrangements and tempo might be a bit overwhelming at first, but it is an appropriate song with which to end the album and one can understand why it was a crowd-pleaser at the Bearsville band concerts.

It was released as a single in the UK and Australia only, containing the non-album track 'England'.

Despite the song being quite popular live in its original form with the Bearsville band, it has only been played live during the 1976 tour.

Introducing Sparks

Release date: 27 September 1977
Produced by: Terry Powell, Ron Mael, Russell Mael
Engineer: Lenny Roberts
Sleeve design: John Kehe, Tom Steele
Photography: Bob Seidemann
Recorded at: Larrabee Sound Studios, Hollywood
Duration: 35:58
Personnel:
    Ron Mael: Keyboards
    Russell Mael: Vocals
    Ben Benay: Harmonica
    Alan Broadbent: Piano
    David Foster: Keyboards
    Ed Greene: Drums
    David Paich: Keyboards
    Mike Porcaro: Bass guitar
    Reinie Press: Bass guitar
    Lee Ritenour: Guitar
    Thom Rotella: Guitar
    Jimmy Haas: Backing vocals
    Nick Uhrich: Backing vocals
    Ron Hicklin: Backing vocals
    Stan Farber: Backing vocals
    Tom Bahler: Backing vocals

Side 1
'A Big Surprise'
'Occupation'
'Ladies'
'I'm Not'
'Forever Young'
Singles from this album:
'A Big Surprise'/'Forever Young'
'Over The Summer'/'Forever Young'

Side 2
'Goofing Off'
'Girls On The Brain'
'Over The Summer'
'Those Mysteries'

On New Year's Eve 1976, Sparks played their final gig at the Civic Center in Santa Monica. It was a sold-out event with support acts Flo & Eddie (formerly of the Turtles) and a promising new band called Van Halen, who had replaced the Ramones at the last moment.

Despite the fairly well-received tour to support the *Big Beat* album, reactions to the album were mixed. From 'At Last: The Real Sparks' to 'The Fall of Two Equilibrists', the album hadn't been unanimously positively received and did not chart anywhere except in Sweden.

After the tour, the Maels returned to Los Angeles. They were disillusioned by the fact that lead guitarist Luke Zamperini had returned to New York, quickly followed by Hilly Michaels and Jim McAllister, the other band members.

Bass player Sal Maida stayed in Los Angeles for a while, residing at the Tropicana Motel and meeting with Ron and Russell on a near-daily basis. They were contemplating their next steps and considering forming a new band. Despite the disappointing sales of their first release, Columbia Records still had high hopes for Sparks, especially now that the record deal with Island was over and they could release and promote the next record worldwide.

It was clear they wanted to focus on the US market with a new record that would appeal to American audiences and feature music that was more recognisable in their home country. Columbia was confident in its success.

Ron and Russell wanted to collaborate with Canadian producer Bob Ezrin, known for his work on successful albums by Lou Reed, Kiss, Alice Cooper and Peter Gabriel. During a meeting with him, the Maels eagerly played some of the new songs they had composed for the upcoming project. However, Ezrin, was unimpressed.

After impatiently listening to the songs, he said, 'Okay, now play me your A-sides.' His reaction ended the Maels' hopes of working with Ezrin and also marked the end of Sal Maida's involvement in the band. He left for New York shortly after the meeting with Ezrin, as the Maels could not afford to keep him on the payroll any longer.

Although only a year had passed since Sparks were one of the most talked-about bands in the UK and at the height of their commercial success, everything felt very different now. Columbia Records took over and decided to make a record in Los Angeles with a selection of top session musicians they had available.

Terry Powell, the A&R man for the West Coast, was chosen as the producer, with Ron and Russell assisting him. The Maels, having no other options, agreed to Columbia's plans. Despite their preference for a different producer, Columbia Records made all decisions and were focussed on creating a commercially successful album. The album was to be titled *Introducing Sparks*.

During an interview with a Dutch music journalist while on a promotional tour for the album in September 1977, Ron said:

> We always try to come up with a nice album title. When the record company asked us about the name of the new album, I jokingly said *Introducing Sparks*. Some memo was sent to every office, and when we returned a week later, the album had that title. Funny. But there's also a deeper meaning behind it, as we really have to introduce ourselves to America. We didn't have a large following there, and this is the record that should be the break-through for us. It's the definitive Sparks album. Over here in Europe, we are slightly better known and I realise it sounds kind of funny here.

Recordings took place at the legendary Larrabee Sound studios in Hollywood. For the first time, Ron and Russell were working with a producer who was unknown in the music industry and had musicians involved who had no emotional connection to their work.

In addition to the many session musicians, some of whom would eventually end up in the band Toto, and another who was the regular bass player for Neil Diamond, the Maels also had to work with a group of backing singers for the first time. This group consisted of Tom Bahler, Al Capps, Stan Farber, Ron Hicklin (and his group The Ron Hicklin Singers, who were the actual singers behind the background vocals of the Partridge Family), Mark Piscitelli and Nick Uhrig. Guitarist Lee Ritenour played most of the rhythm parts, while his colleague Thom Rotella added the solos.

Ron recalled about these recordings:

> Those guys were getting a quarter of a million dollars a year, and they bitched constantly. Most of our songs don't have three chords. They reckoned they couldn't play in the keys we wanted them to or said things like 'Wouldn't it be better to use a sax instead of a guitar', things like that. It was a joke.
>
> I'd never do it again. They are a totally different breed than I was used to working with, and it's a totally different idea of what music is to me. These people are incredibly crafted, but there's absolutely no feelings or personality in anything they're doing. After fifty minutes of recording, everybody said: 'I gotta take a break because of the Union.'

Some years later, Russell was still very firm about this experience. 'It sounds somewhat bereft of personality,' he told *Record Collector* magazine in 2003. 'It was pretty boring using session musicians. These guys come in, get paid $480 for half an hour and they just assume the first take is fine because if it is, they can leave.'

However, after performing the full album for the first time in 2008 during the Sparks Spectacular in London, the brothers were surprisingly more lenient about the album, or at least about the songs on it.

Russell commented:

We almost rediscovered that album ourselves when we did 21 nights in London. Because it comes and goes with little fanfare, in your own head you start to think, 'Well maybe there's something inherently inferior with that album,' and you cast it aside. So for the 21 nights, we were forced to reinvestigate and re-evaluate a lot of our albums which we thought had something wrong with them.

We did songs like 'Goofing Off' and there was an actual audience who were liking those songs on that evening, and so we really thought there was some substance to that album when we rediscovered it. In our heads it's hard to figure out why some things work and some things don't.

Ron added:

One misgiving is that it's the only album we've ever done where we used real session people. They were obviously great musicians, but one guy was from Toto and there were even some backing singers who would be hired to sing on any commercial where they wanted them to sound like the Beach Boys. So the way we went about recording some of the albums wasn't exactly the way we should have, but we were proud of the songs. The event was a great equaliser.

Apart from the nine songs that were eventually released on the album, two additional tracks were recorded: 'Kidnap' and 'Keep Me'. A demo version of the former was included in the 2009 Japanese CD reissue of *Angst In My Pants*. The original versions were never officially released, but were discovered by someone years later and shared with fans.

Something unique was happening during the recordings. In their optimistic enthusiasm, Columbia had decided that a quadrophonic version of the LP should be released if it became a hit. Quadrophonic, or Surround Sound, is a reproduction technique that aims to reproduce sound in three dimensions. Therefore, some of the songs—but not all—were recorded using that technology.

After the LP was released, it became clear that this plan was overly confident, and these recordings ended up in a drawer. Years later, someone stumbled upon them and shared them with fans sporadically. Officially, nothing has been done with them, but under the right circumstances and equipment, the recordings do sound a lot more spacious than those on the album.

The album cover was remarkable as well. Taken in a Hollywood pose, with one of the brothers on each side of the sleeve, it wasn't the type of cover that stood out during the punk era. The portraits were captured by Bob Seidemann, known for his work with Janis Joplin and The Grateful Dead and also responsible for the controversial Blind Faith album cover featuring a half-naked prepubescent girl in a field holding a model airplane.

Russell recalled:

We liked the idea of there actually being no front or back cover, that they were in fact the same image but with a different one of us on each side. We thought it would look cool in shops that randomly, either Ron or myself would be the featured cover. The rings were only a detail that we felt helped better colour-coordinate us with our shirts. There's your symbolism theory shattered.

The album was released in the US on 27 September 1977. Columbia issued the first 7,000 copies as promotional editions, pressed on translucent red vinyl with white labels. Ironically, due to low sales figures, these were for a long time more common than the ordinary version on black vinyl.

For the first single in the US and Canada, they selected 'Over The Summer', with 'Forever Young' on the flip side instead of one of the two outtakes. Perhaps the initial intention was to release 'Forever Young' as the A-side, as a very basic video of that song was shot with Russell in a lumberjack shirt and tight jeans from the brand Fiorucci, which he was very impressed with, according to the fan magazine. He also had an earring on, but that could have been a clip ring, as he only wore it for a very short period of time.

Another video was made for 'Occupation', which may have been chosen as the follow-up. However, both the album and the single took a nose-dive the moment they were released, so a second single was never considered.

The album was released on 21 October in the UK and the rest of Europe. That same month, the brothers left for Europe again on a promotional tour for the album and the single. The single 'A Big Surprise' was released in a few countries in Europe, and several television appearances were arranged to support the single.

In England, they were featured on the BBC children's TV programme *Multi-Coloured Swap Shop*, which aired on 29 October. In Germany, they made an appearance on *Plattenküche*, where the host subtly ended his announcement by making a gesture of a Hitler moustache with his finger, while Russell watched stoically.

In Sweden, where the single wasn't even released, they appeared on the show *Nöjesliv* on 30 September. In France, they were guests on *Ces Messieurs Nous*

Dissent on 2 October and *Musique and Musique* on 16 October, performing 'A Big Surprise'. During both appearances, Ron smashed his piano stool, but during the latter show, he did it in the aisle amongst the audience. He was probably aware that this theatrical outburst had not yet been displayed in Europe. Or perhaps it was a subtle reference to the film *Rollercoaster,* in which he had also performed this act and which was showing in European cinemas around that time.

Upon returning to the US, the Maels discovered that the album had flopped and the deal with Columbia had been terminated. They found themselves without a record label or a band, with a manager who openly criticised their latest releases and began losing interest. It was clear they needed to come up with something completely new. Their next move would create an important template for a new generation of musicians to follow, with the help of a successful collaborator.

Introducing Sparks—The Songs

All songs written by Ron Mael and Russell Mael.

'A BIG SURPRISE'
Duration: 3:42

The very first notes of the opening track clearly indicate that this album is not a follow-up to its predecessor in a purely stylistic fashion. The sound is smoother, almost warm, and contains a well-balanced range of instruments. Ron's distinctive piano sounds are well-placed in the mix and easily audible. Russell's voice even sounds somewhat more polished, and the production unmistakeably aims to achieve a specific sound, accessible to a larger audience.

It also quickly becomes evident that Columbia Records meant business this time, sparing no expenses to create a product specifically fine-tuned for the local market. For the first time on a Sparks album, the vocals are accompanied by a selection of professional session singers who skilfully complement Russell's qualities.

Lead guitarist Thom Rotella immediately showcases his important contribution with a solo that is not too complex but still appealing. This is quite an achievement, especially considering the presence of another great guitarist, Lee Ritenour, who would go on to become an acknowledged talented musician in his own right.

Only in a few countries (the UK, Netherlands, Germany and Yugoslavia) was the single 'A Big Surprise'/'Forever Young' released, in an appealing picture sleeve.

Remarkably, during an appearance on the French show *Musique and Musique* on 16 October, the song was performed live with a large house orchestra.

The arrangements were noticeably different from the studio version. Despite this, the single was never released in France.

> Russell: 'We had no band at the time and attempted an album using LA session musicians. Had we taken a bit more stylised approach to the production, the results may have been more interesting. During a live TV performance of the song in Paris, Ron smashed his piano stool to bits in the eleventh row as a bewildered "middle-French" audience quietly waited for Nana Mouskouri.'

'OCCUPATION'
Duration: 5:17

The next track on the album is back to a more familiar sound, which closely resembles Sparks' traditional style. It embodies all the characteristics typical of the band, adapted to fit this album.

The song is up-tempo, cheerful and sung with enthusiasm, featuring clever sound effects that could easily fit on any other Sparks album.

Driven by energetic guitars and playful pianos, the drums play a vital role, seamlessly blending into the mix. Like many tracks on this album, the backing vocals provide a solid foundation and infuse a distinct California vibe.

The song exudes enthusiasm, leaving one to ponder what could have been if it had been released as a single, as suggested by the accompanying video. The track concludes with a whimsical list of occupations sung in alphabetical order by the backing vocalists. While these are not included in the official lyrics, upon close listening, they appear to be the following:

> Actors, bombers, cut-rate druggists, doughnut makers, elephant trainers, greyhound drivers, hotel keepers, hitmen, knights and dukes of Earle, lady-killers, maids, and nuns, Orson Welles, promo men, quiz show host men, royal family, sailors, trollops, undertakers, vandals, witches, x-rated actors, yes men, yes men, Zorro et cetera.

'LADIES'
Duration: 3:06

With the opening notes of the third track, the first proper nod to the Beach Boys sound becomes evident. The song features plentiful yet pleasant backing vocals and a lively melody driven mainly by piano, bass guitar and drums. With a touch of creativity, one could envision an arrangement including brass instruments, with a zealous tuba leading the way, reminiscent of a marching band performance. The maracas play a prominent role in the song, particularly in the chorus.

The lyrics once again showcase Ron's subtle humour and clever wordplay, with a standout line being, *'Eva Braun is cracking jokes, while Joan of Arc just sits and smokes.'*

'Ladies' appears to be about a man who has illusions of being visited by various famous or historical women, who seem to manifest themselves exclusively for him. However, as soon as his actual wife or friends arrive, the fantasy images vanish. It is a relatively harmless yet intriguing concept, typical of the older brother's uniquely comprehensive imagination. It is rendered in a delightfully tongue-in-cheek fashion.

'I'M NOT'
Duration: 3:26

In 'I'm Not', the narrator expresses his dissatisfaction with life in general, or at least the lack of joy he personally finds in it. The tempo and arrangements suit his chagrin well, giving the song a somewhat dreary quality that immerses the listener in the narrator's general misery. It seems he struggles to find reasons to enjoy his life.

Despite the somewhat cantankerous message, the vocals are once again brightened by the cheerful West Coast backing vocals, which are abundantly present and can be considered one of the main characteristics of this album.

There are no systematic transitions in the verses or choruses, and the structure is based on a jolting arrangement, with the instruments almost pulsating to support the vocals.

The final section of the song starts early and consists of the constant repetition of a portion of the chorus. Particular attention should be paid to the various guitar riffs and solos that are once again very skilfully performed by Thom Rotella.

Like most songs on this album, Russell does not use his characteristic falsetto, opting for a range closer to his speaking voice. It is noticeable that hardly any song exudes enthusiasm or sincere cheerfulness. The songs are certainly not bad, the arrangements are warm and cheerful, and the musicians are more than capable, yet the record exudes a sense of resignation, as if they are caught in a situation over which they had little control. This aligns well with the actual situation the brothers found themselves in. It is rather ironic for them to be listed as co-producers for the first time on a record on which they had the least influence.

> Ron: '"I'm Not" is a song about extreme negativism. It is not a rebellious song but rather takes it a step further. While rebellion is still active, this song embodies complete inactivity.'

'Forever Young'
Duration: 3:27

At the close of side one, life is viewed from a completely different perspective. The singer's almost manically positive declaration is much more upbeat, despite its lack of realism.

The song features prominent drums, clear piano accompaniment and an up-tempo vibe with guitars that vaguely recall the glam sound of the first two albums released on Island Records.

The verses have a building arrangement that leads into the chorus, which amplifies the enthusiasm and is quite catchy.

It is likely that Columbia had anticipated this song being a contender for a single as a video was made for it. The song had the potential for success, as it's quite a pleasant tune and carries a positive message. However, it never reached that level of recognition, although it did appear on the B-side of both the European and American singles.

'Goofing Off'
Duration: 4:26

After the album was released, no tour was organised, so the songs did not receive a live performance. As a result, the songs have rarely been performed live, except during the Sparks Spectacular, where the album was presented in its entirety on a single occasion. During that event, the audience was invited to request songs to be repeated in a second set following the full performance of *Exotic Creatures of the Deep*.

Remarkably, two songs from *Introducing Sparks* were selected and performed a second time. 'Goofing Off' was one of them, being met with great enthusiasm on both occasions.

It is an exceptionally cheerful and infectious song in a style that had not been encountered before in Sparks—Zorba the Greek meets Nagila Hava, topped with a Hungarian gypsy sauce and some Russian passion. Once again, a violin is used to open the song, creating space for a catchy and dominant piano that takes the song in a completely different direction.

You can almost envision Russell singing while dancing around a campfire, accompanied by various members of a slave choir, who enthusiastically contribute to the backing vocals.

'Goofing Off' is a very catchy song that encourages you to let loose on the weekends, putting aside all worries and focussing solely on having fun. The song features a fitting guitar solo by Thom Rotella, showcasing that while session musicians may be expensive, they deliver a great product. Even Russell was impressed with his work.

During the 2025 tour, it was a pleasant surprise to find this song on the set list. It was met with great appreciation, especially due to the virtuosity of guitarist Eli Pearl, who played the solo in question flawlessly.

'Girls On The Brain'
Duration: 3:41

The contrast with the previous song is stark. While 'Goofing Off' exudes cheerfulness and carefree vibes, 'Girls On The Brain' addresses the problem of someone grappling with the newfound awareness of the opposite sex. This slow, drawn-out song features powerful drums and haunting guitar melodies, following a bluesy structure that maintains a consistent tempo with few unexpected twists.

The driving force behind the track is the prominent drums, wailing guitar riffs and solid bass line. The backing vocals also play a crucial role in enhancing the overall sound. There are several different guitar riffs presented, each occupying its own space in the sound spectrum. The mix of the other instruments is well-balanced, allowing the solo guitars to stand out even more.

'Over The Summer'
Duration: 3:50

One of the most notable songs Sparks has ever recorded is 'Over The Summer', which was released as the only single from the album in the US and Canada. However, it did not achieve the success that was hoped for. The immediate comparison that is almost always drawn by everyone is the Beach Boys, and that is more than justified. The surf-sound arrangements, the cheerfulness, the background vocals performed to perfection and, of course, the subject matter all contribute to the feeling that this song could have been released in the mid-Sixties without causing any great unrest or misunderstanding.

Russell explains the subject of the song clearly, so there shouldn't be many debates about it. It's a mystery why this song, with its typical West Coast sound, did not become a hit, even just in Los Angeles. The promotional team at Columbia Records did not seem to put in much effort to promote the song. There were no attempts to get Sparks on local television, and advertisements were scarce. Perhaps for that reason, the brothers went to Europe to promote the album there, even though it was clearly aimed at the American market.

> Russell: 'Our Beach Boys-like ode to summer romance, whereby a guy's girlfriend goes through a radical transformation over the 3-month period. The demo had a naive charm that we never could recreate using the high-priced session backing vocalists. There's a lesson to be learned.'

'THOSE MYSTERIES'
Duration: 5:03

The final track on this album is typically a classic. It is a somewhat austere ballad-style reflection on the mysteries of life, alternating between the profound and the mundane. There is a nostalgic feel to it, and surprisingly, this was the other track from the album that was requested (and played) during the second set of the presentation of *Exotic Creatures Of The Deep*.

It has a minimal but sufficient accompaniment of just piano, backing vocals, percussion and tasteful guitar riffs and bass lines. The guitar is also responsible for the final notes of this song and thus the entire album, with a sensitive, subdued solo that ends in a fade-out.

Arguably not the bombastic, long and deviant closer we find on many Sparks albums, but the dignified restraint and exceptionally low voice that Russell uses certainly make this song worthy of inclusion in this list.

In addition to being performed twice at the Sparks Spectacular, the song was also part of the Revenge of Two Hand One Mouth tour in 2013.

No. 1 In Heaven

Release date:	1 March 1979
Produced by:	Giorgio Moroder
Engineer:	Jürgen Koppers, Giorgio Moroder
Sleeve design:	Steven Barthel
Photography:	Moshe Brakha
Recorded at:	Musicland Studios, Munich; Sound Arts Studio, Los Angeles; Westlake Studios, Los Angeles
Duration:	33:44
Personnel	Ron Mael: Synthesizers
	Russell Mael: Vocals
	Keith Forsey: Drums
	Giorgio Moroder: Synthesizers
	Chris Bennet: Backing vocals
	Dennis Young: Backing vocals
	Jack Moran: Backing vocals

<u>Side 1</u>
'Tryouts For The Human Race'
'Academy Award Performance'
'La Dolce Vita'

<u>Side 2</u>
'Beat The Clock'
'My Other Voice'
'The Number One Song In Heaven'

<u>Singles from this album:</u>
'The Number One Song In Heaven'/'The Number One Song In Heaven'
'La Dolce Vita'/'My Other Voice'
'Beat The Clock'/'Beat The Clock'
'Tryouts For The Human Race'/'Tryouts For The Human Race'
'Beat The Clock'/'Tryouts For The Human Race'
'La Dolce Vita'/'Tryouts For The Human Race'

After completing their promotional tour of Europe, Ron and Russell returned to Los Angeles in November 1977. There, they were faced with some painful and sobering facts. Despite the album's strong focus on the alleged musical preferences of the American audience, it had not made much of an impact. In Europe, the brothers had received warm receptions and the majority of the press had praised the new album, but the public did not share the same enthusiasm.

Ironically, a British-Italian singer named Anita Garbo had recently found success in the Netherlands and Belgium with her single 'Miracles', a song so obviously similar to Sparks that a chart in the Netherlands mistakenly attributed it to the band.

Adding insult to injury, their contract with Columbia Records was cancelled and manager John Hewlett openly criticized their last two releases, displaying signs of losing interest in their work. They realised they once again had to come up with something entirely different.

They recorded six new songs that were sent to several record companies for a possible deal. Those six songs were 'Biggest Party In The World', 'Get Laid', 'I Wish I Could Dance Like Black People Do', 'After Dark', 'Breathe' and 'Trying Day'. The latter three were eventually included as bonus tracks with Japanese CD releases of unrelated albums. However, prior to that, rather poor-quality recordings were shared amongst fans and were commonly known as The *Arista Demos*, although Arista was just one of the record companies which received a copy of those recordings and had kindly declined, just like any other company who heard the songs.

John Hewlett, the same manager who had been very helpful and supportive during their first visit to the UK with the original Bearsville band in 1972 and was there at the arrival of the Maels in June 1973, was now disappointed about the direction Sparks had taken. And he didn't keep it to himself. In all fairness, he had not really been around during the last couple of years. As he stayed in England, he had left most of the manager duties to Joseph Fleury, who was great with the fans and the press but was not really cut out to guide them in musical directions or dealings with record companies.

Hewlett claimed that Ron and Russell were at a desperate stage. In an interview with him by Sparks fan Hamish Ironside for *Sausade Magazine* in January 1990, John said the following:

S: I'd always assumed the cover of 'Introducing Sparks' was a joke…
JH: I suppose it was meant to be a parody of the fifties style of airbrushed photo, but this was our first release on a really big label, and I'd worked hard for that deal [with CBS] and it was all going wrong.
S: Did you try to tell them it was wrong?
JH: Yes, I think it was in Munich in 1978. We were in a hotel and Ronnie broke down and cried and said I didn't care anymore, that I didn't care for his music, which of course I did.

It is unknown whether this meeting actually took place in that form. It is not unthinkable, but Hewlett also claims that it was his idea to completely change directions. He stated that he came up with the idea for Sparks to delve into electronic music and contacted Giorgio Moroder's office to propose a collaboration with the Maels, to which Moroder agreed.

Again from the interview published in *Sausade Magazine*:

S: Whose idea was it to move into electronic music?
JH: Well, I wanted them to move into that direction and we compromised by deciding to use Giorgio Moroder. So I chased Moroder around the world, and then Moroder called them independently and said there was a guy he knew, some big name manager...
S: So they thought if they went with him, they'd get their big break?
JH: Yes, which shows, I suppose, another of their follies. They were all sheepish and quiet when they told me. I said 'that's an extremely unpleasant thing to have done' and I walked out and went to a lawyer. But I did like some of the songs they recorded with Moroder, some of them have got that raw sound, which is good.
S: So Moroder was heavily involved, not just on the musical side?
JH: He's a very clever guy. He writes these sort of two-finger melodies and I suppose in that respect he's the equivalent of Stock, Aitken and Waterman. But I think after a while he realised they weren't going to make it on a huge scale, and he's a very greedy man. He cut me out, and Ron and Russell fell prey to it, he cut their royalties heavily.

The more common story, also highlighted in the documentary *The Sparks Brothers*, is one in which Ron and Russell became fascinated by songs like 'Don't Leave Me This Way' by Thelma Houston and especially 'I Feel Love' by Donna Summer, which was co-written and produced by Giorgio Moroder. They decided that they wanted to work with Moroder.

During an interview in late 1977 with a German journalist living in Los Angeles, they boldly claimed that their new project would involve Giorgio Moroder. The journalist was very surprised as she turned out to be a close friend to Moroder and stated that he had never mentioned anything about it.

Upon being exposed, the Maels had to confess that they had never actually met Moroder or discussed a possible collaboration with him, but they were very interested in the idea. They just didn't know how to contact him. After hearing this confession, the journalist offered to set up a meeting with Moroder to explore a potential partnership, to which the Maels eagerly agreed.

The meeting between Moroder and the Maels went exceptionally well, and they decided to enter into a cooperation. Unbeknownst to them, this collaboration would serve as a crucial blueprint for a new style of music and image that would influence a whole generation of musicians, many of whom are still successful today.

Ron remembers the period of that pivotal decision as follows:

> We didn't have a list of other ideas. That was the only idea we had. A lot of people thought it was a step backwards, that we were entering the disco world. Our sensibility kept it so it was a funny mixture of elements. We were in that area and outside of it at the same time. The lyrics and Russell's singing kept it separate from the wider world of disco. So much of that music was done by legitimate singers. Donna was amazing. Giorgio was uncomfortable with Russell's singing at the start. It was a combination of things that kept it from being as slick and processed as some of the other people who were working in that area at the time.

The album was recorded during the spring of 1978 in Los Angeles and Munich. Moroder wanted full control over the recording of the new project, which involved deciding which songs would be suitable. Only two songs made the cut: 'Beat The Clock' and 'Academy Award Performance'.

Throughout the recording process, Ron would come up with additional new songs but they were all rejected by Moroder. In the end, the other four songs on the album were all co-written with Moroder himself.

Ron reflects on those recordings:

> Anytime we were stuck he would say 'Boys, let me go away for 15 minutes', and he'd go over to an acoustic piano and 15 minutes later he'd have come up with something. Even 'The Number One Song In Heaven' took him just 15 minutes on the piano.
>
> *No. 1 In Heaven* was pretty exciting to make because there were no preconceptions of how a disco producer working with an eccentric rock band would turn out. This was the only album we've ever gone into with almost no material. Only 'Beat The Clock' and 'Academy Award Performance' were written beforehand. Giorgio wrote the music to at least half of the other songs. We tried to get as much of us as we could on *No. 1*, but at the same time we wanted an outside influence. Obviously, we got it.

Apart from the synthesizers played by Ron and Giorgio, the only other instrument on the album was the drums, played by British-born Keith Forsey, a musician from Moroder's stable.

Ron explained:

> There wasn't a choice actually. Keith was skilled at playing the kick drum for 15 minutes at a time. We were purists for live drums. When making *No. 1 In Heaven*, you could use electronic effects that would give it a rhythmic feel

but as far as solid rhythms, it always had to be played. It gave it something different.

With the recordings completed, the next step was to find a suitable record label for the release. This task fell to Moroder. Ron and Russell later claimed that it took over a year after the album was finished to secure a label willing to release it. While this may be true, international music press reports from as early as September 1978 documented a competition amongst several record companies seeking to sign Sparks' new project with Moroder.

According to the official account, a tape of the new album landed on the desk of an A&R representative at Virgin Germany, who was impressed by it. He forwarded the recording to the head office in England, where executives shared his enthusiasm and proceeded to sign Sparks for their upcoming release.

Virgin, the label founded by Richard Branson, featured a diverse roster of artists—from Mike Oldfield, whose *Tubular Bells* (1973) was a commercial breakthrough for the label, to the Sex Pistols, who had been dropped by both EMI and A&M due to their controversial behaviour.

Although Branson founded the label, he was not directly involved in its musical operations. Simon Draper, who oversaw artist signings, quickly recognised the potential in the collaboration between Sparks and Moroder, which he described as unlike anything he had previously encountered.

Virgin Records released the album on 1 March 1979, but they were not the only company that believed in this new kind of music. Independent distribution deals were made with Elektra in the United States and Canada (where the album was released on 17 April), Warner Bros in France, Music Box in Greece, Durium in Italy and Ariola for most other European countries. In Australia, it was also released by Virgin and distributed by the Festival label.

A special yellow fluorescent vinyl edition was released in the United Kingdom on 2 March, and several variations of the singles were issued in a range of colours.

The album cover did not include any images of the band. Instead, it featured what appeared to be nurses—possibly angels—posed against a pale blue background, illuminated by a single fluorescent tube. The inner sleeve included a black-and-white photograph of the Mael brothers, captured during the recording sessions, standing before an impressive array of synthesizers.

Russell reflected in *Trouser Magazine* in 1982:

We went to England and had so much criticism thrown at us that it was terrible. 'Why did you make a disco album?' We thought it had a disco element, but nobody had made an album combining it with other elements. We were put on the defensive.

'I like the album a lot: I think it has an atmosphere that isn't in any of our other albums, and isn't in anybody else's albums. It was a one-of-a-kind situation: people from different areas not having a clue how it was going to turn out. The women on the cover are high-paid fashion models. We wanted a cold feel to the album and to play down our personalities a bit.'

On the mainland, their first single was 'La Dolce Vita', while the UK opted for 'The Number One Song In Heaven'. Sparks' return caused quite a bit of commotion. This was not only due to the surprising new style displayed by the band, but also because of the new image in which there was only the duo involved, sometimes supplemented by a hired session drummer. In many cases this was David Humphrey, who had been involved in PIL's *Metal Box*.

The fact that Ron had restyled his hair with a large curly lock across his forehead only added to the intrigue. Sparks were all over television and present in music magazines. Although a large part of the music press and their fans strongly rejected the new direction and even accused the Maels of selling out, the new collaboration sparked an almost unprecedented movement within the music industry.

Within a year, it was already evident what influence both style and image had on a new generation of musicians, who shamelessly imitated the new Sparks. Bands like Soft Cell, Yazoo, Pet Shop Boys and later Erasure took both image and music as a source of inspiration. Other bands such as Depeche Mode, Bronski Beat, Tubeway Army and The Human League were mainly influenced by the music.

Most bands would go on to achieve far greater commercial success than the artists who had unintentionally influenced them, but the source of inspiration was unmistakable and gave rise to an entirely new musical form. The album's biggest hit was still to come and would not be confined to success in the United Kingdom alone.

Many combinations and variations of nearly all the tracks—excluding 'Academy Award Performance', arguably the most traditionally Sparks-sounding track on the album—were issued globally, achieving varying degrees of commercial success. However, the most significant immediate effect was that Sparks re-entered public and critical discourse.

About a year-and-a-half after the poorly received release of *Introducing Sparks*—an album largely ignored by their earlier fan base—Ron and Russell experienced the busiest period of their career since 1975. Primarily in England and mainland Europe, Sparks were featured regularly on television, beginning with a tour in April 1979. Their television appearances included performances in the Netherlands (13 April), Spain (24 April), Munich (26 April) and Paris (27 and 29 April), with an additional appearance in Italy.

Between promotional tours and televised performances, the Mael brothers remained highly active. Their first side project featured a Los Angeles-based singer named Noël—stylised as Nöel on the UK release but as Noël on most other editions.

They had written several new songs intended for a female vocalist. During a visit to Doug Weston's Troubadour nightclub in Hollywood in December 1978, they saw a performance by a singer who impressed them. After the performance, they approached her and inquired about her interest in collaborating. She agreed, and they recorded demo versions of 'I Want a Man' and 'Dancing Is Dangerous.' The Maels brought these recordings to the Midem music fair in Cannes, France, where they secured a deal for an album with Noël—once again under Virgin Records.

Sounds magazine in the United Kingdom announced the release of her first single as early as April 1979. This early announcement indicated Virgin's confidence in the new musical direction pioneered by the Maels and Moroder, and suggested that the label anticipated a similar success with an unknown vocalist, even before the Maels' own album had achieved commercial traction.

The album *Is There More to Life Than Dancing?*—which included only five of the eight recorded tracks—closely resembled the sonic style of the Maels' own album. However, the lyrics were more conventional, and Noël's sultry, seductive vocals contrasted starkly with the clinical textures of *No. 1 in Heaven*. Nevertheless, the album was unmistakably the work of the same creators.

With this release, Ron and Russell demonstrated that they had paid close attention during their work with Giorgio Moroder. It marked their first serious engagement with production duties—a role in which they succeeded notably. The synthesizer programmer was Gary Chang, for whom this project marked his first professional engagement in the field. He recalled the recordings as follows:

> This is one of my very first recording sessions in LA! It was recorded at the original Larrabee Studios at Larrabee and Santa Monica Blvd in Los Angeles. The entire project was recorded with my modified Yamaha CS-80 and Serge Modular Music System, the CS-80 being gated and processed through the Serge. Ron sat at the CS-80, and me programming and gating the CS-80 through the Serge. Russell provided temp vocals and the creative direction and Bob (Stone—engineer) offered his wizardry with the drums sounds (this is before the sampled drum machines). Thanks to Ron and Russell for the opportunity at the start of my career!

Neither the singles nor the album achieved commercial success, but it later became a cult classic amongst fans of that particular strain of disco.

An even more unusual collaboration occurred with composer Adrian Munsey. Virgin commissioned the Maels to produce his upcoming single, 'C'est Sheep', a tongue-in-cheek reference to Chic's hit 'Le Freak'. Munsey appeared to have a recurring interest in sheep, as his previous single was titled 'The Lost Sheep'. The track is primarily instrumental, incorporating bleating sheep sounds and occasional vocalisations by a female performer, who does not sing any actual lyrics. It consisted of Part 1 and Part 2; both tracks are as peculiar as they are forgettable.

During the same year, Ron and Russell undertook a third project: producing a new album for the French rock/pop trio Bijou. The group, who had previously released two albums, approached the Maels in hopes of revitalising their sound. The resulting album, *Pas Dormir*, was crafted in the band's established style, and the Maels delivered a polished and appealing final product. On a larger scale, however, the music was neither innovative nor particularly impactful.

Overall, 1979 proved to be a pivotal year for Ron and Russell. They returned to the European charts after a four-year hiatus and inadvertently pioneered a new musical style that would influence others. This reaffirmed Sparks' reputation for innovation. Despite criticism from some music journalists accusing them of capitulating to disco trends, the Maels asserted creative control over their musical direction. By trusting their instincts rather than conforming to label expectations, they took a significant artistic risk—one that ultimately proved successful. Their follow-up album would generate considerable controversy, but it would also yield Sparks' most commercially successful single to date.

In May 2024, *No. 1 in Heaven* was rereleased on the Lil' Beethoven label to commemorate its forty-fifth anniversary. The reissue included the album on white vinyl and two CDs featuring earlier single mixes. Concurrently, Noël's album was also reissued. The vinyl edition was pressed on green vinyl, while the double CD included the three tracks omitted from the original release, along with three demo recordings featuring Russell on vocals, serving as guides for Noël. These were labelled as 'Vocal Guide Versions'. In addition, a promotional video for the single 'Dancing Is Dangerous', originally directed in 1979 by Micky Dolenz of The Monkees, was officially released in 2024.

No. 1 In Heaven—The Songs

All songs written by Ron Mael, unless otherwise stated.

'TRYOUTS FOR THE HUMAN RACE'
Written by Ron Mael, Giorgio Moroder and Russell Mael
Duration: 6:05

The opening notes of the first track would have puzzled both dedicated Sparks fans and casual listeners alike. The track begins with a fade-in instrumental introduction lasting over a minute, composed of accelerating electronic beeps and underpinned by what is now recognised as a quintessential synthesizer sound—though highly unconventional at the time. The drums also fade in, executed with meticulous precision, and are followed by Giorgio Moroder's trademark machine gun-like synthesizer rhythm, which dominates the remainder of the song.

Russell's vocals provide a familiar anchor, although the backing vocals are distinctly not his. The song conveys a euphoric energy that is both overwhelming and exuberant. Despite the clinical appearance of the album sleeve and the dominance of electronic instrumentation, the track remains uplifting and full of promise. The lyrical subject matter is also highly unconventional: the narrative unfolds from the perspective of sperm preparing to fertilise an egg.

Although Moroder contributed to the songwriting, the lyrical content—replete with puns and conceptual wit—can be confidently attributed to the Maels. The song was released as the lead single in the United States by Elektra, but it failed to make an impact on the charts. In the United Kingdom, it was released as the third single from the album on 19 October 1979, peaking at number 45.

Like previous singles from the album, it was released in a 12-inch format with a playable label that included a comedic spoken-word segment by Peter Cook. The UK 12-inch version was issued in ten different colours, with both edited and extended mixes appearing on various official releases. Numerous unauthorised remixes have also circulated.

The song was not performed live by a full band until the 2006 tour, which featured new arrangements for guitar and bass that enhanced its dynamic character. In contrast, during the 2013 Revenge of Two Hands One Mouth tour, it was performed using only keyboards and vocals.

The song has twice been officially released on DVD: first on *DeeVeeDee*, recorded in 2006, and later as part of the 2018 concert featured on the bonus disc of *The Sparks Brothers*. Both performances were recorded in London.

> Russell: 'Despite the success with the public, the British press crucified us for "going disco" with this LP. We felt we had committed some crime, and Giorgio was our accomplice. Funny how ten years later, "disco" is called "dance music", and it's no longer a pejorative term. A video for "Tryouts" that has never been shown in America was shot at Shepperton Film Studios in London. We were transformed into werewolves by one of Hitchcock's Shepperton based make-up artists.'

'Academy Award Performance'
Duration: 5:00

The energy and intensity introduced in the album's opening track are surpassed by the second song. A loud, up-tempo drumbeat, accompanied by a frantic, full-bodied sound reminiscent of a swarm of electronic bees, gradually fades out and gives way to an enthusiastic vocal entrance by Russell. Synthesizers effectively substitute for the bass guitar, carrying the track's low-end energy. This track clearly demonstrates that traditional arrangements have not vanished, but have instead been replaced by electronic counterparts.

It is the only track on the album solely written by Ron, and this authorship is evident in its distinctly Sparks-like character. The lyrics have been interpreted from a range of perspectives, some of which are speculative or implausible. The simplest reading suggests that the lyrics contain no deeper or ambiguous meanings, and that the song is simply about someone confident in a talented actress finally receiving the recognition she deserves.

The track was first performed live during the Sparks Spectacular and was later featured in their 2009 Tokyo performance, for which a high-quality recording exists. It reappeared in the 2013 Revenge of Two Hands One Mouth tour, performed using only keyboards and vocals—a stripped-down but effective interpretation of the song's complex arrangements.

During the 2025 tour, the track became a well-received and regular feature of the set list. Along with two other songs, it represented half of the album performed live. The addition of guitars contributed to a notably dynamic performance.

'La Dolce Vita'
Written by Ron Mael, Giorgio Moroder and Russell Mael
Duration: 5:56

Borrowed from the title of Federico Fellini's 1960 film *La Dolce Vita*, the song begins with a choral passage. While some listeners believe the opening was synthesized, it was in fact created by a group of twelve vocalists, each singing individual notes in succession before ultimately harmonising together. These recorded voices were then mixed manually, with each vocal track faded in individually via the mixing board.

The introduction features various sonic elements introduced through gradual fade-ins, followed by an up-tempo drumbeat that establishes the rhythm and leads into the vocal section.

A synthesizer solo follows, accompanied by a synthesized bass line. Throughout the track, a rich blend of sounds produces a dynamic stereo image, and the arrangements—though constrained by the available synthesizer technology—are cleverly constructed.

Russell's lead vocals are cheerful and clear; aside from the pre-recorded backing vocals, his voice remains unaccompanied. Like many Sparks songs, 'La Dolce Vita' lends itself to multiple interpretations, one of which suggests that the song portrays a male prostitute or gigolo serving an elderly, affluent woman—a reading that aligns well with the lyrics.

'La Dolce Vita' was the first single released from the album, in February 1979. It was issued in Germany, the Netherlands, France, Italy, Spain and New Zealand, with all versions released in picture sleeves, except the New Zealand edition. The single failed to chart in any of these markets. It was also Sparks' first 12-inch single, released exclusively in Germany, though no extended mix was included. The song has only been performed live during the Sparks Spectacular and at a concert in Tokyo in 2009.

'Beat The Clock'
Written by Ron Mael and Russell Mael
Duration: 4:23

'Beat the Clock' was one of only two songs originally written by the Maels that Giorgio Moroder accepted for inclusion in the recording sessions, although its original version differed significantly from the final product. Ron Mael has noted that the song was initially composed in a slow, Velvet Underground-inspired tempo and arrangement. However, under Moroder's influence, it was dramatically transformed—a change that ultimately proved beneficial, as it became the album's most successful single when released as its second.

The single was issued both as a standard 7-inch black vinyl and in twelve different-coloured 12-inch vinyl editions, each featuring a playable label. This 12-inch release also included a spoken-word monologue by Peter Cook, who, according to various accounts, had likely never heard of Sparks prior to the collaboration. At one point, 'Beat the Clock' held the record for the highest single-day sales in Virgin Records' history, reaching number 10 on the UK Singles Chart and becoming Sparks' third UK Top Ten single. It also peaked at number 16 in the Dutch singles chart and number 10 in Belgium.

Surprisingly, the album itself remained on the charts for only one week, peaking at number 43 before dropping out entirely.

'Beat the Clock' is arguably the most commercially accessible track on the album, featuring an upbeat tempo and an especially catchy chorus. The drums take a prominent role, supported by a programmed synthesizer bass line. More than twenty-five different mixes of the song exist—most of them unauthorised—which attests to its enduring popularity and inspirational quality.

A music video was produced to promote the single and is still occasionally aired on British television. From their early concerts in Los Angeles in 1981 through the Two Hands One Mouth tour in 2013, the song was regularly included in Sparks' live performances. It returned to the set list during the 2025 tour and was notable as one of the few songs in which Russell employed his falsetto live once more.

Russell: '"I Feel Love" had caused an amazing impression on us. Working with Giorgio Moroder, we wanted to see if we could combine some of the electronics and feel of that song with our lyric slant. "Beat The Clock" was the second British hit single from the LP. We were happy to see that the menu was basically the same at the BBC TV-canteen.'

'My Other Voice'
Written by Giorgio Moroder, Ron Mael and Russell Mael
Duration: 4:54

While the previous track may have the most hit potential on the album, the next one is probably the least commercial. However, that doesn't mean it wasn't well-regarded, as many people consider 'My Other Voice' a very appealing tune.

This is largely due to the slightly mysterious production of the song, and the lyrics, which are open to many interpretations. The song begins with a recording of reversed cymbals, slowly fading-in in stereo, while a bass sound with a matching drumbeat guides the intro and takes over. A voice-like synthesizer joins in, adding an almost angelic sound to the song. More synthesizer sounds are gradually added to the mix, preparing the listener for the moment when the actual vocals appear, which doesn't happen until three minutes into the song.

Just before that, a robotic voice can be heard, and the same artificial voice handles the second verse. This arrangement is reminiscent of Giorgio Moroder's use of similar sounds on his albums $E=MC^2$ and *Knights In White Satin* from 1975 and 1976 respectively.

The song was released as the B-side to 'La Dolce Vita' in Germany and Spain, and has only been performed live during the Sparks Spectacular and at a concert in Tokyo in 2009.

'The Number One Song In Heaven'
Written by Ron Mael, Giorgio Moroder and Russell Mael
Duration: 7:26

The final song of the album is the centrepiece. It is often the case that the last track of a Sparks album is special, and this is no exception. One could argue that the album itself is a representation of life and death. The opening song is about conception and the closing song is about death or nearing death. The songs in between handle the actual experiences between those two events.

The closing song is composed of two parts that differ considerably from each other and are separated by a short but powerful drum break, after which the tempo changes. Before that, the first part of the song mainly builds up to that moment, with serene voices and a machine gun-like sound, combined with the electronic beeps heard earlier on the album.

The first single off the album in the UK was an edited version of this track, released in a tasteful sleeve and available as a 7-inch in black and green vinyl. For the first time in the UK, Sparks also released 12-inch singles, which came in black, red and blue.

The single was a hit record. Not nearly as big a hit as 'This Town Ain't Big Enough For Both Of Us' had been, but it peaked at number 14, their biggest success since 'Never Turn Your Back On Mother Earth'. In Ireland, it even reached number 5.

Live, it is one of the songs that has been played the most often. It was included in their first gigs after the release of this album and has been included in all the tours since, including the one of 2025. Most of the time, only the second part is performed, although there have been occasions when the complete song was played, most notably during a short radio performance in the UK in 2008. During the instrumental portion of the song, Ron typically performs his signature Ron shuffle, which generates a lot of excitement from a large portion of the audience.

Russell: 'The combination of Giorgio Moroder's electronics and a dance beat had been intriguing to us. Both Giorgio and ourselves were feeling our way through the recording process, as he had never worked with a band before, and we had never worked with a producer known more for his work with solo artists like Donna Summer. No drum machines were used on the album; none existed at the time. Just Keith Forsey and his steady right foot. Though recorded mostly in Los Angeles, once again the British and European public were the most supportive of what we were doing.'

9
Terminal Jive

Release date: 28 January 1980
Produced by: Giorgio Moroder and Harold Faltermeyer
Engineers: Brian Reeves and Dennis Drake
Sleeve design: Pearce Marchbank
Photography: Gered Mankowitz
Recorded at: Musicland Studios, Munich; Sound Arts Studio, Los Angeles; Westlake Studios, Los Angeles
Duration: 35:55
Personnel: Ron Mael: Synthesizers
Russell Mael: Vocals
Harold Faltermeyer: Synthesizers
Keith Forsey: Drums
William Walden: Guitar
Richie Zito: Bass guitar
Laurie Forsey: Backing vocals

Side 1
'When I'm With You'
'Just Because You Love Me'
'Rock 'n' Roll People In A Disco World'
'When I'm With You (Instrumental)'

Side 2
'Young Girls'
'Noisy Boys'
'Stereo'
'The Greatest Show On Earth'

Singles from this album:
'When I'm With You'/'When I'm With You (Instrumental)'
'When I'm With You'/'Just Because You Love Me'
'Young Girls'/'Rock 'n' Roll People In A Disco World'
'Young Girls'/'Just Because You Love Me'

The year 1979 proved to be a successful one for brothers Ron and Russell Mael. They took a significant risk by following their own instincts and preferences, and with the help of a key collaborator, they created a new genre of music.

On the other hand, they had little to lose. Since 1976, they had lost relevance with the general public and the press, and commercial success had eluded them for almost four years.

Now they were back in the spotlight, particularly in Britain and some countries on the European continent. While their last single did not match the success of previous ones, they were once again significant. All they needed was a strong follow-up to *No. 1 In Heaven* to solidify their comeback. There were warning signs, though.

After Island Records released *The Best of Sparks* in various countries, following their move to Columbia, they did the same in the UK on 24 November 1979. This was clearly motivated by the return of attention and the commercial success of Sparks. However, the compilation flopped, just as it had in other countries before. Apparently, many of the early fans had abandoned them, and the old music was not interesting enough for the new fans. Even a reissue of 'This Town Ain't Big Enough For Both Of Us', backed by 'Looks, Looks, Looks', did not have any impact.

Recordings began in Los Angeles in late 1979. The new album had a significant change, with Harold Faltermeyer taking over most of the production work from Giorgio Moroder.

Ron had brought around twenty new songs, but only one, 'When I'm With You', was selected by the production team to be on the album. Other songs were discarded, and new ones were written during the recording process. Three new songs were written by Ron and Russell; the rest were co-written with Moroder, Faltermeyer and even drummer Keith Forsey. Faltermeyer played most of the synthesizer recordings.

Afterwards, Ron remarked bitterly that he was not allowed to play on his own record, but that is probably a bit exaggerated. Nevertheless, his role during the recording was less prominent than on any previous album.

> Ron: 'Harold could play better than me or Giorgio, but the songs were more heavily screened. We submitted twenty songs, and only one passed muster. And even then the middle eight was changed. I was hurt.'
> Russell: 'Recording *No. 1 In Heaven*, we got so into it that we suggested guitars were obsolete. This time however, there's a whole load of guitars and any other suitable instruments that came to hand. We considered what to use carefully, and decided that it would be ridiculous to close off everything but synthesiser possibilities. The big danger was making *No. 1 In Heaven, Volume Two* and I think we've avoided that.'

The photos for the cover were taken by Gered Mankowitz, who had also worked on the back cover of *Indiscreet*. He and the Maels had met a few times in the summer of 1979, and in August, a photo session was held at his studio in Great Windmill Street. The photos from that session were used as press material and would also be featured in reissued CDs in the future.

For the actual sleeve, the Maels, Mankowitz and art director Pearce Marchbank went on two sessions of 'guerrilla photography' in west London, on 22 October and 6 December 1979.

Gered Mankowitz said: 'Ron was up for anything. He just relished the grotesquery, and Russell loved this style. They worked beautifully together—they were so visual, such fun, so inspiring.'

The album included eight songs, one being an instrumental version of the lead single. It was released in late January 1980. There are indications that the original title of the new album was suggested to be *Tokyo Bombed*, not *Terminal Jive*. Since the early 1980s, an image of an Asian man smiling on the phone, holding a piece of paper with the words 'Tokyo Bombed' and the LP's catalogue number handwritten, was circulating.

Recently, Sparks' management denied this, claiming that the design was actually created for *Kimono My House*. However, in late 1979 someone from record company Virgin gave the photo, along with a cassette of the newly recorded LP, to British Sparks fan and collector Paul Mauger. He was informed that this would be the new record and cover, but Virgin had not made a final decision.

Reviews for the album were mixed. Some believed it was Sparks' best work, while other music magazines were less impressed with this new direction. Leading music magazine *Oor* in the Netherlands, which had traditionally favoured Sparks, was unforgiving about *Terminal Jive*:

> After the relative success of 'No. 1 In Heaven', a strong follow-up could have brought Sparks back in the saddle. But that's when they come up with their weakest record. Terminal Jive, like its predecessor, was created under the care of mother hen Giorgio Moroder, and you have to admit that at least something happened on No. 1 In Heaven. This new one lacks any adventure and has the vitality of a dishcloth. What were they thinking with Terminal Jive? In its dullness, even Ron Mael's satirical pen has lost its edge, and the record had to be completed with an instrumental repeat of the new single 'When I'm With You'. And what's with the guitars on 'Stereo'? Principles are not always as consistent as claimed. 'Young Boys' and 'Noisy Boys', how is it possible that a mind as creative as Ron Mael's could have produced such an exasperatingly annoying, devoid of every ounce of inventiveness, godawful record? The answer: What record? We consider Terminal Jive non-existent.

However, Harry Doherty wrote in *Melody Maker* on 9 February 1980:

> The inclusion of the instrumental version of the single seems superfluous until placed in the overall context of the album. The album's intention is defined for the first time, with the hard rock guitar chopping ferociously alongside the mannered synthesizers. *Terminal Jive* is given further depth via the quality of the Maels' song-writing, with additional credits to various members of the Moroder entourage. Still obsessed with adolescence, Ron and Russell emerge with a series of memorable pop tunes, any of which would make fine singles. 'Young Girls', 'Noisy Boys' and 'Stereo', the three tracks that open side two, are persuasive arguments in favour of their best-ever album.

The first single taken from the album was 'When I'm With You'. The single was released in a surprising variety of countries, including several European ones, as well as Canada, Argentina, Mexico and even Madagascar, where it was available in a limited edition on green vinyl. In Mexico, the album was released under a different name, *When I Am With You*, with a completely different cover. The single had the biggest impact in France, reaching the top of the charts at the end of 1980 and staying there for several weeks.

In addition to their busy promotional activities in France, the Maels also connected with the Belgian band, Telex. Telex, a trio from Brussels consisting of Marc Moulin, Michel Moers and Dan Lacksman, were well known in Belgium and had even participated in the Eurovision Song Contest that year (1980), where they finished second from last. Their music came purely from synthesizers and rhythm boxes, and there were certainly similarities with the music Sparks were making at the time.

Telex were also involved in producing an album for Lio, a popular teenage singer from France. Lio, originally from Portugal, was quite successful in France at a young age with a few singles that had a fresh and cheerful sound, coupled with an image that bordered on a somewhat naïve view of budding sexuality. Ron and Russell were asked to write the English lyrics for Telex's new LP, titled *Sex*, except for the UK, where it was given the slightly less confrontational title *Birds and Bees*. Years later, the Maels would also write English lyrics for Lio as she aimed for the international market.

Her album *Suite Sixtine*, released only in Canada in 1983, contained six songs with English lyrics and is now quite rare and remarkably expensive. The reissue on CD, in 2005, included four more English versions of the original songs interpreted by Ron and Russell.

More importantly, on a personal level, was the fact that Marc Moulin and Ron became very good friends. Moulin passed away in 2008, and at a tribute concert in Brussels in 2013, Sparks were invited to perform and covered the Telex song 'Tell Me It's A Dream'. On that occasion, Ron shared with the audience that Moulin had been his best friend since they met.

In 1983, Sparks recorded their album *In Outer Space* at the private studio of Telex in Laken, Belgium. Telex also did a cover version of 'The Number One Song In Heaven' on their 2006 album *How Do You Dance?*

Another remarkable thing happened to Ron in 1980. Paul McCartney, whom they had seen performing at two concerts with the Beatles in the US in the 1960s, released a new single called 'Coming Up'. In the video accompanying this single, McCartney was seen dressed up as a number of highly acclaimed musicians, including Hank Marvin (The Shadows), Buddy Holly, John Bonham (Led Zeppelin), a version of himself during the Beatles' heyday and none other than Ron Mael on keyboards!

> Ron: 'That was really strange for me. The oddest thing was going into a dry-cleaner the day after they showed the "Coming Up" video on Saturday Night Live, and the guy who was working there said, "Hey, I saw you on television last night", and I was like, "Oh yeah." It was really flattering because it was Paul McCartney and also because of the other people he had chosen to pay homage to in the video. It was pretty amazing.'
>
> Russell: 'To have a Beatle acknowledging your existence is the goal of any musician.'

More recently, in the Edgar Wright documentary *The Sparks Brothers*, Russell says: 'I started respecting Ron a lot more after Paul McCartney gave his tribute to Ron, and I realised, God, I'm working with somebody that Paul McCartney likes.'

Meanwhile, television presenter and former model Paula Yates, who was married to Bob Geldof and had a relationship with INXS's singer Michael Hutchence, selected the Maels to be featured in her book *Rock Stars in Their Underpants*, published by Virgin Books. There was little to criticise about Russell, who likely wore his usual underpants, but Ron appeared in the photos wearing white boxer shorts and a torn undershirt full of holes and rips.

It is worth noting that the English press had already reported in July 1980 that the Maels had a new band and would be performing six concerts in the UK that autumn. The band members, who would indeed play on the next LP, were mentioned by name, but the concerts were not listed until late 1981, and they only took place in Los Angeles, France and Belgium. For British fans, it would be another fourteen years before they would see Sparks perform live again—nineteen years since their last gig in the UK.

Despite experiencing a special year that brought Sparks their biggest local hit, years of close friendship from an unexpected angle and tribute from one of the greatest musicians of the past sixty years, it must have been a disappointing period for Sparks. They had the opportunity to finally push through and make their mark after the success of their previous album (or rather, the success of the singles), but they still failed to achieve a commercial breakthrough.

Commercial success is by no means the yardstick for which the Maels aim, but they were also very disappointed on an artistic level. When the author of this book met them in March 1981, they were very clear that *Terminal Jive* had replaced *Introducing Sparks* as the record they were least satisfied with. Once again, they had to reinvent themselves. It had been four years since they had worked in a band format, and they had not played live during that period, despite releasing three complete albums and their first *Best Of* compilation. Their next move, which apparently was already in the making in the summer of 1980, would bring them back to the old format and slowly capture the attention of the American audience.

While the world—and France in particular—was still regularly confronted with the concept of a duo and a corresponding sound, the Maels, in their hometown, were already busy returning to a band format. This time, they did not enlist the help of individual musicians who had to be formed into a close-knit band, but seamlessly added an existing band to form the new Sparks, which would mainly focus on their home country in the coming years.

Terminal Jive—The Songs

All songs written by Ron Mael and Russell Mael, unless otherwise stated.

'WHEN I'M WITH YOU'
Duration: 5:45

A gentle gust of wind introduces the first song of the album, accompanied by a mid-tempo drumbeat and a synthesizer with a warmer tone compared to the previous record. An unexpected guitar melody develops, creating a soothing atmosphere. The inclusion of guitars is surprising, as the brothers had previously indicated that guitars were a thing of the past.

The synthesizer riffs are catchy, creating a romantic and slightly sultry atmosphere. The French audience embraced the song, but most other nations did not. Russell's vocals are pleasant and accessible, with minimal use of falsetto or backing vocals. A mid-song solo, resembling a synthesized trumpet, adds to the variety of sounds used. It is clear why this song was chosen as the first single.

'When I'm With You' was released in the UK on 18 January 1980. A video was shot by Brian Grant of the Millaney-Grant production team (with Scott Millaney, who had also done the video for 'Beat The Clock'). It features Ron as a ventriloquist with Russell as the ventriloquist's dummy. This representation of the inseparable brothers, while undoubtedly tongue-in-cheek, fails to fully capture Russell's importance. This theme would later be revisited in the cover of the album *Pulling Rabbits Out of a Hat*.

The single failed to make an impact in the UK, which was surprising for both the band and Virgin Records. However, in France, the record garnered significant attention, selling over 750,000 copies and topping the charts for several weeks. It remains Sparks' biggest commercial success to date.

However, the album or any singles weren't even released in the USA, which must have been rather disappointing for the Maels. After all, that was their home country, and so far they had never succeeded in establishing themselves properly there.

Nevertheless, the Maels stayed in France for several months in 1980 because they were extremely popular on television shows and were regularly invited. The single also became a minor hit in Australia, reaching number 14, and the LP even entered the album chart, peaking at number 96.

Although 'When I'm With You' was released as a 12-inch single in Germany, the Netherlands and Mexico, it only included the regular album version and the instrumental version on the B-side, showing a lack of creativity from the record company.

Not surprisingly, this song was performed live during short tours in France and Belgium in 1981, as well as in concerts in 1994, 1995 and 1997. It made appearances in 2003 and 2006, where it was only performed in Paris, with a regular spot on tours in 2017 and as recently as 2023.

> Russell: 'Ron had played Giorgio scores of songs before recording "Terminal Jive" and all had been rejected with the exception of "When I'm With You", which Giorgio still felt needed a new middle section. In commercial terms, this was the biggest single Sparks has had to date, and it was never even released in America. The majority of the sales came from France where we stayed for nine months as a result of the large number of TV shows we appeared on. A video of Ron as a ventriloquist and me as his dummy (no comments please) was shown to death in France. As a result, we could walk into virtually any couscous restaurant in Paris and get the best table in the house.'

'JUST BECAUSE YOU LOVE ME'
Duration: 4:36

The rather generic sound that dominates this album is also evident in this second song, characterised by guitars that are not necessarily dominant. It is a milder form of rock 'n' roll with refreshing disco influences. As a result, the arrangements are not as striking as on the previous LP, but they produce a sound that is more accessible to the listener. This also makes it a bit less exciting and more predictable.

In that regard, the lyrics are closely aligned with the chosen musical arrangements. They lack depth, with no clever wordplay or subtle humour, and the topics themselves are somewhat less than fascinating—fairly clichéd approaches to love stories, which is not the kind of approach you would usually expect from Ron.

The vocals seem to be mixed somewhat in the background and are not as prominently present as on most Sparks albums. Backing vocals are provided by Laurie Forsey, the brother of drummer Keith. This song appeared on the B-side of the French single.

As with most tracks on the album, this song was only performed once during the Sparks Spectacular.

'Rock 'n' Roll People In A Disco World'
Duration: 4:47

The mix of guitars and synthesizers in the next song is well-balanced but somewhat flat. The guitars are prominently featured without being overpowering, as they are complemented by the accompanying synthesizers. It's as if they use distortion in a refined manner, avoiding a harsh and aggressive sound.

The chorus is catchy and quickly becomes memorable. A synthesizer-led solo is present but the guitar is added to maintain a balanced sound. Rarely does a Sparks song include a drum solo, which serves as the conclusion of the song. The drum sound is reminiscent of the drums on 'Number One In Heaven', but aside from that there are few similarities to the predecessor.

The song was never performed live during regular concerts.

'When I'm With You' (Instrumental)
Duration: 5:45

What is remarkable, and rather unfortunate, is the fact that out of the meagre eight songs on the LP, an instrumental version of one of these songs has been included. This is particularly disappointing when you consider that Ron came up with twenty original songs before recording began, and the majority of them were discarded. It is hard to imagine that amongst all these songs, there was not a better alternative to repeating a song in instrumental variation.

This instrumental is two minutes shorter than the original, and although the arrangements are slightly different, it does not really add anything significant to the album. Perhaps it would have been better to replace this song with one of the tracks that were not accepted and only use it as the B-side of the single, as was the case in most countries except for France.

'YOUNG GIRLS'
Duration: 4:49

Side two opens with 'Young Girls', a topic that is not entirely unfamiliar to the Maels. Based on some of their other songs, such as the earlier 'Throw Her Away (And Get A New One)' and the later 'Rockin' Girls', they seem to have a preference for 17-year-olds. At least that's the impression they give when addressing the subject. Poetic freedom and all lead us to believe that this should, of course, not be taken literally, but it is somewhat striking.

An instrumental intro of about twenty seconds starts the song, which is set at a mid-tempo. The vocals seem to be a bit more mixed to the front and even contain some falsetto parts. There is an instrumental break of nearly half a minute that really doesn't add much to the song, and it ends in a fade-out.

Although only released in the UK on a 12-inch single, the A-side consists of an extended 'disco version' of over six minutes. The B-side contains an edited version of 3:53 as well as the album version of 'Just Because You Love Me'. The 7-inch single, which was released in the UK, France, Germany and Italy, also features the edited single version.

> Russell: 'Yes, Your Honor, it is a song about being a dirty old man.'

'NOISY BOYS'
Written by Harold Faltermeyer, Keith Forsey, Ron Mael and Russell Mael
Duration: 3:55

The lack of authority the Mael brothers had in the execution of this album is evident from the significant involvement of external individuals in writing the last three songs. The band actually only consisted of Ron and Russell, despite retaining the same drummer who had played on the previous album. Now, this drummer also had a role in writing a song.

In addition, it appears that Harold Faltermeyer played a significant role in writing this track, as the style and arrangements bear a striking resemblance to his later solo work. 'Noisy Boys' is a high-tempo song, and like most tracks on this album, the arrangements are very well balanced.

There is no specific instrument that dominates, and no unexpected breaks or tempo changes are used. The song flows in a fairly predictable pattern; pleasing to the ear but not very exciting. It also features something that could be considered a solo, but it has a somewhat obligatory nature.

Lyrically, it appears to be about a man in a relationship who desires occasional moments of wildness to alleviate the monotony of his current situation.

Apart from the Sparks Spectacular, this song has never been performed live.

'Stereo'
Written by Giorgio Moroder, Ron Mael and Russell Mael
Duration: 4:01

'Stereo' begins with a drum intro and is another upbeat song with a catchy melody. The song's appeal is further enhanced by a somewhat predictable stereo mix of guitars.

Some parts of the song are reminiscent of songs that Duran Duran would later create. In hindsight, this is not surprising, considering that Nick Rhodes and John Taylor were fans of Sparks. However, the somewhat clumsy attempt to insert a break where the vocals happily dart from left to right is predictable, illustrating the scarcity of original ideas that may have been present amongst the twenty songs the Maels initially presented.

The listener is treated to an album with songs that, individually, are not bad at all. However, they are plagued by a generic and predictable sound, where the tracks are almost interchangeable in terms of arrangements, and the lyrics are quite substandard. Since the release of the record, Ron and Russell have always unequivocally distanced themselves from the final product, and that is not entirely incomprehensible.

'The Greatest Show On Earth'
Written by Giorgio Moroder, Harold Faltermeyer, Ron Mael and Russell Mael
Duration: 4:17

The final track of the LP is upbeat, lively and fast-paced, much like the majority of the songs on the album. It does not reach the same level as '(No More) Mr. Nice Guys', 'Equator', 'Bon Voyage' or the later closing songs that would follow. However, this applies to most tracks on the album.

Pleasing to the ear, the production is fitting for the team's desired outcome. Yet it is a consistent characteristic of this LP that the song lacks a unique or remarkable quality.

Perhaps this album would have been better received if created by different artists. However, the Mael brothers have a distinct standard and approach to what they want to share with the world. In this case, their creative input was hindered—or at the very least subdued—by the producers. This album generates cheerful, danceable and easily digestible music, but it does not stand out as an exceptional achievement as Sparks fans have come to expect.

The irony of scoring their first number one hit in this context highlights why music closer to the Maels' creative vision may not be understood by the general public.

10

Whomp That Sucker

Release date: 3 July 1981
Produced by: Reinhold Mack
Engineers: Brian Reeves and Dennis Drake
Cover concept: Ron Mael
Sleeve design: Larry Vignon
Photography: Liz Sowers
Recorded at: Musicland Studios, Munich
Duration: 38:38
Personnel: Ron Mael: Synthesizers
Russell Mael: Vocals
Reinhold Mack: Synthesizer programming and glass shattering
David Kendrick: Drums
Bob Haag: Guitar, backing vocals
Leslie Bohem: Bass guitar, backing vocals

Side 1
'Tips For Teens'
'Funny Face'
'Where's My Girl'
'Upstairs'
'I Married A Martian'

Side 2
'The Willys'
'Don't Shoot Me'
'Suzie Safety'
'That's Not Nastassia'
'Wacky Women'

Singles from this album:
'Tips For Teens'/'Don't Shoot Me'
'Tips For Teens'/'Wacky Women'
'Tips For Teens'/'Funny Face'
'Funny Face'/'The Willys'
'Funny Face'/'Don't Shoot Me'

In the late spring of 1980, Ron and Russell frequented the Farmers Market in Los Angeles, a habit they probably still have, where they would grab coffee and pastries of unmatched quality. It was there that they met Leslie Bohem, David Kendrick and Bob Haag of the band Bates Motel, who were there for the same reason.

Although Bates Motel did not have a record deal, they regularly played in Los Angeles. After meeting, Ron and Russell went to some of their gigs and were impressed. Since they were considering returning to a full band format, they decided to integrate Bates Motel into the new Sparks.

The decision was made easier by the fact that the fourth Bates Motel member, guitarist Dave Draves, wanted to move away from the city into the desert. It was a case of either finding a new guitarist or joining Ron and Russell. For drummer David Kendrick, the decision was simple, as he had been a Sparks fan since 1974 and even had 'Talent Is An Asset' in his earlier band's live set list.

Rehearsals began, lasting about six weeks, with all new songs. For most of them, the lyrics were not yet written so Russell would sing random words. Surprisingly, the titles of the songs were already decided. After rehearsals, the band flew to Musicland Studios in Munich, Germany, owned by Giorgio Moroder, which was located in the basement of the Arabella High-Rise Building. The band stayed there during the recordings, where hits like 'I Feel Love' by Donna Summer and albums by T. Rex were recorded.

The album was produced by Reinhold Mack—or just Mack—an associate of Moroder. He had worked with artists like The Rolling Stones, Scorpions, ELO and Deep Purple, and later produced several Queen albums.

When they entered the studio, Ron brought in the lyrics he had written for each song the night before in his hotel room. One song, 'One Nut', with the line 'One nut is all it takes', was rehearsed but likely not recorded. Its fate remains unknown, as it was not performed live either. Despite David Kendrick's belief that it was a great song, Ron and Russell might have decided it was not up to par.

At Moroder's insistence, they left Virgin Records and signed a new deal with RCA, represented in the UK by the subsidiary company Why-Fi, a small and brand-new division. *Whomp That Sucker* didn't make an impact in England, despite Why-Fi's efforts to promote it with advertisements in local music magazines and a truly unique event to officially launch the album in the UK. There were attempts to tour with Robert Palmer, but that never materialised.

On 6 May 1981, a genuine boxing match was arranged between the two brothers at the Hilton Hotel on Park Lane, London. The Maels were quite serious about it and Ron apparently won the bout but suffered a rib injury. Some say his rib was broken.

As sensational as this launch event was, the album didn't make an impact on the record-buying public in the UK. However, Sparks still had some credit in France and decided to focus on that. A tour was offered, and after consideration, they decided to go for it. It would be the first time since 1976 that the Maels would be playing live again, and they wanted to hold on to the modest success they were enjoying in that particular country.

Then something completely unexpected happened in their home town. LA radio station K-ROQ picked up the album and played songs from it continuously. They started with 'Tips for Teens' and 'Funny Face', later adding 'Upstairs' and 'I Married a Martian'. Interest in Sparks suddenly increased on a very local level.

Upon their sudden success, manager Joseph Fleury thought it would be a good idea to give a concert in Los Angeles, at the Whisky A Go Go, before their tour in France. Ron and Russell were initially reluctant but eventually agreed. When the show was advertised, it sold out immediately, and two more were added—both of which also sold out.

The shows, held from 20 to 22 October, were a huge success and garnered a lot of attention from the press, especially the *Los Angeles Times*. The crowd was enthusiastic, but very few reacted to songs such as 'This Town Ain't Big Enough for Both of Us' or 'Beat the Clock'. Most of the audience viewed Sparks as a new band, emerging alongside the growing interest in New Wave music.

Meanwhile, the album was generally well received all over the world. *Rolling Stone* magazine's Parke Puterbaugh concluded a highly favourable review with the following words:

> Wake up, America. This is Sparks' tenth album of lovable loony tunes. These guys should be someone's heroes by now. With their own cartoon show and everything.

Even Alfred Bos from *Muziekkrant Oor*, who had harshly criticised the previous LP, was full of praise for the new album, as evidenced by his conclusion:

> They can still do it, so why delay for five years? And they are also up to date, because 'Upstairs', if you forget the unmistakable alto of Russell Mael, could have been from This Heat or The Normal with its mechanically pounding synth beat. As bad as *Terminal Jive* was, that's how entertaining *Whomp That Sucker* is, the best Sparks LP since *Propaganda*. Welcome back, guys. Make yourselves at home.

Sparks left for France just as they were gaining serious attention and success in their home town—more than ever before—which must have felt strange. 'When I'm With You' had been a major hit in France, and while some audience members were familiar with their earlier songs, many came just to hear that particular track. However, it had been a full year since the song had charted.

There is not much documentation about that tour in France. Eight shows are known to have been arranged, with four being cancelled due to low ticket sales. The final night at Le Palace in Paris on 13 November was a success, but the others were not sold out.

A similar situation occurred in Belgium. Someone decided to extend the tour with six dates there, but four were also cancelled, with the first two being cancelled at the last minute. The Belgian shows that did proceed were received with great enthusiasm, being attended by fans from France, the Netherlands, England and even the US. The highlight was the concert in Brussels, which surely left the musicians with a good feeling afterwards.

The band must have had mixed emotions about leaving some venues without having played a single note while their popularity grew in Los Angeles during their absence. Nevertheless, they stayed a little longer after the Belgian tour to participate in an event that was broadcast on German television: the *Rock und Klassiknacht* in Munich at Circus Krone, where they were part of a show that included various other acts such as OMD, Tangerine Dream and John Miles. During this short gig, Sparks played four tracks from their latest album and 'This Town Ain't Big Enough for Both of Us'. At the end of the event, Ron and Russell joined the other artists and performed a rather unfortunate version of 'Give Peace a Chance', during which Russell played the maracas and Ron some bananas. The song was performed exactly one year and one day after the murder of John Lennon.

During the live gigs, Sparks had been augmented with an additional keyboard player. Jim Goodwin, a friend of Joseph Fleury from New York, joined them during the Los Angeles shows and the French/Belgian tour. Before that, he had been in John Cale's band.

After the tours in France and Belgium and the performance at the *Rock und Klassiknacht*, Sparks headed back to Los Angeles, where the momentum was still going strong.

K-ROQ continued to play songs from *Whomp That Sucker*, and local interest in Sparks was growing. It was a good moment for the Mael brothers to return to their home town, as the other band members were also sharing in their newfound fame.

Videos for 'Funny Face' and 'Tips for Teens' were made, but they were only shown in Europe. The latter video was a re-enactment of the London boxing match in May of that year, and once again Ron ended up winning despite being cornered by his younger brother several times.

Sparks' success was not limited to Los Angeles. For the first time since 1975's *Indiscreet*, they landed on the US album chart, reaching number 182.

The attention for Sparks in America also began to reach the band itself. In an article in the magazine *Bam*, dated 20 November 1981, we find the following passage written by David Gillerman:

> A few minutes before the scheduled interview with Ron and Russell Mael, the brothers behind Sparks, I happen to meet Ron on the ground floor of the RCA building. Instead of proceeding upstairs however, we are detained by a bumbling security guard who thinks that Ron and I are a journalist team there

to interview an RCA publicist. He insists on calling the publicity department upstairs, and, getting no answer, tells us that we'll have to come back another day. Ron rolls his eyes, then quietly tries to explain the situation to the guard, who, still uncomprehending, starts to call upstairs again. At this point, the normally soft-spoken Ron declares quite firmly, 'Look, my name is Ron Mael and I'm in a band called Sparks.' Pause. 'I'm a rock and roll star, goddamit!'

The situation must have been confusing. They had their first number one hit ever in a European country, but the subsequent tour had to be largely cancelled. At the same time, they were starting to see some success in their home country for the first time in six years.

They thus decided to focus on their home market, and with the new record company Atlantic and the addition of Jim Goodwin on keyboards to their team, they worked on a new album that would bring them even more fame and chart success.

Whomp That Sucker—The Songs

All songs written by Ron Mael and Russell Mael.

'TIPS FOR TEENS'
Duration: 3:33

For those who prefer to experience Sparks' authentic sound, the opening notes of 'Tips for Teens' are a true delight. At 19, the author of this publication might have lifted the needle off the record after hearing the vocal introduction accompanied by keyboards. He may have jumped around his bedroom, feeling a light sense of ecstasy, and exclaimed to no one in particular that 'they were back'.

It soon becomes clear that the Mael brothers had a greater influence on the production and arrangements of this record. It may also be the case that producer Reinhold Mack himself wanted to return to the sound for which Sparks were known. Regardless, this song gave many fans a feeling of coming home, despite the previous LP's number-one hit.

Sparks were a real band again, and that is how they sound—not only on this song but throughout the album. It is evident that some of the earlier frustration was alleviated during the recording of this album, resulting in a more spontaneous, enthusiastic and authentic sound. This is a band that clearly enjoys its work and believes in it. The instrumental break, which includes the sound of a fairground attraction, reinforces this impression.

The high energy of the opening track appears to set the tone for the remainder of the album. Also significant is the fact that the lyrics meet the high standard that listeners have come to expect from the Mael brothers, replete with clever wordplay and subtle humour. It is understandable why this track was selected as the first single, even though there were several other viable options on the LP. Despite Wi-Fi's fairly intensive advertising campaign and the positive reviews in the UK, the single did not chart. It also appeared on 12-inch vinyl in the UK, backed by 'Don't Shoot Me', but both tracks were the regular album versions.

The song was frequently performed during various tours throughout the 1980s. It resurfaced during the 2022 world tour, where it received much appreciation.

Russell: 'We were once again performing live a lot, though now mainly in America. A new young audience was attracted that was virtually unaware of our British and European past careers. We were a brand-new band with nine albums that few of our new fans were aware of. Dick Clark welcomed us back.'

'Funny Face'
Duration: 3:24

The second song on the record was also released as the second single, which is not an uncommon practice for the band. It is a mid-tempo track that is just as cheerful as its predecessor. Here, too, the listener is almost immediately treated to a sound that appears to be inspired by a fairground attraction.

However, the song is driven by the guitar's riff and the accompanying bass. As with the first song, there is no piano in this one. However, Ron primarily uses one (or more) of the five keyboards mentioned on the inner sleeve.

The track tells an unusual tale of a model who only feels appreciated for his looks, yearning for a situation in which people see beyond that, taking drastic measures to alter his appearance.

RCA did not release any singles from the album in the US, despite the noticeable interest in the band in the greater Los Angeles area. In fact, when they returned home, they were informed that RCA would not extend their record deal. Perhaps the prank that the Maels had pulled earlier had something to do with it.

Earlier that year, Ron and Russell were given an undisclosed budget to produce a video for what RCA considered to be the potential first single, 'Funny Face'. The Maels presented a video tape with four minutes of a pornographic movie, over which the song had been dubbed. When it was presented at the meeting with all the executives in attendance, they did not find it remotely amusing.

The video actually made for 'Funny Face' is a bit unusual, somewhat dark even. Ron initially hides behind the bushes, watching three young girls dancing happily. During his hideout, he wears various animal masks, eventually mustering up the courage to offer some candies to the girls, who are not particularly impressed. Eventually, the girls' mother shows up, clearly disapproving of Ron's antics, and knocks him to the floor. What Russell couldn't do in three rounds of boxing, a suburban mum managed without a hitch.

> Russell: 'We again were using a permanent band, having enlisted L.A. group Bates Motel to become official Sparks members. After rehearsals with the band in L.A., we recorded in Munich. Mack (co-producer of many of Queen's albums) produced. Harmonies were back again, as were songs about girls who suffer overly beautiful exteriors and their ensuing suicide attempts, followed by newfound happiness as a result of their total facial disfigurement.'

'Where's My Girl'
Duration: 3:14

The characteristic Sparks sound continues in this mid-tempo track, featuring a slightly hysterical Russell who wonders who has run off with his girlfriend. The acapella opening is surprising but very appealing to the average fan. It becomes apparent halfway through side one of the record that it no longer resembles the previous release. It becomes clear that the Maels wanted to retaliate against the excessive influence of the producers on the last album.

In addition to the synthesizers, which complement the guitar riff in a pleasing manner, we are introduced to Ron's distinctive short piano strokes for the first time on the album, which sound pleasantly familiar.

Attention has clearly been paid to the arrangements, but the songs themselves are also made more interesting with tempo changes, unexpected breaks and Russell's falsetto vocals. In addition, the lyrics are tongue-in-cheek again, which is a relief. Ultimately, the panicked singer appears to have worried about nothing.

'Where's My Girl' was played at the very first concerts in 1981 in both Los Angeles and France/Belgium, but it was not included in any other tours until its one-off performance in 2008 at the Sparks Spectacular.

'Upstairs'
Duration: 3:40

This up-tempo track begins with a standard rock drum sound, accompanied by a frivolous synthesizer. The bass guitar gradually fades in, producing a tone that resembles a synthesizer, likely due to the addition of an effect. Notably, the vocals are at times shouted in a subdued manner, which may seem paradoxical; however, Russell demonstrates that this effect is indeed possible. The guitar is subtly embedded amongst the other instruments, becoming audible only upon close listening. There is also an infectious two-beat thump that evokes a metal-like aesthetic.

The song's lyrics initially appear to describe a physical location, with some interpretations suggesting that it refers to heaven. However, the song actually alludes to the brain, where every conceivable thought occurs and plans are formed that may carry significant consequences. The vocal break is reminiscent of other up-tempo tracks in which Russell attempts to deliver a large volume of lyrics in a brief span of time, thereby showcasing his vocal dexterity.

The song was well received at live performances due to its infectious tempo and energetic vocals. However, it was not performed again after 1983 until the Sparks Spectacular, and has not reappeared in the live set since.

Russell: '"Upstairs" became the new Sparks live encore anthem. Back in London to launch the LP, we staged a 3-round boxing match at the Hilton to tie-in with the LP's cover photo.'

'I Married A Martian'
Duration: 5:12

Side one of this album ends with a humorous anecdote about extra-terrestrials, a topic that Sparks would revisit multiple times. However, each time, their angle is quite different.

The song is up-tempo, featuring a driving guitar, accompanying bass, characteristic short piano strokes and a classic drum rhythm. Processed vocals brighten up the song before the actual vocals kick in.

Three-and-a-half minutes in, there is a brief yet valuable guitar solo by Bob Haag. The song concludes with a fade-out, during which Russell expresses doubt about his decision regarding a close encounter of the fifth kind.

While the song was occasionally performed at American concerts in 1981 and 1982, it was more often omitted. It was recorded for the promotional LP *BBC Rock Concert*, which was distributed to radio stations in 1982.

'The Willys'
Duration: 3:58

The opening song of side two addresses the feeling of someone experiencing something going on without knowing the exact cause. This is a subject that the Maels have explored before and would revisit later.

Unusual sound bites, generated by synthesizers, accompany the introduction and first verse of the song. When the guitar joins in, the song takes on a more conventional arrangement, while the odd sounds continue to appear throughout. The background vocals at the end are a nice addition.

This song clearly demonstrates a greater sense of confidence during the recording of the LP. The songs are powerful, played with bravado, and the arrangements show a willingness to think outside the box. It seems the Maels wanted to prove to the world—and their new record company—that they were far from finished. Perhaps their tremendous success in France had boosted their confidence.

The song was rarely performed live. It was included in the first concert on 20 October 1981 in Los Angeles, but omitted the following day. The same applied to the two concerts in Belgium that year; it was played in Verviers but omitted in Brussels.

'Don't Shoot Me'
Duration: 3:56

It is nice how the previous song flows almost seamlessly into the bombastic opening of 'Don't Shoot Me', with a traditional guitar riff and accompanying drums. The mid-tempo intro lasts for half a minute before the vocals come in. The song leaves little room for keyboards, and even traditional piano sounds are absent, making it fairly conventional in terms of arrangements. However, halfway through the song, a subtle keyboard contribution is added during the instrumental part.

This is the second song on the LP that discusses possible infidelity in a relationship. This time, the narrator seems to have gotten it right, which is a less favourable outcome for the person in question.

The song was released as the B-side to both 'Tips For Teens' and 'Funny Face' in select European countries.

Besides its presentation during the Sparks Spectacular, there is only one known performance where this song was played: on 21 October 1981 in Los Angeles. Fortunately, an audio recording of this concert was made by someone in the audience.

'Suzie Safety'
Duration: 3:57

The fresh and cheerful tones of Ron's piano introduce the next song, which features a delightfully humorous lyrical structure and a beautifully captivating melody. Most of the sounds are produced by the keyboards, but throughout the song the guitar is seamlessly mixed in. The bass sound also appears to come from the keyboards, but Leslie Bohem's contribution is clearly noticeable if you listen closely. It has a slightly warmer tone than the keyboard that runs parallel to it.

The singing is solid and is complemented at well-chosen moments with excellent backing vocals, also performed by Russell.

The subject is easy to understand, with no hidden messages. It's about a man talking about his girlfriend, who has dedicated herself to protecting the narrator in every possible way. This song was never performed during regular concerts.

'THAT'S NOT NASTASSIA'
Duration: 4:57

A captivating melody is presented through a blend of traditional instruments, with the bass guitar taking the lead and the twinkling piano providing a solid foundation and wonderful embellishments.

The middle eight is an almost dreamy rendition, where the vocals and backing vocals are used very cleverly. This is followed by a break that introduces an elongated ending, which may not be easy for everyone to swallow as it concludes with a cacophony of vocals and prominent piano that once again emphasises the earlier theme. Some might categorise this as organised chaos, but it all fits together. It bears resemblance to the ending of 'Achoo' from the *Propaganda* album. Live, it has only been performed once during the Sparks Spectacular.

> Ron: 'We had met Nastassia Kinski through Giorgio. We used her name, although the song isn't about her.'

'WACKY WOMEN'
Duration: 2:47

The closing song on this album does not fit into the stately or remarkable category, as is the case with many other Sparks albums. However, it is a lively and energetic track that highlights the LP's overall intention: dynamic, slightly chaotic, but above all cheerful with a catchy melody.

It is a dynamic rock song with a recurring riff played on the synthesizer, while the rest of the song is performed by traditional instruments. Russell's enthusiastic vocals shine through, and besides the French-language song 'Je M'Appelle Russell', it is the only song in which Russell introduces himself.

During live performances in 1981, it served as the opening number of the concert, with Ron playing the guitar riff (open E major for the completists). This song was also recorded during the only concert in Germany in 1981, at Circus Krone in Munich. The last time it was performed during a regular concert was in 1982, when it was recorded for the promotional LP *BBC Rock Concert*.

11

Angst In My Pants

Release date: 29 March 1982
Produced by: Reinhold Mack
Engineer: Reinhold Mack
Cover concept: Ron Mael
Sleeve design: Larry Vignon
Photography: Eric Blum
Recorded at: Musicland Studios, Munich
Duration: 35:31
Personnel: Ron Mael: Synthesizers
Russell Mael: Vocals
David Kendrick: Drums
Bob Haag: Guitar, backing vocals
Leslie Bohem: Bass guitar, backing vocals
Jim Goodwin: Synthesizers

Side 1
'Angst In My Pants'
'I Predict'
'Sextown U.S.A.'
'Sherlock Holmes'
'Nicotina'
'Mickey Mouse'

Side 2
'Moustache'
'Instant Weight Loss'
'Tarzan And Jane'
'The Decline And Fall Of Me'
'Eaten By The Monster Of Love'

Singles from this album:
'I Predict'/'Moustache'
'Angst In My Pants'/'Moustache'
'Eaten By The Monster Of Love'/'Mickey Mouse'

While in Germany in December 1981, the band continued recording the follow-up to *Whomp That Sucker*. They had to return to Los Angeles by the end of January for three double gigs at the Whisky A Go Go.

In the official fanzine, a hand-written letter from Ron was published:

> The sun is making a brief appearance here in between the snow flurries. Fortunately, bad weather is still a novelty for us California folk. Russell and I are in the last week of the recording of the nouveau Sparks album. David (on drums) and Bob (on guitar) flew back to L.A. yesterday and Les (bassist) took a train to Paris so he could relive his youth. Jim, the additional synthesizer player when we tour, returned to N.Y. two weeks ago after the tour. And here we are.
>
> The new recording has gone quickly. We've felt the pressure of trying to finish the album before Russia invades Germany. We went to East Berlin on a break in our recording schedule here and didn't see too many recording studios there, so you can imagine our concern. Mack is producing this album and is basking in his room-ambiance glory. Russell and I have found a salad bar here in Munich, so we're all right. What can I say of the new album? Maybe some of the poppy-buoyancy of *Whomp That Sucker* is gone, replaced by a heavier beat and slightly darker mood. This is 1982, after all. We're planning on doing a tour of the U.S. upon release of this album (later March or April) and later tour Europe, if it's still there. Bye, Ron.

Like its predecessor, *Angst In My Pants* was recorded at Musicland Studios in Munich, Germany, and produced by Mack from the Giorgio Moroder stable. During the recordings, the band occasionally played a few rehearsal gigs at small clubs in Munich, but these shows were not advertised and very few local fans were aware of them.

The recording of the new album in Munich took about six weeks. Similar to the previous album, most of the lyrics were written in the hotel where the band was staying.

The album was released on 29 March 1982 on their new label, Atlantic, which made serious efforts to promote it by running full-page ads in various music papers and even in the *Los Angeles Times*.

For the first time since *Indiscreet* in 1975, the entire band appeared on the cover, with the addition of Jim Goodwin, who had joined for live performances. It is unclear whether he actually played on this album. Drummer David Kendrick claims that only Ron played the keyboards, although Jim is mentioned on the sleeve as playing synthesizers.

Their first American tour since 1976 began in San Diego on 29 April at the University of California, followed by three performances at the Whisky.

They then played in over thirty cities across North America, including a concert in Toronto, Canada.

The tour took them to places such as Oklahoma City and Washington DC, and it ended victoriously at the Magic Mountain theme park on 30 October. One of the three gigs at the Whisky was recorded by the London Wavelength company, which released part of the concert on a radio promotion album of the *BBC Rock Hour* series. The eleven songs featured were all taken from the last two albums, although the band did play 'Something For The Girl With Everything', 'Amateur Hour', 'Beat The Clock' and even 'Propaganda' on some occasions.

On 15 May, the band was given an extraordinary opportunity when they were invited to perform on the highly popular coast-to-coast television show *Saturday Night Live*. They were introduced by actor Danny DeVito, who had apparently attended some of their concerts. They flew to New York to record the show between gigs in Minneapolis and Cleveland, playing two songs live.

It was not the only major television appearance that Sparks made that year. Seven years after their last appearance on Dick Clark's *American Bandstand* in 1975, they made a comeback on 28 August 1982. This time, 'I Predict' and 'Eaten By The Monster Of Love' were performed, although they were not played live.

Dick Clark was clearly pleased to see the Maels again, approaching them during the break between songs for a short interview. When asked, 'How long has this been going on?', Ron said, 'Much too long.' When Clark asked who the older one was, Ron replied, 'You are.'

It made sense that these two songs were played, as 'I Predict' had been released as the new single on 11 April and had reached an impressive number 60 on the Billboard Hot 100. This was the highest position a Sparks single had reached up to that date. 'Eaten By The Monster Of Love' was released in June but did not chart at all.

The reviews were varied, and the records did not reach any charts in any European country. The brothers could probably live with that realisation because, for the first time in their careers, they were finally being taken seriously in their own country.

Nevertheless, European fans who were still paying attention were treated to a release for which the local American aficionados would have to wait a few more years. Sparks were enlisted by screenwriter Larry Wilson to compose a theme song for a proposed TV series based on Modesty Blaise, the female James Bond of a vintage comic book series. The show didn't materialise, but the French record company Carrere heard the recording and thought it would be a good single.

For legal reasons, the song was renamed 'Modesty Plays' and released with an extended version on the B-side, lasting two minutes longer. There was even a 12-inch single of the extended version, featuring 'Angst In My Pants' on the B-side.

Meanwhile, in the United States, Ron was suddenly offered an audition for the sequel to the blockbuster movie *Airplane!*, playing villain Joe Salucci, but he was beaten to the role by fellow musician Sonny Bono, of Sonny and Cher fame.

Nonetheless, Hollywood kept calling, and if it wasn't for the acting talents of the Mael brothers, it certainly was for their music. *Valley Girl* was a movie that starred a young Nicholas Cage and featured a lot of contemporary music, including 'Mickey' by Toni Basil. Sparks were approached to contribute 'Angst In My Pants' and 'Eaten By The Monster Of Love', songs which appeared on separate soundtracks for the film.

The revenue generated from the rights to these songs was a welcome addition for the Mael brothers, and the film's popularity introduced Sparks to many teenagers who had not seen them on *Saturday Night Live* or *American Bandstand*. Meanwhile, their live performances grew increasingly exuberant, with audiences that matched their energy and evoked memories of European fans during the heyday of 1974 and 1975.

Russell's stage attire became ever-more striking, and Ron also began to take a more active role in shaping the band's live image. Thus, the first tentative steps were taken towards what would become the famous 'Ron shuffle', a choreographed movement that he still manages to incorporate into live performances to this day.

On other occasions, Ron was not hesitant to reprise the striptease act featured in the 'I Predict' video. He would also appear in dungarees, a white t-shirt and bowler hat. At times, he lip-synced to 'You're the One That I Want' from *Grease*, using a large stuffed dog as his duet partner. This tour also saw Ron cleverly modify his Roland keyboard to display the name 'Ronald'.

During this period, the other band members launched a side project and recorded an album under the name Gleaming Spires. *Songs of the Spires* was released, with sleeve notes written by the Mael brothers. While Russell took his time to write a lengthy recommendation, Ron simply contributed the line: 'This is the best Gleaming Spires album … ever.'

More popular than they had ever been in their home country—and far more commercially successful—Ron and Russell had every reason to believe they were on their way up. After more than a decade, they were finally being recognised for their exceptional creative talents. The album reached number 173 on the Billboard chart, nine places higher than its predecessor and the highest position of any Sparks album to date. It was clear that Sparks were ascending.

Angst In My Pants—The Songs

All songs written by Ron Mael and Russell Mael.

'Angst In My Pants'
Duration: 3:25

The style introduced in *Whomp That Sucker* seems to carry over into 'Angst In My Pants'. This tightly arranged opening track is quite appealing, despite its somewhat monotonous initial impression. Notably, guitar and bass are absent from this song, as it was recorded solely by the Maels. The sound is open and spacious, even though the instrumentation is limited to synthesizers and a drum loop. It feels surprisingly full, despite the absence of backing or double vocals.

The subject of the song is clear and leaves little room for interpretation. It evidently addresses the physical side-effects that a man experiences during arousal, presented with a tongue-in-cheek approach. In 2016, the company Tommy John recognised this and incorporated the song into a commercial for men's underwear.

'Angst In My Pants' was one of two songs from this LP featured in the film *Valley Girl* and included on the original soundtrack.

Although 'Angst In My Pants' was released as a single in Germany, it did not chart. The song is frequently performed live and was included in the setlist in 1982, as well as during concerts in 2018 (US only), 2022 and 2023.

Russell: 'We were once again recording at Musicland Studios in Munich with the same band from "Whomp". "Angst" was the final song to be recorded for the LP, having been done after the rest of the band members returned to L.A. We made a tape loop of David Kendrick's drumming and Ron added his keyboard parts on top. Mack encouraged the exaggerated inflection of my vocals. Ron had written another song called 'Angst In My Pants', that we liked lyrically, but weren't too keen on melodically. So, overnight he came up with this alternate melody that we recorded and finished in one day.'

'I Predict'
Duration: 2:50

Led by drums, guitar and bass guitar, the next song is of a completely different nature. While it maintains the same dynamics, it is arranged with an entirely different approach. The vocals soar like a choir, featuring various takes of Russell's voice, along with possible contributions from Leslie Bohem and Bob Haag. The lyrics are straightforward and, above all, very witty.

This song was released as the first single in the US and became Sparks' biggest commercial success to date in their homeland, reaching number 60 on the Billboard Hot 100. Exactly ten years after their first single made its debut on that chart, this position was significantly more impressive.

A video was created for 'I Predict', directed by Frederick Elmes. It showcases Ron Mael in drag, performing a striptease dance in a Los Angeles nightclub, while Russell lip-syncs the lyrics to the song. Although the video is frequently attributed to David Lynch, renowned for his work on *Twin Peaks*, this confusion may stem from the fact that Elmes served as Lynch's director of photography.

Those in power at MTV determined that the video was unsuitable for daytime broadcast due to its content. Controversial topics were occasionally aired at night. One could argue that this form of censorship hindered the single from achieving even greater success, but that would ultimately be mere speculation.

'I Predict' was also released as a 12-inch vinyl record, which included a club mix lasting over six minutes. While Ron and Russell were enjoying the attention and the greatest success they had ever experienced in their home country, interest in Sparks in Europe was rather meagre.

Although both the album and the single were released in several countries worldwide, they received very little attention.

'I Predict' was one of the two songs that Sparks performed on *Saturday Night Live*. During the North American tours in 1982 and 1983, it was a staple of the live set. Subsequently, it was only performed during the concert at the Henry Fonda Theater in 2004 and at the Avalon, Hollywood, in 2006. However, during the 2022 world tour, it unexpectedly re-emerged as a permanent fixture in the setlist.

> Russell: 'Our ode to the "National Enquirer". ("Lassie Will Prove That Elvis And Her Had A Fleeting Affair"). Ron's striptease to his boxer shorts usually accompanies this song live.'
> Ron: 'I like reading the Enquirer and the Star. Nice, inspirational things. I like all those kind of things. So carrying that to a bit of an extreme was really the inspiration for that song.'

'SEXTOWN U.S.A.'
Duration: 2:56

This song explores a theme that likely reflects one of the singer's greatest passions—if not that of the broader human experience. It is an up-tempo track that maintains the same energetic tone established by the two preceding songs.

It opens with cheerful synthesizer sounds, supported by a steady bass tone generated by the keyboards, which is soon complemented by a bright guitar riff. The bass guitar is barely audible, and the same applies to a subtle secondary vocal line that runs parallel to the main vocals. This secondary voice, slightly higher in pitch and mixed at a lower volume, becomes perceptible only upon close listening. For the first time, bassist Leslie Bohem contributes vocals, adding the phrase: 'Never mind, just sing the tune.'

From the chorus onward, the bass guitar becomes more prominent in the mix, though the average listener may still not perceive it. The addition of a second vocal line in the chorus provides a pleasing enhancement. Also notable is the creative use of stereo effects applied to the drums, synthesizers and guitar. The song concludes with a final guitar note accompanied by an almost inaudible vocal addition, which most listeners are likely to miss.

With this track, it becomes evident that the album is a clear product of its time, lacking the timeless atmosphere characteristic of many Sparks releases. The lyrics are once again mischievous, offering a playful nod to the audience: cheerful, nonsensical, somewhat juvenile—yet unmistakably humorous.

Remarkably, the song was never performed live during regular concerts, with the exception of the 1982 American tour.

> Russell: 'Another one of the Disney Corporation's favorite Sparks songs. Originally the song had been rehearsed with a long middle instrumental breakdown section that had unfortunately been edited down leaving only the vocal phrase "there's a whole lotta fish in the sea." On any given night, the song would gain a good 10 to 15 beats per minute causing one of the fastest renditions of a song known to Western music. To keep us off the streets one night while in Munich, we played a show at the tiny Domicile Club on Leopoldstrasse.
>
> 'Out of frustration for an intermittent power transformer on one of Ron's synths, he trashed the sucker. The audience thought it was part of our show, but soon learned otherwise as we left the stage for one hour while our roadies returned to Ron's hotel room to get his spare keyboard. The club thanked us later as their beverage sales skyrocketed due to the lengthy impromptu intermission.'

'SHERLOCK HOLMES'
Duration: 3:34

A completely different mood is established in 'Sherlock Holmes', creating a nostalgic and romantic atmosphere. It is one of the few songs, if not the only one, that had been written beforehand.

Originally titled 'Midnight Rodeo', it had completely different lyrics. The theme closely resembles that of a later song, 'Lighten Up, Morrissey'. In both, the narrator grapples with a girlfriend who idolises a public figure (regardless of whether he truly exists) and feels inadequate, knowing he will never be able to impress his partner on that level.

It features rolling drum rolls and atmospheric synthesizer sounds that evoke the feeling of being on the moors, almost making one think they can hear the Hound of the Baskervilles in the distance. This is complemented by a beautiful, somewhat wistful vocal performance, which makes this song one of the strongest on the album. It is no surprise that it was also featured on the Two Hands One Mouth tour, where the stripped-down version was nearly as compelling as the studio recording. Some even preferred the live rendition.

The song was included in the setlist of several concerts by FFS during their 2015 tour and was occasionally performed live during the world tour in 2017. Mini Mansions, who served as an outstanding backing band for the Maels during the 2017 world tour, recorded a beautiful live version of this song in 2014, which is still regarded as one of the best interpretations of a Sparks song.

'NICOTINA'
Duration: 3:26

Leave it to the Mael brothers—fervent opponents of smoking—to write a song about a cigarette that ultimately evokes sympathy for its central character.

Interestingly, the track features what could be described as two separate introductions. The song opens with a somewhat ominous instrumental introduction that would not be out of place in a 1970s James Bond film. A loud guitar riff, accompanied by drumbeats and synthesizer, is followed by a brief instrumental segment in which staccato-like keyboard notes signal the arrival of the vocals. Subtle stereo effects are skilfully employed during this passage. The narrative that follows is deliberately trivial, filled with ironic puns and an almost exaggerated arrangement.

The verses carry a vaguely menacing undertone but are balanced by an exceptionally captivating melody. In the chorus, Russell Mael subtly employs his falsetto. As the song nears its conclusion, the phrase 'On and on and on and on' is repeated, evoking a resemblance to traditional Russian folk music.

The track concludes at a slower tempo, with vocals accompanied solely by drums, bass guitar and a single synthesizer note that gradually fades out.

The almost hysterical intensity of the guitar riffs contributes to the dramatic effect, at times nearly distracting from the song's underlying meaning.

In Germany, this song appeared as the B-side to the single 'Modesty Plays'.

Like the preceding track, it was performed live at selected shows during the Revenge of Two Hands One Mouth tour and again on the 2017 world tour.

> Russell: '"Nicotina" is a story about a female cigarette who, like all cigarettes, will eventually meet her end from a smoker who will give her one puff, turning her into a cloud of smoke. There's been a lot of songs about male cigarettes through the years; this one's about a female.'
> Ron: 'There are so many things I think are funny that nobody else thinks are funny. Everything is animated in some way, such as having a really pompous

musical song like "Nicotina" with real frivolous lyrics. That song would have been Wagnerian if the lyrics weren't about a cigarette that meets an unhappy end.'

'MICKEY MOUSE'
Duration: 3:16

A number of songs on this album are dedicated to various acquaintances from diverse backgrounds, so it is not surprising that an American icon like Mickey Mouse also receives this tribute. His partner would later be honoured in a similar manner.

This up-tempo track features a driving guitar riff, complemented by synthesizers and tight drums. It embodies the same energy and enthusiasm that defines the album.

Those who believe the subject was chosen for the purpose of mocking or belittling it are mistaken. It was a sincere tribute to this cartoon character.

This was the first song the band performed during *Saturday Night Live*, and was introduced by Ron. He stood calmly, though undoubtedly very nervous, as he uttered the words:

> The mouse is a member of the rodent family, distinguished from the rat in that it is smaller in size. It usually measures six inches in length—approximately 15 centimetres—and weighs one ounce, which is, of course, approximately 28 grams. The mouse is responsible for much of the world's pestilence and destruction. When the mouse is not scaring women, eating saltine crackers from cupboards, or ingesting huge amounts of saccharine in laboratory experiments, the mouse has been known to enter the world of entertainment. One such mouse ... was named 'Mickey'.

'Mickey Mouse' was released as the B-side of the second single from the album, 'Eaten By The Monster Of Love'. It was performed occasionally during the tours of 1982 and 1983, then appeared sporadically at concerts in 2004 and 2009 in both the United States and Japan.

> Ron: 'I love Disneyland. I'd love to live there. The Electrical Parade on Main Street is a religious experience. Everybody writes about those characters so cynically. I tried to do something about Mickey Mouse which isn't a ho-ho-ho situation, just really liking him and not feeling superior by having anything snide in it. It's a real caring thing: the tears are coming to my eyes.'
> Russell: 'The intention of "Mickey Mouse" was an uplifting tribute to Walt Disney and Disneyland. It's a totally non-cynical view of Mickey Mouse.'

'Moustache'
Duration: 3:28

Loud, bombastic and filled with exuberant enthusiasm, side two maintains the same energetic momentum. Once again, the Maels transform an ordinary object into a captivating subject, eliciting smiles from listeners at various moments. With a robust accompaniment from the guitar and drums, the song is primarily driven by the synthesizers. The chorus is especially catchy, making it hard to resist singing along.

There is an opportunity for a basic guitar solo that consists of nothing more than an extended riff and a strikingly pleasant break, where the guitar transitions into a rapid staccato sound. The phrase, 'But when I trimmed 'em real small, my Jewish friends would never call', is not only very witty but also noteworthy because the writer maintained the same style of moustache being referenced. It would be just a few years later that he would change it.

'Moustache' was featured on the B-side of the single 'I Predict' in all countries where it was released.

The song was performed live only at select concerts in 1982 and 1983. In 2008, it was, of course, part of the Sparks Spectacular. Surprisingly, it was also chosen by the audience to be performed again during the second set of the live presentation of the then-new LP.

'Instant Weight Loss'
Duration: 3:27

In terms of dynamics, this song is distinctly different from its predecessor.

It is a mid-tempo piece primarily sung in falsetto, narrating the story of an overweight man who encounters a beautiful woman who points out his excess weight. This encounter motivates him to embark on a disciplined weight-loss journey, which he ultimately succeeds in completing. However, during a later attempt to impress the woman, he discovers that she has developed feelings for another man who, although not slender, possesses significant financial resources. Disillusioned, he reverts to his old habits and regains the weight he had lost.

The song has never been performed live during regular concerts.

> Russell: 'Weight is an obsession with both of us. Ron carries a scale with him on tour; he takes it about as far as you can get without seriously damaging your health. I really like sweets so there's a real dilemma 'cause I also want to maintain the same appearance I had 11 albums ago.'

'Tarzan And Jane'
Duration: 3:18

'Tarzan and Jane' narrates the tale of a group of students who engage in chaos and rebellion without any clear motivation.

It is possible that Ron drew inspiration from the 1955 film *Blackboard Jungle,* which captivated him as an 11-year-old and left a lasting impression. Yet although he may have been influenced by the film when naming the song, there are no other references to these fictional characters in the lyrics.

Percussion reminiscent of African drums, accompanied by a vocal introduction, underscores this piece. While the synthesizers dominate the sound, the distorted bass guitar fills in the gaps.

The melody is less accessible than most other tracks on this LP, and this song was never performed live during regular concerts.

'The Decline And Fall Of Me'
Duration: 2:53

This song, like most tracks on this album, is quite accessible, featuring a catchy melody with lyrics that are not easily interpreted unless taken literally. The instruments are well-balanced, each contributing distinct elements that together create a cohesive whole.

The melody is primarily driven by the synthesizer, accompanied by drum patterns that vary and occasional guitar riffs that add flair to the song. The bass guitar plays a modest role, primarily following the notes of the melody line.

The middle eight, occurring halfway through the song, is a delightful addition and is sung entirely in falsetto. Many listeners have indicated that this is one of their favourite tracks from the album; however, it is notably strange that it has never been performed live during regular concerts.

'Eaten By The Monster Of Love'
Duration: 2:58

The final act of this LP may not be as memorable as the closing songs of other Sparks albums, but within the context of this particular record, it serves well as a concluding piece. Cheerful, dynamic and performed with great verve, this song illustrates the consequences of falling in love, albeit focusing solely on the negative aspects of this experience.

This song was also featured in the movie *Valley Girl,* but did not appear on the original soundtrack. It was later included on a double LP released exclusively in Japan in 1989. The song was performed live during several concerts in the United States in 1982 and 1983.

A vocal introduction featuring Leslie Bohem and Bob Haag effectively sets the tone for this song, which is driven by a tight guitar and bass. The keyboards playfully weave in and out, providing a delightful counter-melody.

The chorus is incredibly catchy, and it is no mystery why this song was selected as the second single in the US. What remains puzzling is that it failed to make an impression on American audiences, as it did not enter the charts, despite arguably sounding more commercial than the first single.

12

In Outer Space

Release date: April 1983
Produced by: Ron Mael and Russell Mael
Engineers: Dan Lacksman and Brian Reeves
Cover concept: Ron Mael
Sleeve design: Larry Vigon
Photography: Jim Shea
Recorded at: Synsound Studios, Brussels
Duration: 36:37
Personnel: Ron Mael: Synthesizers
Russell Mael: Vocals
David Kendrick: Drums
Bob Haag: Guitar, backing vocals
Leslie Bohem: Bass guitar, backing vocals
James Goodwin: Additional concert keyboards
Jane Wiedlin: Vocals

Side 1
'Cool Places'
'Popularity'
'Prayin' For A Party'
'All You Ever Think About Is Sex'
'Please, Baby, Please'

Side 2
'Rockin' Girls'
'I Wish I Looked A Little Better'
'Lucky Me, Lucky You'
'A Fun Bunch Of Guys From Outer Space'
'Dance Godammit'

Singles from this album:
'Cool Places'/'Sports'
'Cool Places'/'Lucky Me, Lucky You'
'All You Ever Think About Is Sex'/'I Wish I Looked A Little Better'
'All You Ever Think About Is Sex'/'Dance Godammit' (12-inch only)
'Please, Baby, Please'/'Rockin' Girls'

At the end of 1982, Sparks found themselves in a different position than they had been a year earlier. By focusing solely on their home country, they finally reaped the rewards of their efforts.

With the support of local Los Angeles radio station K-ROQ, which had extensively played their songs from *Whomp That Sucker* and *Angst In My Pants*, and nationwide appearances on *Saturday Night Live* and *American Bandstand*, they achieved greater success in the US than ever before. Coupled with a rigorous touring schedule, Sparks were on the rise.

'I Predict', the first single from the previous album, peaked at number 60 on the Billboard Hot 100, significantly higher than their last charting single a decade earlier, 'Wonder Girl', which reached number 112. Meanwhile, the band travelled to Europe again, not to tour or promote anything, but to record their next album. Ron and Russell had previously collaborated with Belgian musician Marc Moulin and the other members of the band Telex, and they now went to the Synsound studio in a residential area of Brussels to record the new album.

For the first time, Ron and Russell produced the album themselves, but the sleeve was once again designed by Larry Vigon, who had also created the previous one. As anticipated, the cover was humorous and served as a precursor to the unpretentious and somewhat juvenile fun that is expressed in musical form throughout the album.

On the album, the same band, augmented by keyboardist Jim Goodwin, joined the Maels. Upon their return to the US, a letter arrived at their fan club from rhythm guitarist Jane Wiedlin of The Go-Go's. This all-female band from Los Angeles was at the height of its success, and it turned out that Jane, a long-time Sparks fan, wanted to get in touch with Russell, on whom she had harboured a serious crush for years. In addition to their brief love affair, Jane also collaborated with Sparks on two songs for the new album, one of which was set to be released as the first single. Both songs were recorded in Los Angeles.

The fact that Sparks were invited to perform on Dick Clark's *American Bandstand*, where they were joined by Jane Wiedlin, significantly contributed to their success. The Go-Go's were likely one of the most, if not the most, successful all-female bands of that era.

'Cool Places' reached number 49 on the Billboard Hot 100, marking the highest position any Sparks single has achieved to date. The 12-inch single climbed to number 13, while the album itself peaked at number 88, significantly higher than its predecessor and the highest ranking since *Propaganda*, nine years earlier. In France, the album included an additional track, 'Modesty Plays', which had been released as a single the previous year.

Aside from *American Bandstand*, Sparks had a more significant presence on US television. Their live concerts, including *Rock 'n' Roll Tonite* and a performance at the Palace in Los Angeles, were broadcast. The Mael brothers also appeared in several programmes featuring interviews, such as *NBC's Live at Five*, *MV3's World Rock Report*, the *Stanley Siegel Show* and, most notably,

Andy Warhol's TV. During their appearance in the latter, they were interviewed by Maura Moynihan, while Warhol himself mostly listened in silence with interest.

As early as March 1983, the same month the first single was released, Sparks began performing live. Their inaugural show took place at Bronco Billy's Concert Hall in Palm Springs on 26 March, and the final performance of the year occurred on 31 October in Riverside. In mid-July, Sparks started a nationwide tour with Australian-born musician and actor Rick Springfield, who had already achieved several top ten hits and was immensely popular in both Australia and the USA. Springfield personally selected Sparks as his opening act, stating that he had been a fan of their very first album while still living in Australia, and particularly liked 'Wonder Girl'.

Sparks performed over forty concerts as the opening act for Springfield, taking them to venues they had never before played and exposing them to audiences they had not previously encountered. At the end of the tour, their position was filled by Quarterflash.

The reviews from the music press and local newspapers were quite mixed. Most reviewers praised the remarkable performance by Sparks, while others expressed disdain, possibly because Ron continued his striptease act during 'I Predict', which was not well-received by everyone in rural areas.

In the midst of touring and television appearances, it was Russell's turn to seize an opportunity in the film industry. After Ron's unsuccessful audition for *Airplane II*, Russell was recruited for the cast of the movie *Get Crazy*. This film was a rock 'n' roll parody produced by Embassy Studios, starring Malcolm McDowell as fictional English superstar Reggie Wanker, a name that likely holds more significance in England than in the New World. Russell recalled:

> Originally, Malcolm McDowell was the lead character. Troubles over his contract dragged on until they were forced to start shooting without him, and to seek a replacement. I was given that role. After several weeks of shooting, however, the studio came to an agreement with McDowell and replaced me with the person that they had originally sought for the role. After seeing the film, I was quite happy that they gave the part to Malcolm McDowell. It was no *Clockwork Orange*.

Sparks wrote the main theme of the movie, and the song of the same name was released as a single in the United States, Canada and several European countries. However, it did not chart in any of these locations. The song also appeared on the soundtrack album.

Just like the previous year, a promotional live album for the *BBC Rock Concerts* series was released, featuring nine songs from a performance at Hollywood's

Palace, recorded in early April 1983. The album was distributed exclusively to radio stations in June of that year. Remarkably, one of the songs performed live was 'Modesty Plays', which was completely obscure on that continent.

Meanwhile, the Maels were approached by the Walt Disney Company to contribute to the soundtrack of the upcoming movie *Splash Dance*. They discovered Sparks after hearing the songs 'Mickey Mouse' and 'It's Kinda Like The Movies' from the unreleased *Bad Manners* soundtrack. Although the Maels had indeed written the latter, it was recorded by Gleaming Spires, the backing band for Sparks, and sung by bassist Leslie Bohem. In 2008, during the Sparks Spectacular in London, Sparks performed it themselves for the very first time, with Russell as vocalist. This performance served as a bonus track at the end of the concert for the 1988 album *Interior Design*.

1983 was also the year when Ron finally bid farewell to his signature trademark: the Chaplin moustache, which some misinterpreted as resembling that of an Austrian-born dictator. The new style he adopted during that time more closely resembled the moustache of Hollywood movie star Ronald Colman, giving him a much more distinguished appearance. Ron has mentioned on more than one occasion that he was actually named after this actor. Russell maintained his styled curls but had them cut in a typical Eighties fashion, which now seemed quite outdated.

Joseph Fleury, one of the earliest fans of Sparks since 1972, now officially served as their manager. However, the primary decisions were made by the Mael brothers, while Joseph focused on logistical arrangements, setting up interviews and assisting Ron and Russell's mother, Miriam. She had relocated to Los Angeles and was now managing the official fan club under the pseudonym Mary Martin.

At the end of 1983, Ron and Russell acknowledged Jane Wiedlin's contribution to their album by co-writing with her the song 'Yes Or No' for the upcoming Go-Go's album. Although the song was written and recorded in 1983, it was not released until March 1984 on the album *Talk Show*.

A remixed version of the song was released as a single in September 1984, reaching number 84 on the Billboard Hot 100, which was considerably less successful than 'Cool Places'. The album also featured the single 'Head Over Heels', which became a major hit in the United States.

Although the second single had not been successful for Sparks, they achieved their first top 50 hit single in the USA and a top 100 album. Now all they needed was one final step: another hit single or a remarkable album to propel them into the major league.

Everybody involved with Sparks, including Atlantic Records and the other band members, was quite convinced that their next album would achieve exactly that. The future seemed bright for the Mael brothers as 1984 approached.

In Outer Space—The Songs

All songs written by Ron Mael and Russell Mael.

'Cool Places'
Duration: 3:23

After a failed attempt to record a duet with singer Marianne Faithfull, a collaboration finally materialised approximately seven years later with two songs on this album. Jane Wiedlin's contribution is quite prominent, resulting in a track that strays from Sparks' typical style. While the song is undeniably cheerful and catchy, its light-heartedness and somewhat simplistic lyrics do not meet the high standards that the Mael brothers usually pursue. Ironically, this became their most successful single in their home country.

'Cool Places' was released as both a 7-inch and 12-inch single. The 12-inch version included a remix that was approximately one minute longer than the album version, though it was not significantly different. It was distributed by Atlantic Records in several European countries, as well as in distant locations such as Australia, Japan, the Philippines, Peru, Brazil and, closer to home, Canada. A music video for the song was directed by Graham Whiffler, featuring Ron, Russell and Jane.

The single included a delightful bonus: the non-album track 'Sports', which was the first time since 1976's 'England' that an additional song was added to an album release. The single also came with a picture sleeve featuring Russell and Jane. The photo on the Japanese single's sleeve featured another portrayal of the duo.

In the Philippines, the local record company opted for 'Lucky Me, Lucky You' as the B-side, the other song to which Jane had contributed her vocals. Unfortunately, the single did not generate much reaction in any of the countries mentioned, except for the United States, where it quickly began to climb the Billboard Hot 100, peaking at number 49.

Russell commented:

> Jane Wiedlin had once been President of her own non-authorized L.A. Valley Sparks fan club. Rather than sue her and since we were fans of The Go-Go's, we asked Jane if she would like to do a duet together. We had proposed a bunch of songs from which she picked 'Cool Places' and 'Lucky Me, Lucky You'.
>
> We recorded the two songs very quickly in Giorgio Moroder's home studio in L.A. The only thing debated on was the tail end of 'Cool Places', as Jane and I tried ad-libbing the name of every possible place we thought was cool in L.A. Once the first [of us] reached Canter's Deli, we knew the idea was really

lame, so we scrapped it and added the present endings. Jane performed with us on many of the concerts during the 'Cool Places' tour, and had a keen eye for Tijuana pottery and black velvet paintings. The video was shot in San Francisco by The Residents' regular video maker.

'POPULARITY'
Duration: 3:52

A cheerful and light-hearted melody accompanied by matching lyrics. The sound is primarily produced by synthesizers and a tight drumbeat, leading one to wonder if these elements are also generated by the keyboards, as the overall sound is somewhat flat. The bass guitar is barely perceptible, and the guitar appears to be absent.

The lyrics are intentionally superficial, depicting a person who revels in the hedonistic aspects of life, accompanied by a charming partner and a circle of friends with whom they can share enjoyable moments in comfortable settings.

There are no ambiguous quips, just a straightforward account of someone enjoying life—an excellent combination of a simple yet appealing melody paired with matching, uncomplicated lyrics. The arrangements have clearly been crafted with this in mind. Ron has consistently stated that this is one of his favourite Sparks songs.

The song was played regularly during the 1983 US tour and made a sudden reappearance at both concerts in England in 1997, as well as at Los Angeles' Key Club in 1998. It was last performed on the Revenge of Two Hands One Mouth tour in 2013.

> Ron: 'With "Popularity", one of the better songs on the new album, I think, the song had different lyrics until the last day of studio work in Brussels, and I was forced to re-write it in 20 minutes so I could go with the rest of the guys to our favourite restaurant.
>
> 'I want to write as people talk. But some audiences are used to hearing things in a song kind of way, phrased with language that's specifically for songs. It's a Catch-22. "Popularity" I think is very successful in capturing speech, doing away with convention, except maybe an occasional rhyme. Especially on that song, it might seem poorly written to radio programmers, I don't know. That sort of thing excites me. I wanted to strip away everything poetic, everything that sounded like lyrics. It's kind of too easy to understand, and people will be suspicious because it's too simple.'
>
> Russell: 'Ron whipped it [the lyrics] out in the studio one day when we were looking for one more song for the album. He wrote that while I was in the next room doing overdubs on another song. I think that lyrically it might be the best

Sparks song there is. It's really difficult to come up with things that are just real simple and obvious.'

'PRAYIN' FOR A PARTY'
Duration: 2:59

A song of an entirely different nature. While there are virtually no guitars audible in the two preceding tracks, this song is dominated by a distorted guitar and a complementary bass line. It features a mid-tempo sing-along, which is literally performed in the chorus by Bob Haag and Leslie Bohem, with the latter contributing a small portion of the lead vocals. Russell's vocals are double-tracked, radiating the enthusiasm that the instruments also convey. The quiet interlude provides a refreshing contrast to the full sound.

Lyrically, there is no significant change, and the content is confined to celebrating a good life without any complications. The interpretation of such a life is fervently expressed in this song, this time by an adolescent who feels constrained by their parents' house rules and thus turns to a higher deity. With a bit of imagination, the chorus could be envisioned in a church setting, accompanied by a full choir—though it would likely feature different lyrics.

The song has never been played live at regular concerts.

Ron: 'Songs like "All You Ever Think About Is Sex" or "Prayin' For A Party" are not put-downs. If you're that kind of person, then love of sex and parties is a good thing. You see, I don't consider what we do satire—maybe I'm missing my own joke. It can get a little weird when I'm writing the words that have to go in Russell's mouth, so it looks like they're his opinions. But I'm not trying to set priorities for anyone, say they should get more interested in Central American relief—I'm not using reverse psychology. And I don't target the songs.

'Once you do that, and someone says "Oh! I see the point of that song", then you've kind of finished with the value of the tune. That lyric approach is just too limiting, even if the music stands up. My songs just pop up—I don't decide what to write about.'

'ALL YOU EVER THINK ABOUT IS SEX'
Duration: 4:09

A fifty-second instrumental introduction featuring a blend of drums and synthesizers sets the stage for the song. While the lyrics remain as superficial as those in earlier tracks, they are infused with humour and ambiguity this time around.

They are quite clear and direct; it may also be that the lyrics sung in the last verse serve as a reproach to the tendency of people to focus excessively on the physical pleasures of life, neglecting the importance of developing deep emotional connections with one another.

The arrangements consistently centre around the synthesizers, accompanied by a prominent bass guitar; however, the guitar is once again absent.

After the success of 'Cool Places', Atlantic released it as the second single in July. The 7-inch single was only available in the United States, but a 12-inch version was also released in France. This version included a Club Version that was a full minute longer than the album version and featured an attractive picture sleeve. Surprisingly, it showcased Chynna Phillips, the daughter of Michelle Phillips, who is famous for being a member of the Mamas and the Papas.

In the fan club newsletter, Ron discussed the origins of the remix version:

> In the beginning, there was the seven-inch. But lo, the people said, prithee, why so short and so light on the bass drum? The Lord responded, 'I shall satisfy your earthly desire. I shall extend the hymn by several minutes and unleash the full power of the rhythm section. Now get off my back.'
>
> The people cheered and knew that not only was their Lord a good Lord, but that he could also get recording studio time at a very low rate. When the new twelve-inch creations arrived, the people sensed the dawning of a new era in all things carnal. They rejoiced and rejoiced and rejoiced a little more to the new sounds. Then went to an after-hours club. Unfortunately, on Sunday the people were too tired to properly thank the Lord for what he had given them but instead remained in bed and read the Sunday papers.

As with the previous single, a video was created to elaborate on the theme of the album cover. The video, produced by Marcus Peterzell and directed by Pat Warner, features the entire band performing the song while Ron is bombarded with a multitude of cream pies, all while he continues to play his keyboards.

The song was occasionally performed during concerts in 1983, 1984 and even 1986. It was a total surprise when the song was part of the set list of 2025. The addition of the extra guitar made it an exceptionally dynamic and energetic version, which was greatly appreciated by the astonished audience.

> Russell: 'We were once invited to perform a special year-end concert at Disneyland, this song had been a big radio hit in Los Angeles. However, the Disney officials requested that in keeping with the squeaky-clean image of their park, and since apparently none of the Disney characters ever have sex, we did not perform this song. Our fans were not happy.'

'PLEASE BABY, PLEASE'
Duration: 3:42

Another mid-tempo song featuring arrangements similar to its predecessor, which means, once again, the guitars are absent. The melody is quite pleasant, and stereo effects are effectively utilised in the lead vocals. The chorus includes an appealing staccato-like keyboard touch, and the instrumental section in the latter part of the song is well-constructed.

It is quite challenging to identify a double meaning in this song. It appears to be about what the lyrics suggest: a man who is unfortunate enough to have fallen for a woman who does not reciprocate his feelings, despite his best efforts to win her affection.

The song was released as a single in France, which is not entirely surprising, and was accompanied by a beautiful picture sleeve. Despite this, it faded from public attention almost unnoticed.

It has never been performed live at regular concerts.

'ROCKIN' GIRLS'
Duration: 4:42

The second side of the album opens with a captivating and familiar sound centred around the A major chord. The verses adhere to a standard blues structure but take an intriguing deviation as the song unfolds.

The introduction to this track is minimalistic, featuring only a subtle synthesizer and percussion. Adding more instruments to this arrangement would likely detract from its appeal. One notable aspect is how Russell himself announces the beginning of the song, which contributes to its charm.

The subject matter of this song may not be particularly difficult to explain; however, it ironically reveals the narrator's preference for post-pubescent girls. Despite the potentially controversial theme, the lyrics are cleverly crafted and often infused with humour and subtle hints. This showcases the exceptional intelligence and wit of the songwriting duo behind this piece.

In terms of musical composition, this track incorporates guitar work that beautifully complements the overall sound. The guitar delivers a pleasant riff that seamlessly integrates into the mix. The bass also stands out alongside the guitar, carving out additional space in the arrangement. As the song progresses, the percussion evolves into drums, gaining more freedom halfway through.

The song was featured as the B-side of 'Please Baby, Please' and was frequently played during the 1983 US tour.

'I Wish I Looked A Little Better'
Duration: 2:58

As a contrasting theme to the track 'Funny Face', the narrator this time grapples with his own physical appearance and inability to attract attention from the opposite sex.

The introduction is once again created using synthesizers and drums, although the latter have a distinct sound reminiscent of a drum machine, particularly evident during the drum breaks. The bass guitar plays a crucial role in enhancing the overall composition, but there is little space for the guitar. This changed dramatically during live performances, where the distorted guitar delivered a powerful sound that bolsters the rhythm. At times, Russell's voice has a slightly hoarse quality.

The track appeared on the B-side of the single 'All You Ever Think About Is Sex'. Atlantic also released the song as a double A-side promotional single, using the same catalogue number as the original single.

'I Wish I Looked A Little Better' was performed regularly in concert, although it was only a consistent part of the 1983 tour. After that, it became an occasional inclusion in the setlist. It was last performed in 2018 during concerts in Los Angeles and Mexico City.

'Lucky Me, Lucky You'
Duration: 3:26

The second song on the LP featuring a vocal contribution from Jane Wiedlin, which some may argue is superior to that of the first single, although opinions on this matter may vary.

The track begins with Jane's bold announcement, 'Hit it, buddy', after which the drums open the song. Once again, the drum sounds suspiciously like those generated by a computer, a characteristic that applies to all instruments in this track, including the bass loop. The guitar is more prominent this time, but it is played on a Roland guitar synthesizer, which is undoubtedly also used in other songs where the traditional guitar sound is not evident.

The song narrates the tale of a couple who find themselves stranded on a deserted island following a fierce storm. They feel fortunate to have each other's company and remain hopeful that they can endure for as long as possible before they are rescued.

It was performed live once during the Sparks Spectacular, with all vocals sung exclusively by Russell.

> Russell: 'The president of Atlantic suggested at one point for that to be a single. Maybe someone should have listened to him!'

'A Fun Bunch Of Guys From Outer Space'
Duration: 4:00

This track is fairly straightforward and quite clever, sung from the perspective of a group of cheerful aliens who have settled on Earth and are enjoying every moment of their experience. It also serves as the sole reference to the title of this album.

The synthesizer that opens the song resembles something that could have been played by Vince Clarke during his time with Yazoo. Synthesizers continue to dominate the remainder of the track, with the other instruments—except for the drums—being difficult to discern. From the second verse onwards, Russell effectively employs double vocals.

Overall, it is an upbeat song that is invigorated by the diverse contributions from the synthesizers. The song was rarely performed live, with the exception of the 1983 concert for *Rock 'n' Roll Tonight*, where it was introduced by Ron with the words, 'This is a song called "A Fun Bunch of Guys From Outer Space". Now back to your host, Russell Mael.'

'Dance Godammit'
Duration: 3:26

The closing track of this album begins with a mid-tempo drumbeat accompanied by a staccato attack from the synthesizers. These remain the only instruments featured in the song.

Russell's vocals are not exuberant; instead, they convey a narrative quality, a style he employs in several tracks. It is not uncommon for Sparks to deliver a danceable song with a monotonous and somewhat disinterested vocal performance. They excel in creating apparent contradictions.

While this song may not possess the grandeur typically associated with closing tracks on previous Sparks albums, it nonetheless has an appealing melody that becomes more enjoyable once you get past its monotonous presentation.

Only in the final section of the song do the vocals become brighter, enhanced by a second voice that is sung at a much higher pitch, making it an excellent addition. The song appears on the B-side of the single 'All You Ever Think About Is Sex', but only on the 12-inch version. It has been remixed to extend its duration by a full minute. The introduction has been lengthened, featuring a drum intro that gradually accelerates.

The song was rarely performed live, except for the 1983 concert in Riverside, California.

> Russell: 'We sometimes take great pleasure in writing songs about dancing which are totally unsuitable for dancing.'

Ron: 'In my new song "Dance, Godammit", I write "I like clubs/I like girls/I like music/And that's it". In my lyrics, I talk about real things but in a fantasy kind of way. That's the way I'd like to be—if I only cared about girls, clubs and music. To be honest, I don't always know what my relationship is to the character of the song.

I have strong opinions about what we do and what I want in music, but I assume my opinions are the way things actually are. I've been in the world of these songs so long now, I re-write my own past, write from an adolescent's point of view, making it a real groovy world out there. One reason we've had success amongst young people is it comes out genuine—I'm not writing down to them. When you say I'm a satirist, that works against that feeling.'

13

Pulling Rabbits Out of a Hat

Release date: June 1984
Produced by: Ian Little
Engineer: Steve Bates
Cover concept: Ron Mael
Sleeve design: Larry Vigon
Photography: Jim Shea
Illustration: Stan Watts
Recorded at: Oasis Recording Studios, Los Angeles
Duration: 39:47
Personnel: Ron Mael: Synthesizers
                  Russell Mael: Vocals
                  David Kendrick: Drums
                  Bob Haag: Guitar
                  Leslie Bohem: Bass guitar
                  John Thomas: Additional concert keyboards

Side 1
'Pulling Rabbits Out of a Hat'
'Love Scenes'
'Pretending To Be Drunk'
'Progress'
'With All My Might'

Side 2
'Sparks In The Dark (Part One)'
'Everybody Move'
'A Song That Sings Itself'
'Sisters'
'Kiss Me Quick'
'Sparks In The Dark (Part Two)'

Singles from this album:
'Pretending To Be Drunk'/'Kiss Me Quick'
'With All My Might'/'Sparks In The Dark'
'Progress'/'Sparks In The Dark'/'With All My Might' (12-inch only)

In early 1984, Ron and Russell took a holiday in Japan, where they primarily spent their time sightseeing and shopping. However, they were also featured on Japanese television in Yokohama on a programme called *Funky Tomato*. They appeared live in the studio to introduce the video for 'All You Ever Think About Is Sex', in which Ron is bombarded with pies. Additionally, they visited several radio stations to discuss potential future promotions for upcoming releases.

After the success of *Sparks In Outer Space* and the single 'Cool Places', Atlantic Records was poised for Sparks' final breakthrough in the US and sought a successful producer to collaborate with them on the follow-up album.

They approached Ian Little, who co-produced the recent Duran Duran album *Seven and the Ragged Tiger* and their hit single 'Is There Something I Should Know?' in collaboration with Alex Sadkin. Presumably, they were seeking the same sound as heard on these records.

Recording duly commenced at Oasis Recording Studios in Westlake, Los Angeles. However, according to then-manager Joseph Fleury, this collaboration was quite disappointing; so much so that after just one week, Ron and Russell took over the production and completed the album themselves. However, this has never been officially confirmed.

The sound of the album is predominantly characterised by synthesizers typical of the era, leaving little room for guitars. Released in June 1984, the album did not chart at all. The album was not available in the UK until its rerelease by Repertoire Records in April 2021, at which point it was offered on yellow vinyl. This was at the insistence of Fleury, who stated in *Goldmine Magazine* in 1995:

> I knew it would be our last album for Atlantic, and I had a good idea of what we wanted to do next, so I asked the company not to release it in Britain. The reasoning was, the two albums before it had done absolutely nothing in that country, Atlantic had just put them out quietly, not advertised them or anything, and I knew that too many flop albums would work against us eventually. And I think I was proven right. Rabbits sold as well on import as Angst and Outer Space had on domestic release!

It was released in countries such as Portugal and Argentina, the latter of which is quite remarkable as it is the only Sparks album to be released there.

Unlike the previous album, the backing band was not featured on the cover or the inner sleeve. For the first time, the Mael brothers were represented through a drawing. Continuing the theme from the 'When I'm With You' video, Ron was portrayed as a ventriloquist, with Russell as the dummy, a representation of the collaborative dynamic between the brothers that might have been a little out of balance. Even though Ron is responsible for the larger part of the songs, Russell's contribution within their working method should not be underestimated.

In addition to the new album, several other recordings were released that year. A track specifically written at the request of the Disney Company for the movie *Splash Dance* called 'Minnie Mouse' appeared on the original soundtrack album. Additionally, the song 'Mini-Skirted', which was composed for the remake of the movie *Where The Boys Are*, was included in the respective soundtrack album.

The soundtrack for the movie *Bad Manners*, sometimes referred to as *Growing Pains*, was composed by the Maels. It did not receive an official release and remains unavailable; however, copies have been circulated amongst fans since the early 1990s.

Also released in 1984 was the official soundtrack for the movie *Heavenly Bodies*, which featured the Maels' original 'Breaking Out Of Prison'.

Although Sparks did perform some concerts in 1984, it was nothing compared to the extensive tour they had undertaken the previous year, during which they had partly supported Rick Springfield. This time, only a handful of performances were held in California and New York City. However, on 5 May, a segment of a performance from an earlier concert was broadcast on television. The programme was hosted by actor Dan Akroyd, and three songs from *Sparks In Outer Space* were featured.

Two performances were held in August, opening for the British band Psychedelic Furs. On 19 August, Sparks headlined an event, with rising stars the Red Hot Chili Peppers serving as the opening act. The latter concert took place at the Greek Theatre in Los Angeles.

Despite the disappointing record sales, a memorable event took place in 1984. Once again, following their very first performance in 1972, Sparks were invited to *American Bandstand*, where they mimed to 'Pulling Rabbits Out of a Hat' and 'Pretending To Be Drunk'. This episode aired on 6 October and host Dick Clark conducted a brief interview between the songs, during which he donned Russell's infamous cactus jacket. In a playful twist, Russell seized the microphone and welcomed the audience to the *Sparks Bandstand*. Clark remarked that it was the first time in his career that he had lost control of his microphone.

Being a good sport, Clark sent a letter to Ron after the show, thanking him for his appearance on Ron's show. Sparks would make one more appearance on this iconic television show during the 1980s, following the release of their 1986 album *Music That You Can Dance To*. However, this performance did not provide the much-anticipated breakthrough for the band in their homeland.

It almost felt like a curse for the Mael brothers. Each time a situation arose where just a small final push could have secured them the attention and appreciation of a mass audience, they followed up with a release that undermined everything they had accomplished up to that point.

Indiscreet dismantled everything they had established with its two predecessors, while *Terminal Jive* failed to deliver the success that had been meticulously paved by *No. 1 In Heaven*.

Following their major hit with 'Cool Places', they released a commercially disappointing album that closely resembled the sound of many bands from that era.

To remain relevant, Sparks needed to stay true to themselves and distinguish themselves by being unique. By following a fleeting trend, they failed to stand out; they became just one of many artists producing the same sound. The disappointed record label chose not to prolong their contract, prompting Ron and Russell to once again focus on Europe for the upcoming year.

Pulling Rabbits Out of a Hat—The Songs

All songs written by Ron Mael and Russell Mael.

'PULLING RABBITS OUT OF A HAT'
Duration: 4:07

As is often the case with Sparks albums, the opening track is quite strong and immediately establishes the tone for what listeners can expect. In terms of arrangements, this song does not differ significantly from the previous album; however, one could argue that this track is slightly darker than the more frivolous sounds of its predecessor.

Once again, the song is dominated by synthesizers. Although a bass guitar is clearly present, a guitar does not seem to play any part. The exception is the final rendition of the chorus, where the guitar makes a modest contribution, cleverly concealed by the other instruments.

The song appears to revolve around an individual who strives to impress someone and persuade her of his importance, yet he seems to fall short. While it lacks profound content, intricate layers or clever wordplay, it undeniably possesses a certain dynamic and energy reminiscent of 'Angst In My Pants', another opening track.

Remarkably, the song was never performed live in the 1980s. The 1997 album *Plagiarism* features a rerecorded version of this song, which was played during both concerts in England in 1997 and at the Key Club in Los Angeles in 1998.

It was also featured in concerts in December 2014 in London and February 2015 in Los Angeles, where it was performed with the London Heritage Orchestra. After that, it has not been performed live again.

'LOVE SCENES'
Duration: 4:20

The same guitar sound that appeared in the final section of the opener is now presented in a similar fashion, resembling a somewhat subdued and understated rhythm guitar, distorted in an almost gentle manner.

This time, the bass guitar appears to have been replaced by a synthesizer, which, not surprisingly, dominates most of the arrangements. The song is somewhat lighter than its predecessor and features the typical arrangements employed by many artists of that era, including Duran Duran, Spandau Ballet and ABC. This is hardly unexpected, considering the producer involved.

The lyrics are sung from the perspective of an actor who takes pleasure in the upcoming scenes that emphasise physical collaboration. They were written by Russell.

The song was never performed live, except for the presentation of the complete album during the Sparks Spectacular.

> Russell: 'Love Scenes is okay, but a little bit conservative in its approach. I think it sounds more like a hit song, but also at the risk of losing a lot of our character. But it sounds alright!'

'Pretending To Be Drunk'
Duration: 3:38

This lively, mid-tempo tune features a catchy opening created by synthesizers, with the guitar once again being overshadowed by the other instruments. The sound effect used by the guitar closely resembles that of earlier songs, making it challenging to determine what producer Ian Little contributed compared to the previous record, produced by the brothers.

The arrangements show little variation, with an increasing reliance on synthesizers in place of traditional instruments. Halfway through the song, Russell's backing vocals are utilised quite effectively. The addition of a keyboard-generated variation of a trumpet towards the end of the song is reminiscent of the arrangements in 'Looks, Looks, Looks' and adds a nice touch.

The title of the song accurately reflects its lyrical content. It tells the story of an individual who, much to the chagrin of his girlfriend, struggles to make a meaningful impression on those around him. His choice to present himself as someone who is intoxicated positively alters his behaviour and, consequently, the attitudes of others towards him.

In an interview in *Blitz Magazine,* Russell stated:

> We are often listed as being co-authors, when in fact Ron writes the bulk of the material. On the new album, I wrote the lyrics to 'Pretending To Be Drunk' and 'Love Scenes'. Apart from that, Ron did everything else. My capacity is as an editor. I get rid of the excess or make an arrangement better.

The second single from this album (US only) was released in both 7-inch and 12-inch editions. The 12-inch edition included an Extended Version of 5:37, featuring clearer guitar sounds. Although the song was released as a single in the US, it has never been performed live.

It was showcased during an appearance on *American Bandstand* on 6 October 1984, but was not performed live.

'Progress'
Duration: 4:43

Another mid-tempo song with an instrumental intro lasting half a minute, built around drums and synthesizers. The arrangements and vocals aim to evoke a futuristic vibe, which is partially successful but ultimately sounds dated.

The lyrics seem to revolve around a robot or someone with artificial intelligence and a synthetic body, where continuous enhancements are considered as progress.

This song was included as the B-side of the 12-inch single 'With All My Might', in an Extended Club Mix lasting approximately five-and-a-half minutes. Like most tracks on the album, it was never performed live during regular gigs.

'With All My Might'
Duration: 4:06

Three singles were pulled from the album, with the most successful being the first one, 'With All My Might', which peaked at number 104 on the Billboard Bubbling Under chart. It was also released in France and Peru, but failed to make an impression in either country.

While Todd Rundgren had been informed in 1971 that the band did not want to make slick ballads, this song likely fits that description. Despite its sugary-sweet production and accompanying lyrics, the track possesses a distinct quality and an appealing melody. Unfortunately, the public's perception did not align with this, leading to disappointing sales figures.

It is an utterly romantic song in which the narrator expresses his determination to do everything in his power to reach his loved one. Despite its somewhat clichéd perspective and sentimental arrangements, the song succeeds in conveying its message and is definitely a strong track.

The 12-inch version, which featured Extended Club Mixes of both the A-side and the B-side tracks—'Progress' and the instrumental 'Sparks In The Dark'—reached number 28 on the Dance Charts. Oddly enough, the 12-inch version listed those latter two tracks as the A-side, with 'With All My Might' as the B-side.

A video directed by Graham Whifler, who also worked on the previous 'Cool Paces' video, was equally tongue-in-cheek and imaginative as its predecessor. It featured a model, Lisa Accomando, who joined them on a stuffed horseback.

'With All My Might', strangely enough, has never been played live at regular concerts.

> Russell: 'We thought this could have been really successful commercially, but for whatever reasons it didn't get played a lot. Even the stations that would support us thought it was too soft-sounding. For once in our career, Ron tried to make a song acceptable for an American mass audience—not being overly clever, trying to make them real palatable.'
>
> Russell: 'When we would do a song which was softer in tone, people often wondered what our motive was. They wanted to know what the punchline was for Sparks doing such an atypical type song. There was no punchline. We think "With All My Might" got caught in this dilemma. Another Graham Whifler video with a highly stylized fake western motif which had Ron doing some trick equestrian riding accompanied the song.'
>
> Ron: 'We wanted to do a song that had all the irony removed and was just a "song" song. I really like it, but people look for the motive behind it and then we can't get accepted. People are waiting for the punchline, and there isn't any.'

'SPARKS IN THE DARK (PART ONE)'
Duration: 0:28

A fairly insignificant instrumental track of less than thirty seconds opens side two. The fact that the title is supplemented with 'Part One' suggests the worst: there will also be a Part Two.

While Sparks cannot normally be faulted for their frequent use of filler material, presenting two instrumental versions of the same song leans heavily in that direction. This is particularly disappointing because there was undoubtedly a wealth of other songs available. Even if that were not the case, the Maels could have easily composed a new piece that would have been more surprising than this offering. It feels like a missed opportunity.

'EVERYBODY MOVE'
Duration: 2:58

The previous instrumental seamlessly transitions into 'Everybody Move', giving it the feel of an introduction. This was confirmed during the only performance of the song at the Sparks Spectacular, where it indeed flowed directly into this track.

The arrangements are playful and varied. While it may not be a masterpiece or even an exceptional song, it is a lively piece with appealing and diverse melodies.

Lyrically, it does not offer content that encourages deep philosophical reflection. Initially, it appears to be an ode to fitness, but later in the song, there is a reference to someone driving too fast and nearly colliding with the car in front of them.

'A Song That Sings Itself'
Duration: 4:29

Now, this is more like it. An instrumental introduction featuring twinkling sounds gradually fades in to open the song. After twenty-five seconds, drums and a synthesizer bass guitar are introduced to enrich the composition. The melody is straightforward, yet the chord changes are delightful, and Russell's relatively low vocals align perfectly with the expectations that have been established.

After a minute, the guitar joins in, echoing the sound found in some of the previous tracks. It remains a pleasant complement to the arrangements. The chorus is catchy, encouraging listeners to sing along, which not only elevates this song amongst the best on this LP but also places it in a category where it can compete with other high-quality Sparks songs. It is quite curious that this song was never released as a single.

Lyrically, this song exceeds the quality of most others featured here, which is almost a prerequisite for a composition by the Maels. There do not appear to be any hidden double meanings in the lyrics, suggesting that this is a variation of a love song in which the singer occasionally engages in profound reflection. It has never been performed live during regular concerts.

'Sisters'
Duration: 3:53

The Maels' rather distinctive sense of humour is once again evident in this mid-tempo song, which narrates the story of a man who becomes entangled with two sisters, both of whom are interested in him. The lyrics suggest that he ultimately manages to engage in a sexual relationship with both of them at the same time. It appears that they have overcome their jealousy, and he demonstrates greater physical prowess than initially anticipated.

The instrumental section, which features the guitar's debut, is not necessarily an enhancement, but neither is it disruptive. The chorus is exceptionally catchy and delivered with multiple layers of vocals, prominently including a female singer. However, her identity remains unknown.

Like many songs on this album, this track is mainly driven by a variety of synthesizers, which also generate the bass line. The drumbeats are rather monotonous, lacking any significant breaks, and seem to be produced by the keyboards as well.

Despite Sparks playing over ten concerts in 1984, this song has never been performed live.

'Kiss Me Quick'
Duration: 4:07

Several synthesizer sounds with a pronounced stereo effect introduce this tranquil song, accompanied by percussion and bass that are clearly generated by keyboards. Russell's voice begins at a slightly lower pitch than usual and is soon complemented by a second voice, also from him, which leans towards falsetto in the subsequent verse. A sound resembling a guitar strum is employed, but it is evident that, like all the other instruments in this song, it originates from a synthesizer.

Not much can be said about the meaning of the lyrics, other than the fact that the narrator appears to be sharing his experiences and desires regarding his preference for being kissed. This evokes a range of emotions and experiences for him.

The song was released as the B-side of the single 'Pretending To Be Drunk' in the USA. It features a new mix with a duration of five minutes and forty-five seconds. This version includes primarily instrumental segments, enhanced by additional sounds generated solely by the synthesizer.

Furthermore, there is an extended instrumental section midway through, which adds greater depth and interest to the composition.

'Kiss Me Quick' was never performed live at regular concerts.

'Sparks In The Dark (Part Two)'
Duration: 2:58

Instrumental songs by Sparks are quite rare and it's even more uncommon to find both a short and a long version of the same instrumental track on the same album. Originally, the music for this piece was intended to serve as the foundation for a vocal track. However, this concept was never fully realised, and the music was subsequently rearranged as an instrumental.

There isn't much to say about it. A consistently recurring theme is accompanied by numerous additional synthesizer sounds; however, it remains quite predictable. While it is cheerful and somewhat amusing, it fails to evoke any emotions, contemplation or analysis—elements that are characteristic of most Sparks songs. Some might argue that it is merely filler.

It was one of the B-sides of the 12-inch single 'With All My Might', where it was over a minute longer and did not significantly enhance the album version. This song is not the type Sparks typically use to conclude their LPs; perhaps there was another motivation for including it.

Russell: 'It was the backing track to another lyrical song that we had. But the song was not coming out so well. Ron added a few instrumental lines to it and it began to sound good as an instrumental. I said that he should not worry about me singing on it, because it sounds good just like it is.'

14
Music That You Can Dance To

Release date: September 1986
Produced by: Ron Mael and Russell Mael
Engineer: Dan Lacksman
Sleeve design: Michael Diehl
Photography: Rocky Schenck
Recorded at: Synsound Studios, Brussels
Duration: 37:17
Personnel: Ron Mael: Synthesizers
Russell Mael: Vocals
David Kendrick: Drums
Bob Haag: Guitar, synthesizers
Leslie Bohem: Bass guitar, backing vocals
John Thomas: Additional keyboards, assistant production

Side 1
'Music That You Can Dance To'
'Rosebud'
'Fingertips'
'Change'/'Armies Of The Night'

Side 2
'The Scene'
'Shopping Mall Of Love'
'Modesty Plays' (New Version)
'Let's Get Funky'

Singles from this album:
'Change'/'This Town Ain't Big Enough For Both Of Us'
'Music That You Can Dance To'/'Shopping Mall Of Love'
'Rosebud'/'Theme For Rosebud'
'Fingertips'/'The Scene'/'Fingertips' (12-inch only)

Hello again. It's that time of year again when a young man's fancy turns to 24 track tape recorders. Yes, new product. A sense of deja vu hit us as we landed at Brussels International Airport and Waffle Stand. Soon we realized we had recorded the 'Sparks In Outer Space' album in this loveable land of NATO nubiles and Common Market cut-ups. Off to the hotel for a quick shower, then directly to the studio for two months.

Our intentions were to be a little more elaborate on the new material. I think you will hear the difference. Acting as our own producers, we spent as much time on one song [as] we usually spend on an entire album.

The new tracks (three completed as of this date) seem to affect people in the way that Kimono My House or Number One In Heaven affected people at the time, that is to say to shock and amaze. We hope you have the same impression.

To go along with gussied-up sound, there will be a change in the new release pattern for the new stuff. Thus, the first single, a song called 'Change'" will be released first in Britain, then the rest of Europe, New Zealand, Australia and Japan. Then in America and Canada. Those of you living in trendy cities, not in the UK will no doubt be able to purchase the song soon after its release, in import shops. Others will have to wait a short time, I'm sure you will be able to find something to occupy your time in the interval. June is the probable UK release date. It would make a lovely wedding gift. Especially the twelve inch.—Ron

The message above that Ron shared through the fanzine of the official fan club in early 1985 pertained to the new material they were recording in Brussels at that time. The recordings were once again conducted at Synsound Studios by Dan Lacksman, a member of Telex, who also managed the engineering. This time, Ron and Russell took on the production themselves. Two years earlier, Sparks had recorded *Sparks In Outer Space* in that very studio.

Sparks did not have a record company at the time because Atlantic Records had cancelled their contract. However, with the newly recorded track 'Change', they successfully found a British label interested in releasing it as a single.

Ron and Russell travelled to Europe to promote their single, which was released on 5 July 1985. They were guests on various UK shows, including *Breakfast Time*, the *Terry Wogan Show* and *Music Box* with Julie Brown. They had another interview with Julie Brown in the presence of Thomas Dolby, during which they expressed their dissatisfaction with their record company for not providing a budget to create a music video, so they decided to produce it in-house. Ron then held a cardboard cut-out television screen in front of Russell, who sang a portion of the song. Ron and Russell also appeared on a France 3 television show to promote the song, but despite all their efforts, it didn't chart anywhere.

The London Records executive was unimpressed with 'Change' and was not surprised that it had failed to become a hit. He asked the brothers if they could create music that you can dance to, and shortly thereafter they returned with the song 'Music That You Can Dance To'. The individual in question was not amused and decided to terminate the album contract.

Sparks were once again without a record company although a new album of songs had been recorded. Manager Joseph Fleury started looking for alternatives and eventually came back with several contracts. In the US, Canada and France, the album was released on Curb Records, in the UK on Consolidated Allied Records, in Australia and New Zealand on RCA and in Belgium the album was finally released on Magic. However, this release did not occur until June 1986, highlighting the lengthy process of securing a record company—or, in this case, multiple companies.

Meanwhile, the Maels were not idle. Russell had travelled to Japan, where he sang on two songs by local band Salon Music, consisting of Hitomi Takenaka and Zin Yoshida. On their 1987 album *This Is Salon Music*, Russell sang backing vocals on the song 'When She Comes', and on the LP *O Boy* he did a striking duet with Hitomi Takenaka on 'Say Hello, Wave Goodbye', from the duo Soft Cell, the original of which reached number 3 on the British charts in early 1982.

Ironically, Soft Cell epitomised synthpop, with their image and music drawing inspiration from Ron and Russell, as David Ball of the band has repeatedly stated.

In the course of 1986, the Maels also appeared in the music video for the Ramones' single 'Something To Believe In', along with a host of other artists, including Lionel Richie and Weird Al Yankovic.

The LP was released with an atmospheric black-and-white cover featuring photographs by Rocky Schenck, who later created album covers for artists such as Alice In Chains and produced videos for numerous musicians. For the Belgian release, the record company chose to flip the front and back covers, a decision that had also once occurred in Germany for the release of *A Woofer in Tweeter's Clothing*.

On the album we also encounter an earlier song, 'Modesty Plays', which was rerecorded for this release. In 1982, this song had been released as a single in France and Germany, but remained unknown to the rest of the world unless one had managed to obtain an imported copy of the single.

The first actual single intended to showcase the album was the title track, which prompted Ron and Russell to once again travel to Europe to promote the album, accompanied by drummer David Kendrick. The other band members were acknowledged for their contributions but would not be used further. This was one of Kendrick's final jobs for Sparks. He would still participate in the last concerts in the US, before moving on to work with Devo and other bands.

In Europe, Sparks made their television debut with this single in France on the TV6 channel and on the popular programme *Na Sowass* in Germany, where they were accompanied by four half-naked, body-painted German women.

After returning from Europe, they embarked on a brief tour that focussed solely on California. David Kendrick was the only contributor from the album who remained part of the band. The other musicians of the live band consisted of Hans Reunscheussel on bass guitar, John Thomas on keyboards and Pamela Stonebrook on backing vocals, with no guitarist present.

The tour began on 3 August in Los Angeles at the Annual Beach Scene and ended on 25 October in Valencia at Magic Mountain, where they played two gigs at 8 p.m. and 10 p.m. These were Sparks' last concerts on the North American continent for the time being. They would not perform live in America again until 14 November 1998 at the Key Club in Los Angeles. The tour manager involved was a Freddie Galgas.

Meanwhile, a second single was released by the English record company, but 'Rosebud' failed to have any impact.

As had happened so many times before, Sparks had failed to make a definitive breakthrough in their homeland. Things were even worse for them in Europe, where they had been virtually forgotten by the general public and the music press, who paid little attention to them. The various record contracts were not renewed and the Mael brothers were left empty-handed, having to start all over again.

Music That You Can Dance To—The Songs

All songs written by Ron Mael and Russell Mael, except where otherwise stated.

'MUSIC THAT YOU CAN DANCE TO'
Duration: 4:21

Although the title of the opening track and the album was created as a tongue-in-cheek response to an executive from London Records, the message seemed to have resonated with the brothers. It is a light and cheerful melody that has a great basis for dancing, with a clear focus on both the lyrics and the music.

As expected, the trend continues with arrangements primarily determined by synthesizers, with traditional instruments like guitar, bass guitar and drums virtually absent. A synthesized version of a saxophone is performed instead.

This track was the first single released and appeared in the US, Canada, the UK, Germany, Belgium, France and Australia. It was also released as a 12-inch single with a six-and-a-half-minute club version.

The German single used a photo from the same series taken by Rocky Schenck, this time in colour. The video released with the single was created by the Mael brothers themselves and took about two-and-a-half months to produce.

'Music That You Can Dance To' was also featured in the movie *Rad*, an American sports film directed by Hal Needham.

The club version of the single reached number 6 on the Billboard Dance Charts, outperforming previous singles.

The song was performed live during the 1986, 2006, 2007, 2022 and 2023 concerts as well as during the 2025 world tour, where it actually got the audience out of their seats and dancing.

> Russell: 'We now had spent so many months recording in Brussels, that we were even beginning to understand some Flemish, and that was frightening. We spent longer on the recording of the LP than we had done on any previous one. It was a great luxury for us to be extravagant with studio time, and to be far from home. We also shot the video for this song without any outside assistance. My living room was the set; Ron shot my scenes, I shot his. It took us 3 months to complete. We could ask for help next time. After some promotion for the song in Europe, we made one of several trips to Japan to record with the Japanese group Salon Music.'

'Rosebud'
Duration: 4:37

The female vocalist who modestly opens this song is most likely Pamela Stonebrook, although her contribution is not mentioned on the cover. The opening notes of the strikers, produced by synthesizers, create a somewhat cinematic feel, which is further developed in two additional mixes included on the 12-inch edition of the single.

The song has a slow tempo without being immediately classified as a ballad. In addition to the tranquil setting, there are occasional well-executed additional arrangements that introduce energetic and dramatic elements. This technique is also utilised in some other songs on this album. The dramatic elements are purposefully included to convey the emotional depth of the song. Despite the somewhat sentimental tone, the song portrays the story of someone supporting their loved one after a serious accident that could be fatal.

There is an obvious link to the 1941 film *Citizen Kane*, directed by Orson Welles, which is generally considered a masterpiece, an opinion that the Maels undoubtedly share. During the main character's death scene, his last word is 'Rosebud'. Notably, he is holding a snow globe—an item that Ron has collected for decades.

This song appeared both as a 7-inch with a new 'Cinematic Mix' of over one-and-a-half minute on the B-side called 'Theme For Rosebud'. On the 12-inch release, an extended dance mix appeared on the A-side of over seven minutes, and in addition to the earlier-mentioned 'Theme For Rosebud' an 'FM Mix' of over four minutes was included. The single failed to chart.

'Rosebud' was performed during most of the sporadic live concerts that Sparks played in 1986, but not at regular concerts after that.

'FINGERTIPS'
Written by Henry Cosby and Clarence Paul
Duration: 4:20

For the first time since 1976's 'I Want To Hold Your Hand', a cover was released. Unlike its predecessor, this one was actually included on a regular album. Opinions about this song and the recording vary widely amongst the fan base. The majority find the choice and the execution unappealing and have little sympathy for the fact that it ended up on a Sparks album.

The original song was released in 1963 by a 12-year-old Stevie Wonder, in Part 1 and Part 2 versions. This cover is based on Part 2.

Russell fully utilises his falsetto skills, but the result is not as gratifying this time. In fact, the vocals in this song are not particularly impressive, which is quite rare. In addition to a funky bass line, which once again appears to come from the keyboards, there is actually some space for a guitar this time. The modest contribution of the guitarist, Robert Mache, can be heard as the song approaches the end.

The song was released as a 12-inch single on 15 October, in the US and Canada only. Ironically, it was the song that Sparks performed at their last appearance on *American Bandstand* on 10 November. A humorous conversation then took place between Dick Clark and Ron.

> Dick: 'Why on earth would you record a Stevie Wonder song and not one of your own?'
> Ron: 'What do you mean? I, I …'
> Dick: 'You didn't write that song.'
> Ron: 'I don't know who this Stevie Wonder is but this is my song. This guy is asking for trouble. We have very good lawyers that take care of matters like these.'
> Dick: 'I'm sorry I asked.'

The single eventually reached number 38 on the Billboard Dance Charts, which was considerably lower than its predecessor.

'Fingertips' was performed live during the concerts played in 1986 and on television, on *Rock and Roll Evening News*, on 4 October 1986.

> Ron: 'That's actually the only Stevie Wonder song I ever liked. I'm not partial to Stevie Wonder, but because that's so much of a non-song … I thought since we don't do many cover versions, it would be nice to do a non-song.'

'CHANGE'
Duration: 5:17

'Change' was the song that Sparks had released as a single the previous year. It was completely unknown in America, which is why it was included on the American and Canadian versions of the album. In Europe, it was replaced by another song, most likely due to the rights held by London Records, which prevented Sparks from rereleasing the song there. However, these rights apparently did not extend to the North American continent.

Given the pride the brothers have expressed for this particular song and their usual commitment to consistency, it is doubtful that there is any reason behind it other than legal restrictions.

It was a significant departure from their earlier work and introduced a piece of music that was longer than most other singles at the time, with a duration of 5:12, five seconds shorter than the version on the album. The main distinction was that it was a partially narrative single with no actual singing until the chorus. It bears a remarkable resemblance to the track 'Is That All There Is?' by Peggy Lee from 1969, written by Leiber & Stoller. It touched on the same theme to some extent and shared clear commonalities, particularly in composition and arrangements. Ron has always mentioned this song as one of his favourites, and the similarities are quite noticeable.

The single had been released in the UK, Netherlands, France, Germany, Portugal and Australia, with a 12-inch version in the UK and France, which had an extended mix of 6:12. The British promo edition of the 12-inch even had an extended club mix of 7:12, which was quite different from the extended mix. The single reached number 85 in the British charts. As a B-side, an acoustic version of the song responsible for their breakthrough in the UK and the rest of Europe eleven years earlier—'This Town Ain't Big Enough For Both Of Us'—was rerecorded.

> Russell: 'In terms of personal satisfaction, "Change" is possibly my favorite Sparks song. We went back to Brussels and spent a month each on "Change" and "The Scene". We wanted to try something epic in scope; something that was really involved. The basic song had been written before going into the studio, however we spent weeks and weeks honing the arrangement and recording. The lyrical spirit of everything we had done to this point was probably better conveyed by Ron in this one song than in anything else we had done. And from a sonic standpoint, we couldn't do any better than the instrumental passage in the middle of this song. We're especially proud of it.'

'ARMIES OF THE NIGHT'
Duration: 5:17

This song was released a year earlier. Originally written for the film *Fright Night*, it was included in the official soundtrack, but the version on this album differs slightly. The remixed version is almost a minute longer than the soundtrack version. The movie version was also released as a B-side to the single 'Give It Up' by Evelyn 'Champagne' King.

In addition to the two aforementioned versions, a third rendition was released in 1993 on the French double CD *The Hell Collection*. This mix was different from the previous versions, although all use the same lead vocals and backing vocals. Only the instrumentations are altered.

'Armies Of The Night' is considered by many fans of the film to be one of the musical highlights.

The arrangements for the version on this album have been slightly adjusted to align with the overall feel. The build-up is well executed, and the chorus is extremely catchy. However, Ron and Russell would undoubtedly have preferred the album to be released worldwide with 'Change'.

Although this song is dominated by synthesizers, there is a clear guitar presence, which is absent on most songs on this album.

> Russell: 'Originally recorded for the film *Fright Night*, another one of those horror films that makes Francis Ford Coppola's *Dracula* look better and better by the minute.'

'The Scene'
Duration: 6:11

The explosive dynamics featured in some songs on this album reach a climax in 'The Scene', where the cinematic theme is even more pronounced than in the other songs. A staccato-like guitar rhythm accompanied by a synchronised bass drum opens the song, and is soon joined by an abundance of synthesizer sounds that take over the theme.

A minute into the song, the initial instrumental intro is enhanced with the addition of funky-sounding bass guitars, likely produced by the keyboard. The percussions give way to a crescendo of loud instrumental explosions, after which the drums are extended and the vocals finally join in after about a minute-and-a-half.

The high energy level of the longest song on this record makes it extremely suitable for dancing, aligning well with the album's philosophy. Around the three-minute mark, the cinematic opening notes are reintroduced before transitioning into what could, with some flexibility, be referred to as a middle eight section. This break is signalled by some intense electronically driven drumbeats, not unlike those featured on 'The Number One Song In Heaven'. During the final part of the song, bongos are introduced, and the previously mentioned funky bass lines are used once more. The song concludes with the same notes that were played in the intro, followed by a closing drumbeat.

It's not easy to find a deeper meaning in the lyrics of this song. It seems to be about the shared need—or perhaps the necessity—to let go of daily worries every now and then, and completely surrender to a situation that excites and stimulates. Perhaps it is simply a reference to a place where you can dance without a care in the world.

'The Scene' was released as the B-side of the 12-inch single 'Fingertips'. It was presented to be a special club edit. In reality, it was only a few seconds shorter than the album version, and there was hardly any difference in the mix. The song was performed during some of the few live concerts Sparks played in 1986 but was never part of the set list after that.

'SHOPPING MALL OF LOVE'
Duration: 3:14

Fans of the older Mael brother's vocal style will appreciate this song, as it fearlessly embraces nonconformity and idiosyncrasy, qualities that have never been obstacles for the brothers.

The arrangements are minimalistic, with only a dominant and almost constant drumbeat, occasionally complemented by subtle synthesizer sounds that mainly stay in the background.

The real surprise lies in the presentation of the vocals, performed by Ron in a monotonous manner that is still very captivating. This once again highlights the exceptional nature of Russell's voice and singing abilities, as he skilfully handles the chorus.

The lyrics are witty and can be seen as a romantic ode to an (imaginary) relationship.

Interestingly, the song was never performed live until it was added to the setlist for the world tour in 2022. It remained on the 2023 setlist, giving Ron the chance to shine, which he clearly excels at.

'MODEST PLAYS (NEW VERSION)'
Duration: 3:59

Several official versions of this song have been released, along with some unauthorised mixes.

As mentioned earlier in Chapter 11, it was originally written and recorded for the ABC network pilot of the proposed 1982 *Modesty Blaise* TV series, which never materialised. The French label Underdog heard the song and wanted to release it as a single. This eventually happened in Germany as well. The French release included both a short and a long version of the same song, whereas Germany released 'Nicotina' as the B-side. The singles were not a success in either country, but it did not stop the band from recording a new version for the

LP that was released three years later. Like the original recording, this version was also produced by the brothers and Greg Penny.

Compared to the original recording, the arrangements and mix have been modified to better align with the overall sound presented on this album. The sound is slightly less warm and—for lack of a better term—a bit more industrial. While the original recording was primarily characterised by a driving bass, whether from a synthesizer or not, the sound on the new version is mainly defined by a fast but somewhat thin-sounding drum. It appears that the vocals have not been rerecorded.

The lyrics describe the main character as the female equivalent of James Bond. 'Modesty Plays' was occasionally included in the set list during the 1983 American tour, even though it had not yet been released for the American market at the time. The performance at Magic Mountain in Valencia on 5 June 1983 was recorded and included on the *BBC in Concert* series, which was a promotional live LP created for radio stations.

'LET'S GET FUNKY'
Duration: 6:05

The last song on the album may not be the grandiose and impressive ending that is common on many other releases, but it is undeniable that 'Let's Get Funky' is a remarkable song that leaves a lasting impression in terms of style and execution. It is up to the listener to determine whether this evokes a positive or negative emotion; opinions are strongly divided on this matter.

The captivating introduction, lasting over a minute, is driven by percussion and various synthesizer sounds, making good use of basic but appealing stereo effects. The arrangements are then overtaken by a repetitive theme of thin brass instruments, clearly generated by the synthesizer, which has a familiar sound to it. Contrary to the title, the song's rhythm does not have the slightest hint of funk in it, but that's just a very typical tongue-in-cheek display to be expected of the uncompromising Mael brothers.

The song tells the story of an encounter with a particularly silent young lady who nevertheless leaves the narrator fascinated to the point that he eventually lets her move in with him. Despite the wafer-thin storyline, the words are very well-chosen and give the tale a comic twist.

'Let's Get Funky' has never been performed live at regular concerts.

15

Interior Design

Release date: 26 August 1988
Produced by: Ron Mael and Russell Mael
Engineer: John Thomas
Sleeve design: Donald Krieger
Photography: Christi Haydon
Recorded at: The Pentagon Studios, Los Angeles
Duration: 44:25
Personnel: Ron Mael: Keyboards
Russell Mael: Vocals
Spencer Sercombe: Guitar
Pamela Stonebrook: Backing vocals
John Thomas: Keyboards

Side 1
'So Important'
'Just Got Back From Heaven'
'Lots Of Reasons'
'You've Got A Hold Of My Heart'
'Love-O-Rama'

Side 2
'The Toughest Girl In Town'
'Let's Make Love'
'Stop Me If You've Heard This Before'
'A Walk Down Memory Lane'
'Madonna'

Singles from this album:
'So Important'/'The Big Brass Ring'
'So Important'/'So Important'/'So Important' (12-inch)
'Madonna'/'So Important'
'Just Got Back From Heaven'/'Just Got Back From Heaven'/'Just Got Back From Heaven'/'Just Got Back From Heaven'/'Just Got Back From Heaven' (12-inch only)

After failing to return to the charts and regain the spotlight in the US and Europe with their previous album, *Music That You Can Dance To*, the brothers decided to focus on building their own recording studio.

This initiative was primarily aimed at eliminating their dependence on record companies, which dictated the amount of studio time they received and the producers associated with their recordings. The studio would be set up in Russell's home. From that point forward, Sparks would record their music entirely independently and on their own schedule, presenting the finished product directly to record companies. Ironically, this approach mirrored the method they employed for their very first LP, the self-recorded Halfnelson demo album in 1969.

In the meantime, Russell travelled to Southeast Asia for several weeks, during which he specifically visited Hong Kong and Tokyo. Although the trip was primarily a vacation, he took some time in Japan to contribute his vocals to an album by the Japanese band Salon Music. Meanwhile, Ron remained in Los Angeles, and once his younger brother returned, the two of them began working on their new home studio.

At the time, a record company was lacking. After the release of their previous album, the brothers did not have a contract with any record label. They established Fine Art as a legal entity to serve as the owner of the new material to be recorded. For the actual pressing, distribution and promotion of the new album, they would rely on a record company; however, they would maintain complete control over the recording process.

In the first half of 1987, a message from the Maels appeared in the fanzine of the official fan club, announcing the purchase and construction of their own studio.

Hello from Ron and Russ,

Greetings: We've spent the time since the last album setting up our own studio, so that we can avoid the slings and arrows of outrageous studio bills. This is why you haven't received any news about Sparks lately. We've been working continuously on the next album, though, and have completed ten tracks plus two or three extras that we hope will be covered by someone less hip than ourselves.

Our studio set-up is based on the principle that such recording work can now be done on computers rather than recording everything immediately to tape. The value of this system is that you can change sounds, keys, and tempos without it being such a big deal.

The material for the next album, far from being more mechanical and 'Electronic', is in fact based more on what we feel are strong songs rather than strong conceptual pieces. They are tuneful but still contain that patented Sparks 'Je ne sais quoi' that we can't seem to rid ourselves of. Nevertheless, the songs seem to strike people who have not considered themselves to be Sparks fans (there are one or two), and this fact is especially flattering to us, as we like to pride ourselves on the craftsmanship of our songwriting as well as being what many record company people call 'interesting'.

The album, due to the meticulousness of our recording habits, will probably not be released until middle or late summer. We also plan to tour at that point since the new songs will lend themselves to a live interpretation and also because we miss a live audience. Four walls and an engineer's face don't give you a lot of feedback from your music. Thanks for your patience.

The fanzine's edition published at the end of 1987 was mainly dedicated to photos of the Maels during the recording of their new LP. It also extensively discussed the brands and models of equipment, keyboards and microphones used in the studio, which was named 'The Pentagon'.

Throughout the recording of the new album, the Maels received assistance from John Thomas, who played various keyboard parts and handled engineering duties. John would go on to become a significant figure in Sparks for nearly twenty years. He referred to himself as 'the third brother' and continued to be involved in future Sparks albums and live performances. Notably, he played a crucial role in preparing for the live shows at the legendary Sparks Spectacular in 2008. John was also present backstage during almost every album presentation, managing the computerised aspects of audio and video playback programming. He even joined the band on stage during the presentation of *Terminal Jive,* where he played the solo on 'When I'm With You'.

John contributed to every Sparks album up to and including *Exotic Creatures Of The Deep*. Initially, he played keyboard alongside Ron, but later focused primarily on engineering and mentoring for Russell, who gradually assumed that role.

In addition to John Thomas, guitarist Spencer Sercombe, who also hails from Los Angeles, was brought in to assist. The credits mistakenly spelled his surname as Sircombe. He was a member of Shark Island, a band known for its glam metal sound. In the early 1980s, he auditioned for the band Kiss to replace guitarist Ace Frehley, but did not meet their expectations. After contributing to *Interior Design,* Spencer continued his work with Shark Island. The band released its most recent album in 2020; however, Sercombe was no longer part of the line-up at that time.

The final addition to the album was Pamela Stonebrook, a tall blonde jazz singer from Los Angeles who had made a small, uncredited contribution to the previous LP. She had also worked as an actress, appearing in classic films such as *Sexerella and Prince Erotico* (1977) and *Saturday the 14th Strikes Back* (1988). Following her involvement in this Sparks album, she authored a book titled *A Jazz Singer's True Account of Extra-terrestrial Contact*. In this book, Pamela reflects on her sexual experiences with a reptilian alien and discusses her interactions with several other extra-terrestrial beings. However, it is assumed that she restricted herself to singing only during the recording of the album.

Although she does not perform on the album, special attention should be given to Christi Haydon. She first encountered the band in 1986 when Russell spotted her at Bullock's Department Store in Los Angeles, where she was employed on the Estée Lauder cosmetics counter. Russell had left a package for her during her absence, which turned out to be the 7-inch single of 'Music That You Can Dance To', with a note complimenting her appearance and a request for her to call him.

According to Christi, who shared this information on the blog of Sparks enthusiast Monte Mallin, the Maels were seeking a singer or girl group to produce. This aligns with the announcement in the fan club magazine at the end of 1987, which stated that Ron and Russell were finalising five songs they had written for the female duo Universe Of Love. The duo, Christi Haydon and Pinky Also Known As, were expected to release an LP that year, featuring these five songs. However, that album never saw the light of day, although songs were recorded a few years later with only Christi Haydon. Interestingly, the photos of Ron and Russell used for the inner sleeve were taken by Christi.

'Interior Design' was released on vinyl in only four countries: in the United States by Rhino Records, and in France, Italy and Israel by Carrere. This was a remarkable move.

As for the CD, it was a completely different story. Ron and Russell owned the recordings through their company, Fine Art, so obtaining the rights appears to have been easy or inexpensive. There were likely no specific conditions regarding the choice of cover to be used, but the one selected was quite unusual and made it difficult to identify it as a Sparks album. The CDs released worldwide typically did not feature the original design.

Over the years, the CD version has been released under various titles, including 'So Important', 'Just Got Back From Heaven', 'The World Of Sparks/Madonna', 'Gold', 'Heaven and Beyond' and 'The Magic Collection'. All of these releases featured covers with photographs that were not related to the era in which the album was originally released. Collectors consistently seek out the more obscure editions of this CD.

For the first time since *Terminal Jive,* no live performances were held to support the new album. However, the brothers did appear at a Love-O-Rama Block Party on 15 September 1988, at Tower Records in Sherman Oaks, California. This well-attended event was organised by Rhino Records to officially launch the new LP. It featured a variety of somewhat juvenile quizzes, speeches and an unexpected number of inflatable love dolls filled with condoms. Video footage of this memorable day was captured by a fan.

Despite this, the album did not chart in any country.

Interior Design—The Songs

All songs written by Ron Mael and Russell Mael.

'So Important'
Duration: 4:33

None of the band members who had been part of Sparks' previous four albums and live shows since 1981 were still with the band when this album was recorded. Even drummer David Kendrick was no longer a member of the band, and no other drummer is mentioned. It is safe to assume that all drum parts were performed by a drum machine. Nevertheless, the album opens with drumbeats that sound quite authentic. The Maels had clearly invested in a proper drum machine for their studio.

It is striking that there is no bass guitar either. The lack of this instrument is compensated for by the keyboards, but they are barely audible. The remarkable fact is that a guitar is present again, after a fairly long absence, and it serves as a crucial foundation for the sound. Furthermore, there is an actual guitar solo, which had almost seemed to be extinct on Sparks albums. The entire concept gives the song a somewhat rock-oriented feel.

As for the lyrics, there are no double layers or hidden messages to be found. The singer is in a relationship where he considers his partner to be much more valuable than the other way around, and he expresses his frustrations in the song.

Oddly enough, David Kendrick was still featured in a performance of 'So Important' on *On The Fritz*, KNBC TV Channel 4, in October 1988. Guitarist Spencer Sercombe and keyboardist John Thomas also appear in this broadcast, and the same formation can be observed in other American broadcasts of this song. However, the band ultimately appears without David Kendrick and with the addition of Pamela Stonebrook on backing vocals.

It became the first single and was released in the US, France and England. It was not successful in any of the countries. However, the 12-inch version of the single reached number 8 on the Billboard Hot Dance Music/Club Play chart, which was a very positive outcome. This was due to the two additional mixes that appeared on the single. A promo CD was also released, which was Sparks' first formal CD single. This release is quite difficult to find nowadays.

In France, the song was performed on two television shows, with the Maels being accompanied by the two members of Les Rita Mitsouko. Like most of the songs on this album, 'So Important' was never performed live.

> Russell: 'We have finally put together our own studio after having always been at the mercy of record company imposed recording budgets to determine when

and for how long we would be allowed to record. "Interior Design" was the first LP to christen "The Pentagon". We performed "So Important" on French TV with Catherine Ringer and Fred Chichin of French band Les Rita Mitsouko assuming the roles of the Sparks' guitarist and drummer. We reciprocated by doing 3 songs together for their LP "Marc et Robert".'

'Just Got Back From Heaven'
Duration: 4:09

The gentle sound of a music box, accompanied by a synthesizer, opens the song. A funk-inspired guitar riff and matching bass line come together, establishing a rhythm that has not often been utilised in earlier arrangements. The instrumental version of the verse demonstrates that this song also features a very catchy melody, evoking a cheerful feeling.

The funky guitar remains present throughout the song, although it is quite subtle and only noticeable when you pay close attention. Limited but useful backing vocals from Pamela Stonebrook enhance the song, which was chosen as the second single.

The single, which was only released in the US, contained no fewer than five different mixes, all of which differed from the album version. Two mixes were also released on CD single, but again, only in the US. This 12-inch single performed even better than its predecessor, reaching number 7 on the Billboard Hot Dance Music/Club Play chart.

In terms of lyrical content, it is highly unlikely that the statement in the title should be taken too literally. It seems as though the singer enters a heavenly state when he gazes into the eyes of a lady who evokes this feeling. Not such a strange rationale in itself, considering that most of the songs on the album seem to be primarily a tribute to love. A funny twist, realising that Harley Feinstein once suggested to Ron and Russel in the early Bearsville years that they should record an album dedicated to such a theme, which was then met with deathly silence.

'Just Got Back From Heaven' has not been performed live at regular gigs.

Russell: 'All those wonderful things that you've heard about heaven are 100% true.'

'Lots Of Reasons'
Duration: 3:47

A cheerful, up-tempo song about a self-confessed, rather persistent stalker who seems to have few moral objections to his behaviour. In a nutshell, that is the lyrical content of this song, which, like most on this album, is very catchy.

The song is dominated by a steady, consistent drum rhythm with minimal variation. Once again, the guitar takes on a prominent role, alongside the customary synthesizers, which play a modest part in this song. There is also a clearly artificial tambourine that appears regularly. After a forced chuckle from Russell, a genuine guitar solo ensues, evoking the sound of a rock band that might perform at venues like the one in the film *Roadhouse*.

'Lots Of Reasons' has not been performed live at regular gigs.

'You Got A Hold Of My Heart'
Duration: 4:58

Of a completely different order in terms of arrangement, style and somewhat lazy tempo, this song is undoubtedly amongst the top ten most romantic songs recorded by Sparks. Minimal use of instruments, fully executed by keyboards, and a clearly audible bass line, which also originates from Ron's keys, form the backdrop for somewhat sultry vocals that lament the loss of a great love.

Just like in some other songs, reference is made to the brothers' home environment; the state of California, which they consider to be a place like no other. It is the quietest song on the album, and despite the lyrical content and the sadness that the listener is exposed to, there is something comforting about the whole thing. It's one of the better songs on the album but was never performed live at regular gigs.

'Love-O-Rama'
Duration: 4:44

An acapella introduction with a basic stereo effect and unexpected Caribbean percussion immediately indicates that this is a completely different song from its predecessor. The compelling loud drumbeats, accompanied by synthesizer sounds, create a less captivating melody that is compensated for by the energy and enthusiasm radiated by the song.

The rhythm creates the sensation of listening to a melodious train passing by, and the chorus is once again very catchy and sung in falsetto. It seems like a guitar is involved in this song, but upon closer listening, it becomes evident that it is actually a programmed synthesizer.

The song has never been played live during regular concerts.

'The Toughest Girl In Town'
Duration: 4:16

In keeping with the overall style of the arrangements on this album, this song starts with a specially programmed synthesizer sound, accompanied by artificial cymbals. The vocals, which come in after around fifteen seconds, alter the tone of the song. Sung in falsetto, they create a serene atmosphere. The arrangements are slightly enhanced with additional typical synthesizer sounds, and the drum computer only kicks in after the chorus has been performed.

The demo of this song is slightly faster than the final version and includes a second, lower voice that, although cleverly masked by the falsetto, is still discernible to the experienced listener. The second voice was omitted from the final version.

Only towards the end of the song is the drum machine used more prominently, with an apparently authentic drumroll added, making the song slightly chaotic but also more interesting. Surprisingly, 'The Toughest Girl In Town' was a permanent part of the live set during the 2023 world tour.

During the concert in Utrecht in the Netherlands, Russell dedicated the song to German fan Sandy Debets, for reasons known to those close to her.

Drummer Stevie Nistor seized this opportunity to assert himself and performed his parts with great verve and professionalism. As a result, the song was received with much enthusiasm everywhere. Regarding the song's lyrical content, the title accurately describes it.

'Let's Make Love'
Duration: 4:45

In terms of atmosphere and tempo, this song can be compared to 'You Got A Hold Of My Heart'. The song features somewhat metallic-sounding percussion and various synthesizer sounds. A lower second vocal line, positioned just below the main falsetto, is used very subtly.

The artificial bass is once again utilised effectively, and this time the guitar is absent. The song concludes with an emphasis on the drums, without it being a traditional drum solo.

Like most tracks on this record, it is dedicated to a romantic relationship, and the lyrics are straightforward, without any double meanings or subtle puns. It has never been performed during a regular concert.

'Stop Me If You've Heard This Before'
Duration: 3:41

Despite the somewhat sad conclusion that can be drawn from the lyrics, which involve someone confronting their partner about infidelity, there are still some amusing elements included.

The sound and atmosphere of this song are defined by the loud metallic drums and funky artificial bass that were used previously. As expected, these elements are complemented by a series of tones generated by the synthesizer. The vocals are sometimes delivered in regular bursts, which seems to be an intentional choice. The use of the instruments is aligned with this. Apparently the last song written for the album, it has not been performed live during regular gigs.

During the Sparks Spectacular performance, the focus was primarily on rhythm guitar and bass, with the synthesizer occasionally playing different riffs and even a modest contribution from the lead guitar.

'A Walk Down Memory Lane'
Duration: 4:53

The second-to-last song on the LP is a ballad-like tune with a half-minute instrumental intro that mainly features percussion, synthesizers and bass guitar sounds generated from keyboards. There's no use of the electric guitar this time. This is also the first time that Frank Sinatra is mentioned in a Sparks song.

Russell uses his backing vocals in the choruses in a rather pleasant manner. In line with its title, the song has a nostalgic and somewhat romantic undertone. As is typical of most Sparks songs, it features a melody that lingers in your memory.

The demo version is about forty seconds longer. Apart from some instrumental variations, the vocals are noticeably different, featuring high-pitched backing vocals throughout the whole song.

The content is difficult to interpret. It seems to refer to past failures and how everything could have been different if this had been successful. It has never been played live at regular performances.

'Madonna'
Duration: 4:38

The final song, while not as grand as what is typically expected for a closing song on a Sparks album, addresses a special subject, especially considering the timeline in which it was released. The song opens with an extremely catchy yet simple synthesizer riff that continues throughout. Once again, it features a lingering melody that compels you to repeat it in your head long after the song has ended.

There will undoubtedly be several songs by various artists that have Madonna as their subject, but leave it to Sparks to describe an imaginary affair with an artist who was then just about at the height of her fame.

In line with its content, this song is narrated, rather than sung. An exception is the chorus, which is refreshing, both in terms of the vocals and the melody. It is also the only moment where the very catchy riff is not used.

The US version of the official CD presents versions in French, Spanish and German as bonus tracks. Only the vocals are different, the instrumental parts being unchanged. The song has never been performed live at regular concerts.

Russell: 'Back when Madonna was a wholesome girl, we had written this story about a guy who had an imaginary affair with her. We thought everyone should be able to hear this story in their own language, so we did four versions: English, German, Spanish and French. We've had numerous requests, so maybe one day we'll release versions in Italian, Russian, Swedish, Serbo-Croatian, etc, etc.'

Afterword

The first fifteen LPs by Sparks already showcase a world of differences in the brothers' creative outbursts. Few artists have delivered such a varied range and have consistently maintained a high quality of songs. Of course, not all songs are of equal quality, but the vast majority still command admiration and often amazement.

In the second part of this examination of the talented brothers' career, their other albums will be discussed similarly, with additional focus on the more than 100 songs that did not appear on regular albums. The almost 150 songs that were never formally released will also receive ample attention.

As with many publications involving an element of review, these findings may not always align with those of others. This is inherent in discussing artists who have produced such a wide range of music and who cannot easily be classified into conventional genres. I hope that readers find as much pleasure in reading this work as I did in writing it.